TEACHING JUNIOR HIGH SCHOOL MUSIC

General Music and the Vocal Program

Junior High School Boys' Chorus (Florida High School, Tallahassee, Florida)

TEACHING JUNIOR HIGH SCHOOL MUSIC

General Music and the Vocal Program

Irvin Cooper
PROFESSOR OF MUSIC EDUCATION
THE FLORIDA STATE UNIVERSITY

Karl O. Kuersteiner
DEAN, SCHOOL OF MUSIC
THE FLORIDA STATE UNIVERSITY

ALLYN AND BACON, INC.   BOSTON

Library of Congress Catalog Card Number 65-14918

Printed in the United States of America

First Printing . . . February, 1965
Second Printing . . . March, 1967

FOREWORD

This book evolved in response to the requests of a great many school music teachers, gathered over the past twenty years at various festivals, clinic-demonstrations, and workshops.

Excellent books are available on various aspects of junior high school music, but it appears that school music teachers are in search of a book which will outline clearly and comprehensively a cumulative plan for teaching the basics of music in a general music course. It is not proposed that the various techniques appearing herein constitute the sole method. It is proposed, however, that this method is workable; it has been proved in many school systems.

Information presented herein is structured around a concept that a general music program should subscribe to the intrinsic value of music as a desirable junior high school curricular component. It is suggested that music instruction should be concerned primarily with musical values and that the concern of the school music teacher should be to (1) inculcate a love of music in students, (2) bring students into contact with fine music through performance and listening, (3) bring about an understanding of the printed score, and (4) develop in the students a discriminatory taste in their choice of musical entertainment. This does not preclude the use of the method by a teacher who, being well versed in masterpieces of other arts, wishes to implement the listening program by appropriate references to those arts.

v]

A frequent complaint of junior high school music teachers is that, with responsibilities to various school music organizations, the general music program, homeroom, bus duty, and other duties, there is little time or inclination to engage in research or in the development of original comprehensive plans for general music classes. It is hoped that *Teaching Junior High School Music* will prove to be helpful to these teachers in providing a cumulative lesson-by-lesson plan for all the various aspects of the type of general music program proposed in this book.

This book is not offered as a panacea to all musical ills. In many instances, instruction in the early lessons will appear oversimplified for classes which have passed through a good elementary music program, but this is rare; on the other hand, the most advanced chapters will appear to be beyond the reach of some classes. This book is written in such a manner that any school music teacher with the usual under-graduate training can adapt it to his use, no matter at what level of in-tellectual or musical competence his class may be.

A choral approach to general music has been adopted after careful consideration. While general music is frequently taught by instrumental teachers, the problems involved in an instrumental approach are obvious:

1. A considerable financial outlay to purchase a sufficient number of instru-ments is mandatory.
2. Instrumental balance in a small class group is almost impossible.
3. It requires at least six weeks before a beginning general music instrumen-tal group can acquire sufficient skill to perform the simplest arrangement. The problem is further compounded when it is remembered that many general music classes meet for one weekly period of forty minutes, in some instances for a maximum term of nine weeks.

It is hoped that *Teaching Junior High School Music* may make some worthwhile contribution to the coming of age of junior high school music by helping to prepare the music teacher and potential music teacher for intelligent and satisfying service in this area.

I.C.
K.O.K.

CONTENTS

[viii

CHAPTER ONE

A CONCEPT OF GENERAL MUSIC

Diversity of Practices

There are about as many notions concerning the purpose, objectives, and content of a general music program as there are teachers engaged in this work. Most junior high school systems throughout the country are committed to some sort of music program. There is some general consensus among school superintendents and principals that music is a desirable addition to the basic curriculum. They are not always certain of the educational benefits to be derived by students through participation in music, but they are generally willing to be convinced, if the supervisor or teacher can advance plausible arguments in support thereof. This is reasonable enough, since it is uncommon to find an administrator who has received music training of any consequence. They thus want an explanation for the pursuit of music by the contemporary school population. If administrators are willing to go along with modern practice in this matter and create a place in the school curriculum for music, they are entitled to know what will be taught, and in what manner students will benefit, not only now but throughout adult life. Administrators most often turn to the area music supervisor or the school music teacher to plan the composite music program and in this respect they are completely at the mercy of the planner's musical integrity and competence.

A typical program provides for instrumental and choral performing groups (in which membership is elective on the part of the student
and selective on the part of the music teacher), and general music, in
order to expose the larger portion of the school population to some
sort of music.

Priority for Performing Groups

The general music program does not always enjoy good repute
because some school music teachers give top priority to the development
of superior performing groups and regard general music as a necessary
but undesirable chore. Why?—because there is no widely approved
established pattern of instruction or course content available to which
the teacher may turn. Should this situation persist through the years
it is quite conceivable that a time might come—sooner than is expected
—when school music teachers throughout the country could be challenged strongly about the appropriateness of spending large sums of
money on salary and equipment for such a small portion of the total
school enrollment.

Fine music performing groups are most desirable for students
capable of participating in them, but it is equally important that the
other seventy-five percent of the student body become aware of the
beauty and power of music as a pleasurable enrichment of life. Music
educators are rendering both the students and themselves a singular dis-
service by regarding casually or neglecting entirely this aspect of school
music. There is national concern over the preference of our young
people for trash and vulgarity in music; yet some of the responsibility
for this state of affairs rests securely on those school music teachers
who although having opportunity, fail to bring to their students the
fine literature abounding in music.

Even the select minority participating in performing groups needs
general music instruction. The limited amount of music which school
organizations are able to perform comprises an infinitesimal portion
of the total literature; moreover, a member of a performing organization is often so concerned with his own part that he rarely has any con-
ception of the whole sound to which he contributes. School orchestras
are not numerous, and the only way the prodigious amount of fine

music written for the orchestra can be brought to the students is through a general music course.

The school drama club is a lot of fun for a few people but it assuredly does not encompass the field of literature, and it is not regarded as the basic course in literature for the school. Choral speaking groups fall into the same category: the members concentrate on learning from memory certain select items of literature for performance. Members of school music performing organizations must spend a great deal of time practicing over and over again various sections of the work-in-hand to assure perfection in performance, even committing long programs to memory. This precludes a comprehensive survey of the literature. Furthermore, as the main objective of these groups is performing to please audiences, the musical worth of the materials studied is tempered adversely by generous use of Broadway show music, novelty numbers, and the like. Although such organizations are indeed desirable, there is urgent need for additional musical instruction which will involve a larger number of students. It is a fallacy to assume that music can be enjoyed only by those who are able to perform.

Need for Strong General Music Course Outline

It is perhaps worthwhile at this point to inquire how and why the general music program has fallen into some disrepute.

Administrators are skeptical about general music because there appear to be no plans which will lead to cumulative growth in music understanding. They are also keenly aware that after having taken a semester of a required general music course an alarmingly small percentage of the students go on to take the course as an elective subject. The students have apparently received nothing which would stimulate a desire for further music experiences.

In view of this situation and the music teacher's lack of enthusiasm in demanding time for instruction, the school principal may settle for a token scheduling, sometimes as little as one required period per week for nine weeks in Grade 8, more frequently one meeting per week for one semester only. Less frequently, two or three periods a week for one or two semesters are sometimes available for the more enthusiastic teacher. The crux of the whole situation rests upon the kinds of activities the students are involved in during general music instruction. Widely varied practices exist, although in many instances it requires a considerable stretch of the imagination to correlate what is being taught with the intrinsic and actual values of music.

The most casual method of presenting a general music lesson consists of playing phonograph records, with no cumulative plan of learning in view. Whatever is topical at the moment becomes a subject for interpretation through the medium of a phonograph record. Every listening lesson is a separate experience, and there is no continuity of musical learning envisioned in the course.

Another popular procedure is one which uses the general music period as a supplement to the social studies class. The music teacher consults with social studies teachers to determine what aspects of geography or history are being dealt with and engages in personal research to discover appropriate songs his classes may sing (irrespective of whether or not the melodic range is compatible with the restricted vocal ranges of children passing through early adolescence) and recordings of folk dances. Devotees of the *Core* curriculum heartily support this type of general music program; it probably contributes to the social studies lessons and also has some musical value if it may be regarded as an introduction to further music experiences. When it is realized, however, that this brief interlude may well be the terminal organized school music activity for these children, it seems that the procedure described above scarcely constitutes the kind of instruction which will lead to understanding or love of music.

There is also the *project* type of general music program which has considerable support in some quarters. A class may, for instance, engage in an Indian project during which feathers are collected and painted, a wigwam constructed, Indian songs discovered and learned, Indian pictures are collected and pinned to the bulletin board—all in the name of music. One general music class which met one period a week for nine weeks built a magnificent replica of a full orchestra from match sticks, cut-outs of figures pasted on cardboard, risers, everything, but the group never performed or heard music during this busy-work project.

There are many more types of general music programs. The committee-type of program is one in which the class splits up into a series of committees. Each has its own appointed area of busy-work and reports progress frequently at full class sessions. Another kind of program encourages creative music in the junior high school although this accomplishes little for the whole class in terms of lasting musical growth. It is unlikely that this process will reveal some great composer of the future, and the hours spent in extracting note after note from various members of a class may after careful editing by the teacher produce a class song of dubious musical value.

Lack of Success in General Music Programs

Why has general music fallen into such disrepute? In what ways have music educators failed to grasp the opportunity to realize in fact the fine slogan "music for every child and every child for music"?

Singing, the backbone of the music program in the elementary grades, becomes a veritable nightmare in junior high school because boys' voices start to change and seem to be completely out of tune. It is at once assumed that boys in junior high school are *nonsingers.* Instead of finding what common vocal ranges are available for a combination of unchanged, changing, and changed voices, and selecting appropriate songs in singable ranges, the teacher often decides singing is undesirable and plans some other activity which might be defended as music. This will be discussed more fully in Chapter Three.

Concerning the listening program, again, the teacher may be at a serious disadvantage if he has had an insufficient amount of course work in music literature as an undergraduate. Knowledge of the literature can be obtained vicariously, through attendance at college recitals, concerts, or a personal record collection. But anyone teaching music literature needs, in addition to a basic familiarity with that literature, the ability to present it in an organized cumulative pattern.

Music as a "Fringe Benefit" in Curriculum

Possibly through fear that music might be discarded from the school curriculum as a frill, leading authorities in music education have tried to promote music as a desirable adjunct to many phases of the education curriculum. As a result, the intrinsic value of music has been downgraded in an effort to justify it as an additional resource for any subject it might remotely enrich. Instead of minimizing the stigma of frill, it serves to intensify it. If this is the *raison d'être* of general music in the junior high school, its position must seem very insecure to the music teacher. Should the education administrator at any time decide that this type of contribution does not have sufficient merit or body to justify the necessary outlay of public funds, general music could quite reasonably be eliminated from the curriculum. Performing organizations would probably remain, but the music teacher with teaching time not completely utilized might be required to undertake non-musical work, or to teach in more than one school. As a matter of fact, there is already some evidence of this trend.

Although the situation portrayed is somewhat dismal, it need not be so. Teaching general music can be a most challenging and engrossing activity if a stand is taken for the intrinsic values of music. Children deserve and have a right to be taught to understand and love music as music, for their continued enjoyment throughout life, not as a fringe benefit to geography, history, or other subjects. The general music course can provide the teacher with continuous and enjoyable experiences while he carries out his obligation to the various classes he meets. To ensure this, however, there are certain desirable prerequisites for the music teacher.

Prerequisites for the Music Teacher

The teacher should be convinced that insofar as is possible every student in his school ought to be exposed to music instruction for a minimum of one semester as a required course, with opportunities later as an elective. Active recruiting for general music students is equally important as is recruiting for the school chorus or band. There needs to be some persuasive effort in the first instance because unless they are told, boys and girls at this level have no idea that music can be an engrossing, pleasurable activity. They naturally do not elect a subject of dubious interest or quality, and if the guidance director senses this apathy, the youngsters are frequently counselled away from music. Friendly communication between the music teacher and guidance director are essential in good recruitment for general music courses.

Another prerequisite for the school music teacher is a reasonable acquaintance with music literature, particularly orchestral, for it is in this medium that the majority of great music works have been written. Music with words is more easily understood and much fine choral music has been written. Also, choral music presents only one basic texture of tone color and therefore is not so complex as orchestral music.

Frequently the music education undergraduate program does not emphasize music literature courses. Following prescribed courses which will eventually lead to a degree and legal certification to teach music in the schools, a student usually becomes enmeshed in such required courses as general education, teacher education, applied music, theory of music, history of music, instrumental and choral methods. No time is left on his schedule for music literature courses, even if they were available at this level. As a result the student often loses contact with the very essence which first attracted him to music, the beauty of organized sound in melody, harmony, and rhythm, and his progress through college becomes a mundane task of accumulating sufficient credit points to graduate.

It is unreasonable to imagine that a teacher can bring music literature to his classes if he has but a smattering of poorly organized information on the literature. Introduction to symphonic literature and introduction to choral literature should be required courses for music education students at the undergraduate level, and they should be taught by the music education faculty as quasi-pedagogy courses. If such courses are not available at the institution where the music education student is in residence, he should take every opportunity to use the school library and record-playing facilities.

Perhaps the most important prerequisite is a basic knowledge of what should be taught in a general music class in order to ensure a cumulative learning process. This will provide children with a solid foundation for selecting and enjoying music listening experiences in adult life. The general music program described in the following chapters ensures such a cumulative learning process. It is based on the theory that every phase of the course should emphasize the intrinsic value of music.

Proposal for a General Music Program

Singing. The core of this course will be singing, and arguments in support of this proposal will be developed in Chapter Two. Information based on research concerning adolescent voices is included, along with materials especially written and commensurate with vocal ranges found in the junior high school.

Music reading. Music reading is also regarded as an important activity, and one chapter will be devoted to a discussion of workable methods and suitable materials.

Ear training—listening. Formal ear training used in moderation should be practiced frequently in very brief sessions. The main objectives of this kind of work are to teach the students (1) to listen attentively, (2) to perceive intelligently what is being heard, and (3) to respond to questions concerning what has been heard. This activity should run parallel to the sight-reading program and should precede that part of the listening program which presents recorded musical works. An organized plan for directing intelligent listening to music is necessary. It should provide for the use of attractive, tuneful material which will lead the junior high school student in a cumulative process from the simple to more complex musical compositions. Each lesson should build from the previous lesson, and no new phase of learning should be attempted until it is evident that the class has understood the preceding sequence.

Music history. Parallel with the listening program should come a broad, uncomplicated review of the development of music and master composers who have contributed to this growth such as Palestrina, Bach, Handel, Mozart, and Beethoven. The lives of minor composers should be given brief mention if their works are to be used in the listening lesson.

Written work (theory). Finally, a general music program is not complete without sufficient theoretical written work to implement the sight-reading and listening portions.

It is recommended therefore that the ideal general music course be sixfold in its content and include song singing, music reading, ear training, listening, history, and theory (listed here in order of their relative importance). The following chapters will outline procedures, methods, and materials by means of which this ideal might be reached. The total ideal envisaged is completely unattainable in situations where schedule time and/or materials are not available, but in order to provide for such situations, proposals will be made for modifications of course content in terms of schedule time available. In the future, however, at least some of the concepts and practices presented in this book may find favor with music educators; they in turn may derive the firm conviction that music deserves an important place in child education.

Conviction in Favor of Music Instruction

If the junior high school music teacher is able to present to the school principal or superintendent a sound, defensible teaching plan, obviously cumulative in growth with clearly discernible goals, he will have a better chance of obtaining a more reasonable amount of teaching time for general music than is generally allowed. With so many subjects crowding the school curriculum, time is too valuable to be appropriated for subjects with vague objectives and intangible future value.

The onus for developing a nation of discriminating music listeners lies with the music educator. No other segment of society can combat the baleful influences of radio and television which hour by hour pour out their tawdry tunes and words into the impressionable ears of countless teenage listeners. There seems to be some fear in the hearts of school music teachers that they will lose favor with their students if they attack the short-breathed, coarse-voiced shouters of popular ditties whose products are so often beamed to adolescents for commercial purposes.

Music educators need to rise against this state of affairs. Mass education in music discrimination can in part combat this mediocrity. A general music program with a well-planned course of study should be regarded as a vital part of the child's total learning program. Admirable activities though they be, school chorus, band, and orchestra reach only a small segment of the school population, and even these groups expose their members to a relatively small, specialized portion of music literature. General music should become the basic course of music instruction, but it requires teachers who are thoroughly prepared and who are dedicated to the task of bringing music to the greatest possible school population.

CHAPTER TWO

A SINGING PROGRAM

Core of General Music Program

Singing should be the core of the junior high school general music program. Vocal expression is man's instinctive medium of communication. In moments of exultation, happiness, unhappiness, sorrow, anguish, or any moment of stirring emotional experience, personal feeling is reflected in vocal expression. Deep personal emotion can on occasion transcend the immediate environment so completely that mere words are inadequate for communication, but through music or words wedded to music a more satisfying expression of the emotion becomes possible.

SINGING AS A VALUABLE EMOTIONAL EXPRESSION

In singing, the performer is able to achieve an experience even more sublime than in listening because he is actively participating. There is also great satisfaction in expressing oneself directly with the voice, a satisfaction greater perhaps than through the secondary medium of a mechanical instrument.

Junior high school boys, noisily articulate about anything else, are completely inarticulate about their deeper emotions. These emotions are considered unmanly and are held in check until they are dissipated in rugged horseplay. Choral music in the classroom provides the ideal vehicle for self-expression. Girls and boys experience the emotions reflected in their various songs and through them express themselves. The frequent defense of the non-singing general music class that "boys often dislike singing, and they should not be compelled to sing," is nonsense. Certainly they have little taste for the childish musical fare that is sometimes offered them and resent being considered juvenile. In fact boys not only like rollicking songs but also love songs.

Singing is not merely a quasi-therapeutic activity. It is the most natural and spontaneous of all media of musical expression, and through this simple medium particularly in three- and four-part music, it is possible for participants to realize personal musical experiences of rare beauty. The lasting beneficial influences of such experiences are incalculable. Every boy and girl should be brought to participate in singing and not solely on an elective basis, for they are much too young to understand the values of music in their own lives or its implications for an aesthetically richer adult life.

One additional value of the singing class is the opportunity to participate with a group in the creation of beauty, the feeling of belonging to a successful team which constantly rises to new peaks of achievement.

Types of Activities

There are three different but related phases of the junior high school singing program: learning to read music vocally, class singing, and special performing groups such as choirs or ensembles. Strictly speaking, the latter do not fall under general music, but techniques pertaining to choirs and ensembles will be discussed in this volume in order that the junior high school music teacher may have a more composite body of information at his disposal for the total vocal program.

Learning to read the music score with some degree of reliability is essential in building an adequate vocal program. This does not imply long, tedious drill at the expense of singing songs to aim for perfection in *sight* singing. The objectives of learning to read the score reasonably well are to enable the students to learn songs more intelligently and quickly, and as a visual aid in understanding music literature presented on the phonograph or tape recording.

The more quickly a class can become reasonably proficient in music reading, the easier becomes the teacher's work in teaching new music. The physical resources of the teacher are subject to considerable strain by rote teaching, and if for no better reason than self-preservation, music reading is highly recommended as a regular practice. Teaching music reading solely through songs is not a successful method because there is no cumulative process which leads the student step by step through successively more difficult exercises. Chapter Four of this book will present a system for teaching the reading of music vocally along with a considerable number of reading melodies in which each new step is incorporated and approached in an organized manner.

Obviously, proficiency in reading music vocally cannot be attained within the first few weeks; songs in the meantime will have to be taught by rote. Incidentally this is the most critical period for class and teacher, one during which the teacher can completely capture the group by realizing with them a series of highly successful choral experiences.

Unison Singing, a Fruitless Enterprise

The most natural thought for the music teacher planning his first meeting with a Grade 7 class is "What unison songs have these boys and girls known in elementary school that we can review?" If carried through, this procedure leads to vocal chaos in Grade 7, because during the summer break between Grades 6 and 7 so many boys' voices lose the soprano range and drop into the first phase of the maturation process. Unison songs unless they are contained within this range are

SOPRANO-CAMBIATA

BARITONE

Composite Octave-Unison Range
for Combined Ranges

absolutely unsingable by combined boys' and girls' groups in Grades 7 to 9. This phenomenon will be discussed later in detail. As a result, three- or four-part singing is the only satisfactory type of vocal activity available in the junior high school.

One of the prime requisites for a music teacher starting work in Grade 7 is a thorough understanding of the ranges, scope, and limitations of voices with which he will work. Junior high school is frequently regarded as a problem area for vocal music, but the problem is not the child's. It lies in the teacher's lack of understanding or misunderstanding of the capabilities of voices in early adolescence.

Voices in Early Adolescence

During the past twenty-five years a considerable amount of conflicting information has been circulated concerning the voices of young adolescents. This information contributes to the confusion in vocal practices of rank and file music educators. For example, some authorities subscribe to the opinion that the boy's changing voice has such a limited range and is so unreliable that singing is an undesirable activity at this age. Other texts visualize the range of the boy's changing voice as being very limited, and the pitch location of this range can lie anywhere within

depending on the concept held by any particular authority.

In practice there must be some happy medium commensurate with vocal attributes of most of these boys. Although they do not read music education text books and are unaware of pedagogical problems, boys sing together spontaneously on many occasions.

Early Incidence of Voice Change

Another factor contributing to the confusion is that voice change occurs at an earlier age than was the case twenty-five years ago. Dr. Alexander Comfort of the Department of Zoology, University College, London, England, has been engaged in research on earlier maturation. In this connection he mentions that in England church choir directors have difficulty finding "choirboys old enough to behave themselves who can still sing treble."[1] Limited investigation by the writer has revealed many boys' voices changing in Grade 6, and in some cases, as soon as Grade 4. If the pattern is widespread, new thinking is required concerning appropriate song material in upper elementary grades.

How does the "growing up faster" theory create new problems for the junior high school music teacher? Earlier maturation of girls presents no vocal problem. With regard to boys, in Grade 7 classes there are very few soprano voices and possibly one or two young baritones; however, the majority of boys' voices are in the process of the first change, with a singing range suspended between soprano and baritone. Thus singing materials which were adequate twenty-five years ago are no longer compatible, and new materials being prepared must adhere to the new vocal range criteria or the problem will be compounded. There is at present a lack of music designed to meet the needs of all types of young adolescent voices.

Vocal Ranges in Junior High School

In junior high school there are five basic types of voices: (1) girls', (2) boys' unchanged, (3) boys' in the first change, (4) boys' in the second change, and (5) boys' changed. The working ranges of these voices are:

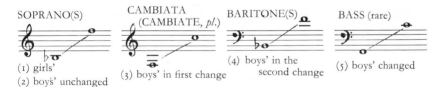

FIG.1

The term "cambiata" refers to the boy's voice passing through the first change and is a device to avoid confusion with the many conflicting ranges proposed for alto-tenor. These range definitions should be thoroughly assimilated by the reader inasmuch as they form the basis for a great deal of further discussion in this and following chapters.

[1] Alexander Comfort, "Growing up Faster," radio address (London, England: British Broadcasting Corporation, June 14, 1960).

It is a gross error to assume that every voice in each category fits the prescribed range boundaries, but it is safe to say that the ranges apply in ninety percent of the cases studied. Some girls, for instance, can sing higher and lower than the range defined above; while a number of boys passing through the first change do not realize the upper portion of their range until stimulated to do so. Similarly, boys passing through the second phase of the change gradually realize their lowest note, Bb, over a period of a few weeks. Confirmation of these ranges is available in a sound-color-movie, *The Changing Voice*.[1]

A study of the above vocal ranges will reveal why unison singing is an unrewarding activity.

COMPOSITE UNISON-OCTAVE RANGE

The highest note of the cambiata range is the top unison limit; while the lowest note of the unchanged soprano voice range is the bottom unison limit, a range which is paralleled an octave lower in the baritone voice.

VOCAL TESSITURA

Unison singing is therefore restricted to songs with a range of a major ninth, and more definitely restricted to the specific major ninth shown above. A further restriction is imposed on unison singing when tessitura is introduced. Tessitura is that portion of the vocal range in which it is comfortable to sing for a considerable time without tiring. Brief vocal excursions outside the tessitura can be very effective, but if the general line of any song lies outside the tessitura, voice strain results.

[1] Irvin Cooper, *The Changing Voice,* sound-color-movie (Tallahassee: Florida State University, 1959).

SOPRANO (girls and boys)   CAMBIATA   BARITONE

TESSITURA WITHIN INDIVIDUAL PART RANGES

The above illustration presents the approximate vocal tessitura of each category of voices under discussion. By applying a procedure similar to that used in finding an overall common unison-octave range, it will be seen that the common unison or unison-octave tessitura of combined mixed voices in junior high school is:

SOPRANO-CAMBIATA

BARITONE

COMPOSITE UNISON-OCTAVE TESSITURA
for COMBINED RANGES

About the only song compatible with this unison range is "Jingle Bells," a pleasant song but not recommended as a steady diet.

It becomes more apparent why unison singing is such an unrewarding activity: if the song moves up into the best part of the soprano voices it eliminates cambiate; while, conversely, a melody favoring the best register of cambiata voices employs the weaker registers of sopranos and baritones. Implications emerging from the situation will be discussed later in this chapter.

VOCAL QUALITY

The vocal quality found in young adolescents presents phenomena which unless thoroughly understood can lead to pedagogic frustration, particularly in the matter of vocal classification.

Girls' voices during this period are inclined to be thin and sometimes shrill; the illusion that they are high voices will lead elementary school music teachers astray. A thin voice is not necessarily a high voice; it could be, of course, but this is not the general situation.

Surprisingly enough, alto voices are rare among the girls, even in Grade 9. A few have been encountered, usually in physically very well developed girls or slow learners who have repeated grades and are older than their classmates. Another phenomenon is that richer, thicker vocal quality does not necessarily indicate a low voice. Among the girls in a class singing group or in the school chorus will be potential contraltos or potential lyric sopranos, but at this age the vast majority of girls' voices lies within one common range:

Generally speaking, girls' voices in Grades 7, 8, and 9 are rather thin and colorless, and girls require greater stimulation than boys to realize their full vocal dynamic potential. Suggestions will be offered a little later how to deploy these voices in choral work so that the best musical interests of the girl and her group are served.

Boys' voices present a fascinating challenge to the alert, conscientious junior high school music teacher. This applies to instrumental as well as vocal teachers, because it is quite a common administrative procedure to allocate general music responsibilities to the band director. The challenge exists because beginning as low as Grade 6 in some instances, boys' voices move downwards in a series of three well-defined levels as illustrated earlier in this chapter.

Elusive Quality of Cambiata

During the first phase of the change which might last anywhere from a few months to two years, the voice has a quality which is very elusive to classification. The difficulty of classifying cambiata voices has misled many music educators with the result that there are few tenor singers in adult choirs. The quality of cambiata voices is rich and a trifle *woolly,* a truly beautiful sound if it is controlled in volume and not permitted to become strident from sheer vocal exuberance of the boys.

The boy's voice during its first change presents the aural illusion of sounding an octave lower than is actually the case, and sometimes his correct classification can only be achieved by comparison with a known bass or baritone singing at the octave. The number of cambiata voices classified in error as light basses is legion. As a result of this, some ridiculous malpractices are perpetrated, because boys so classified actually sing a bass part an octave higher than written, with an upper limit of printed middle C. In such cases the group sings SATB material with boys' voices in the second change (baritones) singing the tenor part, while voices in the first change sing the bass part which in reality sounds higher than the tenor. The sound is most disconcerting. Youngsters sense it does not sound right and appear self-conscious and uncomfortable.

Tenor Music Inappropriate for Cambiata

With regard to voice classification and the choral function of cambiate, these boys are not tenors and cannot cope adequately with a tenor part. The usual tenor part is *too low;* even though the part being performed is apparently contained within the total vocal range presented on page 15, it is wrong in terms of the tessitura defined earlier, compelling cambiate to use only their lower register and denying them any development of the upper or middle registers. A deplorable outcome of this practice is that through disuse the upper register disappears, and this condition carries over into the next level of voice change.

It is a popular misconception that the tenor part is too high for cambiate and that any compromise or adjustment of the part to bring it within the competence of these voices must be in the nature of eliminating high notes. In reality the cambiata voice contains pitches up to four or five notes higher than those required for the average tenor part.

The practice of using the G clef for tenor voice parts is a contributing factor to this mild confusion since the singer in performance actually transposes the part an octave lower than printed, while the cambiata sings his part at the written pitch. Add to this the aforementioned phenomenon of the octave aural illusion, and it is little wonder that junior high vocal work has been designated as a problem area and that many music teachers have resorted to a peripheral general music program as a matter of expediency. A voice classification procedure will be outlined later, which over a period of years has proved reliable in reducing the incidence of error.

Another interesting phenomenon associated with boys' voices during the first change is that very soon after they become established in a part they serve as a *pitch-anchor* for the rest of the group. They rarely waver in pitch and can be relied upon with confidence in achieving quite difficult choral modulations; further, they assimilate their part in a new selection more quickly than other parts and are unshakable thereafter. However, if they have learned a wrong note it is there forever. Incidentally, it is recommended that the cambiata part of any song be taught first unless it happens to be carrying the melody line, in which case the baritone should have preference. All things taken into consideration, working with cambiata voices and responsibility for their amazingly responsive development is a most exhilarating and rewarding experience for the junior high school music teacher.

From Cambiata to Baritone

The second phase of the voice change is usually entered during a summer vacation, and the new status is generally reported with some pride by the boy to the music teacher. Such reports are occasionally premature because some boys might have a friend who sings baritone or might imagine that singing baritone is a more manly activity than singing cambiata. All these reports need to be validated before allocating boys to the baritone section. As a matter of fact, it is good procedure to run a quick voice classification check for the whole group of boys about once a month. There is little need for worry, however, because a cambiata's suddenly singing out of tune usually indicates that he cannot reach the higher notes of the song and is seeking vocal compromise.

Sudden and dramatic transfers from range to range can occur, and a boy may quickly have to learn new music. Occasionally, a voice will take two or three weeks to settle, but this process can be accelerated by transferring the boy to the baritone section immediately upon the change's becoming apparent. As was the case with cambiata, aspects of the new change require careful study in order to understand the voice and realize its full choral potential.

The baritone range indicated in Figure 1, though it does not coincide with popular opinion on the matter, is that of the majority of

Seventh Grade Cambiate (80—Two Front Rows), Elementary School Orchestra (126, with 7 Pianos), Three-Part Seventh Grade Choir (287), (Dallas Independent School District, John Loren Jones, Director)

junior high school boys in the second voice change. Of course an occasional voice is capable of singing lower than Bb, and the potential tenor can reach above F.

There is usually very little difficulty in persuading the boy to realize his total range of the baritone voice if he has previously done a good deal of singing as a cambiata. If, however, he falls into baritone status as an outcome of the first classification procedure in Grade 7, some stimulation will be necessary to realize the upper register with confidence.

Bass Music Inappropriate for Baritone

In view of this range it becomes fairly obvious that baritones cannot cope with the lower notes of the usual SATB adult music; furthermore, the tessitura of the voice does not coincide with that of the music being sung. Here again the upper register of the voice is neglected. Some teachers, perceiving this and anxious to use the voices to best advantage, realize that they can sing tenor parts of some music and use this system. Unfortunately, due to the octave aural illusion, the bass part is often allocated to misclassified cambiate.

One of the most interesting observations about the voices of boys during early adolescence concerns quality. Boys' voices in the second phase of change exhibit two contrasting characteristics. The vocal range ascribed previously to baritones is prevalent in most cases, but within this range will be found voices with an obvious tenor quality, while others display bass quality. It is important to bear in mind these are not completely *changed voices;* they still have the final change into an adult vocal category.

The junior high baritone sound bears not the slightest resemblance to that of an adult singer. It is a pleasing sound but has little body or volume except in the upper register. It is not as flexible as other voices are and except for the octave cannot readily cope with rapid articulation of wide intervals. The augmented fourth presents odd problems, but paradoxically, the diminished fifth correctly resolved is a routine matter.

Evolution from Baritone

Almost every boy passes through the baritone phase on his way to vocal maturity as either tenor or bass. Any rapid change of a voice from soprano to bass should be investigated for a classification error resulting from the octave aural illusion. Frequently during a cursory classification a voice appears to lie within the bass range, but it is more likely that the individual is a cambiata singing in a vocal range which is an octave higher than bass, particularly if he is in Grade 7 or 8. Teachers who have unwittingly classified it as bass may be perplexed when later the voice, instead of remaining stable, apparently *moves higher* to the baritone range. It is small wonder that so many problems appear to exist in this area. Should the ultimate destination of the voice be tenor, there will be no further drop from the baritone range. As maturity progresses it may even shade upwards a little in pitch, and the quality of the voice will become that of a tenor.

Should the ultimate destination of the voice be bass, the range will descend to the level indicated previously, and the quality will become thicker with increasing resonance. This development is rare even in Grade 9, and the frequency of incidence varies from year to year. A Grade 9 class may boast as many as three basses one year, and for the following two or three years classes in the same grade may have none.

CLASS VOCAL BALANCE

The distribution of boys' voices in typical sample classes is illustrated below. These figures are based on an average class enrollment of thirty, evenly divided as to boys and girls, and reflect the situation at the beginning of the school year.

	Soprano	Cambiata	Baritone	Bass
Grade 7	3	10	2	0
Grade 8	1	10	4	0
Grade 9	0	8	7	very rare

There are, of course, deviations from the above pattern and the situation changes during the course of the year, but these changes are utterly unpredictable in their variations. One high incidence of change occurs during the summer vacation and the ensuing football and basketball seasons. During these periods vocal chords are frequently subject to strenuous, even violent, activity which accelerates the change. In view of this, the theory that singing during the period of voice change is likely to injure the boy's voice seems untenable; yet until comparatively recent years this theory found substantial support, particularly from directors of church male voice choirs.

Correct vocal classification is the key to solving problems enumerated thus far in this chapter. Complete understanding and control of this procedure are considered sufficiently vital to merit comprehensive treatment in the following chapter.

Criteria for Selecting Vocal Materials

In spite of efficient and accurate classification of voices in junior high school vocal enterprises, the *problems* will not be lessened unless intelligent consideration is given to the selection of appropriate vocal materials commensurate with the ranges defined previously in this chapter. Range is the prime criterion. The often applied criterion of *simple* SATB music with a few notational compromises is completely unacceptable.

Children are capable of singing difficult and complicated music if ranges are compatible with voices available. For years the youngsters have suffered through expediency. Father's old suits may be cut down for junior, but the result though functional is still sartorially offensive; similarly, adult music altered a little here and there, while perhaps singable, is musically unpalatable.

Vocal Range Criterion

The first criterion, therefore, is that of vocal range. Junior high singing materials should have vocal ranges within the respective range limits defined earlier. This criterion, however, needs further qualification with respect to tessitura; no matter how conscientious the music teacher might be in observing total range limits, unless tessitura limits are also applied serious problems could still arise. For a cambiata voice, constant excursions above the tessitura while singing an alto part (SAB) could result in the traditional and embarrassing *break*. Boys may withdraw from class to avoid such experiences in the future.

Overindulgence in extra tessitura excursions for soprano voices results in loss of pitch and a straining quality for the voice. On the other hand, such voices are capable of exceeding the upper limit of the total range on rare occasions when the song, building up in exhilaration, reaches a peak of declamation on high G. As soon as this is accomplished, however, the melody line should return for rehabilitation within the tessitura.

Little published music is available which challenges the upper register of the baritone. A problem in applying baritone range criterion occurs in discovering music which remains within the lower limit of either the total range or tessitura. Baritones in Grades 7 and 8 are so new to the lower register that it sometimes requires considerable concentration for the boys to realize accurately the lower pitches. Constant vocal activity in the lower register, or vicarious excursions below the lower limit, results in an indiscriminate assortment of indeterminate pitches through which the actual sound of the printed notes never materializes in performance.

The range criteria under discussion apply to singing activity in the general music class, or to the selection of music for a junior high school representative choral group which allows boys with changing voices to participate. The latter practice is commendable because it opens the door for boys who desire to belong to a *peer* group in Grade 7 and to continue in choral development throughout junior high school.

GRADE 9 CHORUS TOO RESTRICTIVE

In some junior high schools with large enrollments, it is possible to organize a Grade 9 school chorus on the basis of SATB grouping. This is not an uncommon practice when the choral teacher wishes to realize an adult sound from the group. Membership in such a group is highly restrictive due to the limited supply of immature basses and true tenors; consequently, to maintain a respectable balance the number of girls selected is relatively small. This school choral group is not really representative, and, however gifted the teacher might be, the adult sound is not forthcoming because none of the voices is sufficiently mature. The alto voices are so immature that the prime qualification for membership in the alto part becomes competent reading, not vocal range or quality. At other times the voices of potential sopranos can be adversely affected if they are drafted for alto parts.

There appears little hope that drafting will be abandoned in the near future. The junior high music teacher is usually energetic, constantly working for higher achievement with his group; until something better can be realized with the singing of Grade 7 and Grade 8 youngsters, his obvious goal lies in a compromise with adult music.

Interesting Parts for All Singers

The second criterion to be observed in the selection of appropriate music for use in junior high school choral activity concerns the lines of individual vocal parts. Boys and girls in Grades 7, 8, and 9 all want to sing a melody line; in fact, when a supporting part becomes dull cambiate or baritones may stray from their own part and associate themselves with the principal melody. To avoid this, it is wise to select music written in a quasi-contrapuntal style. Each part while contributing to the over-all sonority should have something quite individual to say, and phrases should move with some purpose to their own logical cadence points. Sequential-type patterns, either melodic or rhythmic, are most effective. Girls are easier to satisfy on this count than boys who, although possibly subscribing to the team effort, are not prepared to subjugate their strong voices all the time to let a group of girls *show off* on a good tune. The baritone part requires some well-defined intervallic and rhythmic purpose since boys in this part, until they have gained some experience, are the worst offenders of associating their voices with someone else's tune. When this occurs it should be checked at once; if it is tolerated for a lesson, the error becomes permanent and is perpetuated in all further performances of that song. No amount of later corrective work seems to eliminate the error. Sometimes it will appear to have been eradicated, only to materialize again under the stress of a public performance.

Intervallic Progression

Another aspect of part content to be considered in defining criteria for selecting appropriate singing materials is the intervallic progressions contained in any part. Melodic diatonic intervals of the 2nd, 3rd, 4th, 5th, or minor 6th are comfortable to articulate, but a leap of a major 6th is not comfortable unless the music is moving fairly slowly. The leap of a minor 7th falls in the same category, but here a resolution back within the interval is necessary following the leap.

The leap of a major 7th is rarely encountered in any printed vocal music. However, it is sometimes accomplished in two consecutive leaps,

in which case the second leap should be treated in the same fashion as the minor 7th illustrated above. An octave leap is very strong and effective, and quite singable, but the notes preceding and succeeding the leap should lie within the confines of the leap.

Leaps of augmented intervals are almost impossible for junior high singers to articulate, as is the diminished 4th, but the diminished 5th is very effective if resolved immediately.

Consideration of this in selecting music will obviate many potential troubles.

Articulation Speed

The third criterion to apply in selecting appropriate vocal materials for use in junior high schools concerns articulation speeds of young voices. Soprano voices are quite flexible and capable of singing florid passages with ease, and the music teacher need not be concerned with first and second soprano parts. Once the boys' voices move into the first change, however, articulation speed is appreciably slower; consequently, the teacher is advised to ensure that whatever part will be visualized for cambiata moves at a reasonably slow tempo. After the second change in boys' voices, articulation speed is even slower in baritone than in cambiata. Attempts to sing quickly moving passages result in a wandering fog of approximate sound; clean articulation is impossible.

Appropriateness of Words

A fourth criterion applies to text. First, the words should be interesting to junior high school students. Such bright little songs as "A Froggie Would A-Wooing Go" and "Here We Go Round the Mulberry Bush" are an insult to junior high intelligence. Love songs are in order providing the words are not so sentimental that boys become embarrassed. Songs expressing noble or heroic sentiment are excellent, as are narrative songs, songs of achievement, and patriotic songs. Spirituals, religious music, and songs of the early pioneering days are favorites with these youngsters, and the occasional humorous (not silly) song does much to lighten a singing period.

Care should be taken to avoid selecting music in which high notes are to be sung on the difficult vowel sounds, *ee* and *oo;* the former will tend to sharpen and the latter will tend to flatten.

Musical Integrity of the Composition

The fifth and last criterion relates to the musical worth of the items to be selected. No matter what category or style is being favored, the quality of the music should expose the children to fine choral literature. Folk songs are always in order, and some carefully selected melodies from Broadway musical productions add a touch of variety to the program.

Availability of Suitable Music

Choral music which will conform to all the aforementioned criteria is not available in great quantity at this time. A partial list will be found in Appendix A. There is need for a body of new choral literature to be written and published for use in junior high school, geared to the limits and capabilities of voices passing through the changes experienced in early adolescence. The outlook is not bleak, however, because writers and publishers are becoming aware of these needs. Music publishers must rely on the expressed needs of music educators in selecting manuscripts for publication, and as junior high school teachers learn to understand the nature and function of the voices with which they work, their demands for appropriate vocal music will be met. Sheet music and books commensurate with the needs of young choristers will be forthcoming eventually.

CHAPTER THREE

VOICE CLASSIFICATION

Correct classification of voices is the key to enjoyable singing experiences in junior high school classes or representative choral performing groups. This is equally important in the general music class
or in the school chorus.

The first music lesson in Grade 7 often begins by the teacher's
learning what songs had been sung in Grade 6, selecting one or two
which appear to be known to the entire class and spending the remainder of the lesson with a review. This is a fairly common practice.
It results, however, in musical chaos. During the summer vacation
between Grade 6 and Grade 7 voices change a great deal; consequently
the boys are seldom able to sing Grade 6 songs. They are as surprised
as the music teacher and flounder helplessly in an attempt to realize
a once familiar melody. Actually the melody is still familiar aurally, but
changing voices cannot cope with notes in the upper soprano vocal
register.

A music teacher who is unaware of the characteristics of boys'
changing voices, and dismayed by the performance, may be led to
the erroneous conclusion that his class contains a large number of
monotones or nonsingers. Young teachers, particularly, are surprised
when careful plans for singing appear to be useless in the light of
the first lesson. On the other hand, this first lesson can be filled with
pleasurable vocal experiences for both class and teacher if the voices
are classified and the students learn a simple three- or four-part song.
The realization of three- or four-part harmony in the first lesson is a

pleasant surprise to students; it is a new and quickly realized way of making music.

Classifying voices individually is *not* a recommended practice. There are several drawbacks to this procedure, the primary one being that cambiata voices are elusive to detect unless contrasted with baritones at octave pitch. The subject of classifying voices became critical in the early phases of research and experimentation with changing voices in one large city where the music supervisor did not have time for an annual voice classification for each student. To meet this situation various group methods for voice classification were tested. One system was gratifyingly reliable, and during ensuing years this method of voice classification became standard procedure at the beginning of each semester. This method is outlined below.

Steps in the Voice Classification Process

STEP I

Talk to the class about the different kinds of singing voices found in junior high school: girls' soprano, boys' soprano, boys' in the first change, boys' in the second change, and boys' changed voices. Illustrate by diagrams on the chalk board. If you have evidence that these children have been exposed intelligently to the *staff* and *clefs* in previous grades, the above might be superimposed on a combined bass and treble staff system. However, do not waste time and risk inattention by drawing staff lines if they are not already on the board. Discuss very briefly the vocal stages through which the boys may expect to pass before they reach adulthood.

Referring again to the chalk board, draw an imaginary melody line through the range designation already there, add to this a second line, parallel to the first but an octave lower, to illustrate why they are unable now to sing even simple songs with the girls. Draw the obvious conclusion that a new kind of music must be used, music which will suit all their voices no matter where they are in the change.

Explain to them that you are going to use music appropriate to their voices, but that first you have to know what kind of voice each of them has to place them in groups for part singing.

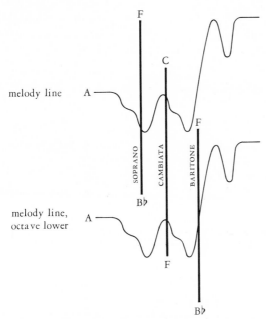

Way down up-on the Swa-nee Riv-er . . . (key of F major)

MELODY-LINE GRAPH OF "OLD FOLKS AT HOME"

Stimulate their interest and expectations, perhaps by mentioning how essential boys are in choral work.

Now, classify the students as baritones, sopranos, and cambiate.

STEP 2

Upon entering the classroom or music room for the first lesson, boys and girls usually take seating positions indiscriminately. Request all girls in the first three, four, or five rows (according to the numerical size of the group) to stand and move to the rear of the room. The vacant places should then be filled by boys from rows six, seven, eight, etc., after which the girls who have been standing at the rear will move into places vacated by the boys.

STEP 3

Tell the boys, all of whom are in the front of the room, that you are first going to listen for baritones only and that they should sing the chorus of "Jingle Bells" in whatever kind of voice feels comfortable. Tell the boys also that you will move among them and that any boy you tap on the shoulder is a baritone and should stop singing when tapped.

Pitch the key of D major, give the starting note F♯, beat one measure of silence to establish a desirable tempo, then lead them in. Immediately it will become obvious that the boys are singing in octave unison.

Determine which boys are *definitely* singing in the lower octave, tapping on the shoulder each boy who will be a baritone. Any voice about which you are uncertain leave alone for further checking later. For instance, you will find one or two voices wandering with no semblance of the melody anywhere. The reason is that sometimes a boy's voice enters the first change during Grade 6, from which time on he can no longer sing unison songs with the rest of his classmates.

Not willing to have a silent observer in the singing lesson, a teacher may encourage the boy with the changing voice to sing anyway. He does this, but usually about a fourth below the others in quasi organum manner. Boys passing through the first phase of the voice change and exposed to this kind of participation for any length of time adjust aurally to the situation and develop skill for singing a fourth lower than the rest of the class.

Boys who have experienced the first phase of voice change in Grade 6 seem to transfer the quasi organum style of singing into junior high school and are generally labelled *nonsingers* because of their inability to match pitches with girls in a unison song.

These are the boys who will be *wandering* in the classification procedure under discussion. Eventually they will become oriented in the cambiata part where the music is too low to pitch a fourth lower. They should not at this stage be considered as baritones. Later in this chapter suggestions will be offered concerning remedial work on these voices.

As the boys sing, one by one, voices obviously singing in the lower octave will be silenced until, very shortly, none of these will be left. It is unwise to spend time on any voice of which you are uncertain. If an error is made at this time it will show up very clearly later in the lesson when a four-part song is taught. Do not mistake richness of quality for depth. When the elimination of the lower voices is complete, instruct all boys who have been *tapped* to stand and move to the rear of the room, explaining at this time that the situation is quite temporary and that they will be regrouped in a few minutes. You will probably find that by this time the boys are more than mildly interested and they follow the ensuing developments closely.

Step 4

The boys still remaining in front are either sopranos or boys whose voices are passing through the first phase of change (cambiate).

Explain this briefly to the boys, and tell them the next step is to locate voices which have not yet started to change, namely sopranos. The reason for selecting sopranos as the next target area is that the sound of these voices is more familiar to the teacher's ear than is the sound of cambiate and will therefore be recognized more easily.

Tell the boys now remaining in front that they will sing the chorus of "Jingle Bells" again, but this time you will give them a different starting note (C in the key of A♭). You will tap all boys who are singing soprano, and each boy when tapped is to stop singing. Stress the fact that they are to sing where it is most comfortable, in a high or low voice.

Pitch the key of A♭ major, give the starting note C, beat one measure of silence to establish a desirable tempo, then lead them in. As was the case in the first phase of classification it will become obvious the boys are singing in octave unison:

Repeat the procedure employed in diagnosing baritones, only this time tap all obvious sopranos. Do not waste time trying to diagnose *wanderers;* tap only those who are without doubt sopranos.

Very soon all sopranos will be silent, and the rest will for the time being be classified as cambiate who have been discovered by a simple process of elimination.

You may be surprised and disturbed at this point to discover very few, if any, sopranos, despite the fact that you were reasonably sure the group contained boy sopranos. Sometimes boys prefer anonymity and shy away from anything that might make them conspicuous. This subtle threat evaporates later when the class starts to sing as a whole, and the true soprano sound comes through an octave higher than cambiata, necessitating a transfer to the boy soprano section.

Complete this phase of the classification procedure by instructing all boys who have been tapped as sopranos to move out of their desks or chairs and take a temporary standing position at the front of the room. There is no need for concern about sufficient space in this move, as a maximum of three or four sopranos will usually be involved. You have now identified baritones and boy sopranos; the boys still seated are cambiate who have been identified by a simple process of elimination. The awkward and frustrating problem of listening to potential cambiata voices in an effort to determine the nature of their classification has been circumvented.

Earlier experimentation with boys' voices showed that in individual testing the elusive quality of the first change precluded reliable classification. The procedure just outlined seems to be the most reliable, the simplest, and the one which may be accomplished in the least time. The entire classification sequence just defined *must not occupy more than five minutes* or you have *lost* the class. With the school chorus, where a greater number of students is involved, it will require a proportionately longer period of time. If, however, voice classification is accomplished in the various classes, boys will know to which part they have been allocated before the first chorus meeting.

STEP 5

At this moment the distribution of the class is as follows: girls seated in the rear half of the seats, cambiate occupying a number of seats in the front half of the room, baritones standing at the rear of the room, boy sopranos standing at the front of the room.

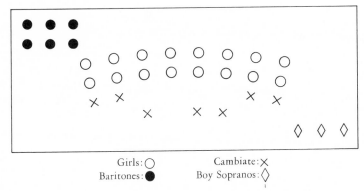

Girls: ○   Cambiate: ✕

Baritones: ●   Boy Sopranos: ◇

Using the chalk board draw the following diagram to illustrate how you want the class to regroup. The seating plan illustrated herewith may need some slight modification according to the distribution of voices you have discovered.

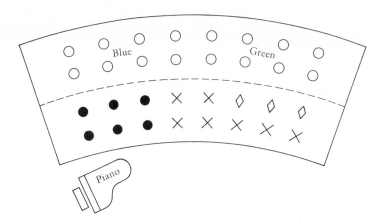

First move cambiate to their new location, then baritones, and finally boy sopranos. Explain to boy sopranos that they are located in this position so that there can be an easy transfer when a voice enters the first change.

Two considerations must be kept in mind. (1) It is unlikely that this initial classification is completely accurate because the need to retain class interest places an arbitrary time limit. (2) This disposition of voices will be subject to periodic change as boys' voices move from soprano to cambiata, cambiata to baritone. As the group continues singing and boys relax, misclassifications become obvious.

In order not to perpetuate a classification error, and also to validate the vocal ranges prescribed on page 15, baritone boys should be asked to sing "John Brown's Body," using the key of D♭. This will exploit the higher vocal register and immediately destroy the theory that junior high school baritones cannot sing above middle C. Pitch the key of D♭ major, beat one measure of silence to establish tempo, then lead them in.

John Brown's bo - dy   lies   a   mould - 'ring in   the   grave,

The degree of success which may be anticipated in this is in direct ratio to the amount of stimulation developed by the teacher. A languid beat will realize minimum response, whereas an enthusiastic beat will realize the full vocal range. In any kind of vocal music performance junior high school youngsters will reflect the attitude of the director.

It may be that the initial effort appears to fall short of your expectation. If so, transpose the song downwards a major second and try again. Owing to a long layoff during the summer vacation, singing voices have not been used, and a week or two of conditioning may be required before the complete vocal range is realized.

Now quickly check the cambiate. Using the same song, this time pitch the key of A♭ major, beat one measure of silence to establish tempo, then lead them in.

John Brown's bo - dy   lies   a   mould - 'ring in   the   grave,

Almost immediately it will be noted that most of the previously discovered "out-of-tuners" are no longer out of tune. The tessitura of the melody being coincident with cambiata tessitura is responsible for this favorable change. While one or two out-of-tuners may not yet have merged with the rest of the group, this is not the time to initiate remedial measures. More will be said of this matter later in the chapter.

STEP 6

The final step is not absolutely necessary, but it contributes to a happy class. As yet the girls have been silent, an unnatural state at any time, so to bring them into the orbit, ask them to sing with the boy sopranos using "John Brown's Body" key of D♭. Usually there are so few boy sopranos that they are most reluctant to sing alone, but with girls joining in, the boys feel less conspicuous and often try to show off by outsinging the girls.

Pitch the key of D♭ major, beat one measure of silence to establish tempo, then lead in sopranos, girls and boys. It will be found that girls need just as much stimulation as boys, unless there is a strong, experienced singer in the group who acts as a leader. It is quite possible some girl out-of-tuners may be discovered. They will be subject to remedial work later. This recheck procedure must be expedited in order to retain interest and preserve concentration.

GIRLS' VOICES

What about girls' voices? How does one classify sopranos and contraltos? Most girls' voices fall within the range,

and there are very few true altos in junior high school grades. Because of this girls should be moved arbitrarily into two equal groups. In the case of the school chorus they should be balanced in such a manner that an equal number of Grade 7, 8, and 9 students are allocated to each group, ensuring a balance of vocal maturity between the two groups. What designation is to be given to identify each group? To these girls the term "second soprano" appears to imply inferiority, so a safe and simple solution which satisfies the girls is to refer to them as the *Blue* girls or the *Green* girls. In singing activities which involve three parts, soprano, cambiata, baritone, all girls will obviously sing soprano, but in four-part singing where the girls must sing in two parts the duties of singing first and second parts might be alternated song by song between *Blues* and *Greens*. Two benefits accrue from this practice: all the girls exploit the total range of their voices during every singing lesson, and they all have equal opportunity to sing and enjoy melody lines. Every girl has the opportunity to develop naturally into whatever category is appropriate to her vocal maturity. No girl is forced into a part incommensurate with her natural vocal range. Consistent use of SATB music, where the alto tessitura is low, can ruin young girls' voices.

The method defined above for allocating parts with respect to girls' voices would be incomplete without some provision for those rare young people who display unmistakable high soprano or alto quality potential. Such voices will not be noticed for a week or two at the beginning of the year, but as time passes and confidence rises, these girls will start to sing out and will quickly be recognized. The accompanying seating diagram will illustrate how these voices may be placed in order that they may sing at all times the part appropriate to their needs.

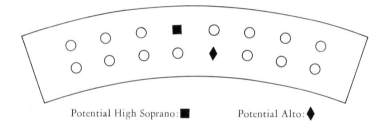

Potential High Soprano: ■   Potential Alto: ◆

As a result of this placement, potential high sopranos can sing the top choral line in every song, alternately singing with *Blues* or *Greens;* similarly, potential altos are able to sing the second choral part in every song.

A composite seating plan, therefore, for a classroom or school choral group is shown on page 39. The piano is so placed to give baritones maximum support from piano bass notes.

The First Song

The voice classification and regrouping processes should not occupy more than fifteen minutes of the first lesson; sufficient time

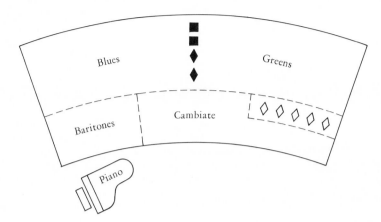

should be left to teach a song. This is most important for the future success of the class, although you may find that *difficult* voices remain to be checked, and remedial work must be undertaken.

Neither is unison nor two-part singing likely to be successful, because even in a two-part song (girls and boys), the unison problem (previously described) arises for either a soprano, cambiata-baritone distribution, or soprano-cambiata, baritone distribution.

The ideal choice for the first song, which must be taught by rote, is one which contains four easy-to-sing parts, each of which consists of a simple melodic line with something interesting to say. Preferably each vocal part of this first song should contain a short musical figure reiterated in simple sequence.

The song which has proved easiest to teach in clinics given by the writer is a four-part arrangement of "Santa Lucia."[1]

Music for "Santa Lucia" is presented herewith.

At this stage it must be assumed that most of the youngsters do not read printed music. A few may have taken private piano lessons or studied some other instrument, but this experience differs from reading a melody line and producing it vocally. Many fine instrumental readers have difficulty reading vocal music.

Each of the supporting parts of the music is so contrived that it presents simple sequential patterns which are easily learned by the singers. It can be taught by a combined rote-diagram method and the following teaching routine.

[1] Irvin Cooper, "Santa Lucia" from a collection *Teen-Age Songs* (Niagara Falls, N.Y.: Gordon V. Thompson, Inc., 1944).

Santa Lucia

Neapolitan Folk Song
Arr. by Irvin Cooper

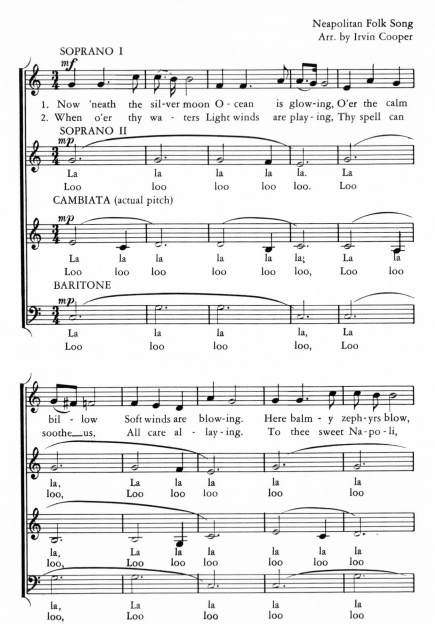

SOPRANO I

1. Now 'neath the sil-ver moon O - cean is glow-ing, O'er the calm
2. When o'er thy wa - ters Light winds are play-ing, Thy spell can

SOPRANO II

La   la   la   la   la.   La
Loo   loo   loo   loo   loo.   Loo

CAMBIATA (actual pitch)

La   la   la   la   la   la;   La   la
Loo   loo   loo   loo   loo   loo,   Loo   loo

BARITONE

La   la   la   la,   La
Loo   loo   loo   loo,   Loo

bil - low   Soft winds are   blow-ing.   Here balm - y zeph-yrs blow,
soothe_us,   All care al - lay-ing.   To thee sweet Na-po-li,

la,   La   la   la   la   la
loo,   Loo   loo   loo   loo   loo

la,   La   la   la   la   la   la
loo,   Loo   loo   loo   loo   loo   loo

la,   La   la   la   la
loo,   Loo   loo   loo   loo

From *Teen-Age Songs.* Copyright U.S.A., 1942, Gordon V. Thompson Ltd., Toronto, Canada. International Copyright. Used by permission of Gordon V. Thompson, Inc.

Santa__ Lu - ci - a! San - ta Lu - ci - a! Home of fair poe - sy,

La la la la, La la
Loo loo loo loo, Loo loo

La la la la la la, La la la
Loo loo loo loo loo loo, Loo loo loo

La la la la, La la
Loo loo loo loo, Loo loo

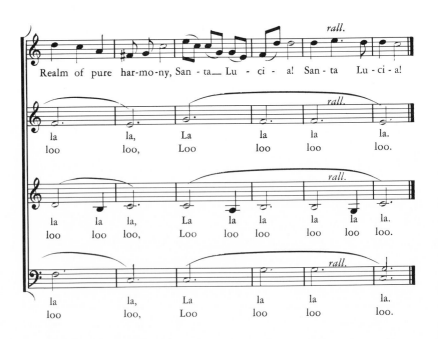

Realm of pure har-mo-ny, San - ta__ Lu - ci - a! San - ta Lu - ci - a!

la la, La la la la.
loo loo, Loo loo loo loo.

la la la, La la la la la la.
loo loo loo, Loo loo loo loo loo loo.

la la, La la la la.
loo loo, Loo loo loo loo.

Inasmuch as boys tend to follow a song melody-line, even wandering from their own part to do so, teaching the melody line contained in singing part one might be deferred until the last step. By the time this stage is reached, the boys hopefully will be so entrenched in their own part that nothing will shake them loose.

In most cases it is best to teach baritones first, but in this first song, best results are obtained by teaching the parts in this order: cambiata, second soprano, baritone, and first soprano. Explain this to the class so that the boys and girls know what is about to take place. Write the following cambiata pattern on the chalk board.

Pattern 1 (sing four times)

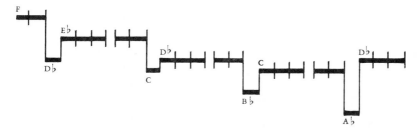

GRAPH FOR CAMBIATA LINE

The melodic line gives the cambiate a picture of what their voices will do. If you find that the class is familiar with music *syllables,* you could use them here. This practice has been successful in such situations. The cambiata pattern would then appear as follows:

Play the chord of Db major on the piano and, beginning on F, sing the cambiata line, vocalizing on a neutral syllable such as *loo* or *lah,* pointing to the pattern on the board as you progress. Pitch syllables can be used rather than the neutral syllables. Male teachers *must* sing this pattern at concert pitch; otherwise, cambiate will try to come down an octave, with disastrous results. After this pattern has been sung twice you will find the boys are secure, except for the occasional tendency to sing only the first two figures of the pattern, repeating them over and over, instead of proceeding through all four figures. These temporary out-of-tuners will be helped later.

When the cambiate know their part, turn your attention to that section of the girls' group designated as *Green*. Using a technique similar to that used for teaching the cambiata part, draw the following patterns on the chalk board. This will represent the second soprano part.

Pattern 1 (sing four times)

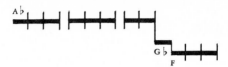

Pattern 2 (sing four times)

GRAPHS FOR SECOND SOPRANO LINE

or if you prefer to use syllables:

s — — | s — — | s — f | m — — ‖

s — — | f — — | f — — | m — — ‖

Play the chord of D♭ major on the piano and using *loo* or *lah* (or music syllables), sing Pattern 1 only, then teach it to the girls in the *Green* section. They will need more stimulating than did the cambiate. When Pattern 1 is reasonably secure proceed to Pattern 2 and teach it. Tell the girls the song will be complete for them when they have sung Pattern 1 four times, followed by Pattern 2 sung four times.

The moment the *Green* girls know their part, combine them with the cambiate, not only for practice but also as a device for keeping the boys as busy as possible.

Next teach baritones their part, using the same technique as before.

Pattern 1 (sing four times)

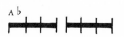

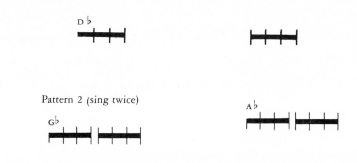

Pattern 2 (sing twice)

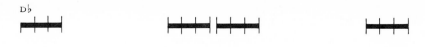

GRAPHS FOR BARITONE LINE

Or if your prefer to use syllables:

$$\begin{array}{c|c|c|c} d \;-\;- & \overset{s}{} \;-\;- & \overset{s}{} \;-\;- & d \;-\;- \end{array}\Big\|$$

$$\begin{array}{c|c|c|c|c|c|c} d\,-\,- & f\,-\,- & f\,-\,- & d\,-\,- & d\,-\,- & \overset{s\,-\,-}{}\;\overset{s\,-\,-}{} & d\,-\,- \end{array}\Big\|$$

Explain to the baritones that singing Pattern 1 four times and Pattern 2 twice will be the complete baritone part for the entire song. Play the chord of D♭ major and sing Pattern 1, pointing to the figures on the board as you sing. Follow this immediately by asking baritones to sing Pattern 1. Do not teach Pattern 2 until Pattern 1 is well in hand.

The use of hand signs (see Chapter Four) for music syllables is most effective here. Hand signs not only save your voice, they also impart a strong visual stimulus. An occasional out-of-tune singer may appear among the baritones, but do not apply remedial measures at this time. The objective of this part of the first lesson is to teach a four-part song in quick order so that the youngsters will have an exciting choral experience.

When baritones are reasonably sure of both patterns, combine them with *Green* girls and cambiate, but make certain all parts have their own starting notes. During this performance the group may start to realize their potential as a choral group.

Only the song melody remains to be taught, and of course the girls in the *Blue* section will sing it. Many of the girls will have sung this song in elementary school, and they will remember it if you play or sing it once. The melody is in simple two-section (binary) form, and it is wise to teach each section separately, using *loo* or *lah*. Chalk board diagrams are not necessary for the melody as it is fairly easy to teach by rote.

When the *Blue* girls are certain of their melody, combine all parts, being careful to assure each part of its own starting note. The youngsters will be more than delighted with their achievement. Although the tone is rough and far removed from a smooth, adult sound, here is the nucleus of a choral group which is likely to have many pleasurable hours of good choral singing ahead.

The first song should be taught in approximately twenty to twenty-five minutes, or customary junior high restlessness will set in.

For a couple of minutes talk to the class or group concerning what they have accomplished, express pleasure and satisfaction, and tell them finally that to prove it was not a temporary success, they are going to sing the song again. Do not give any starting notes. Beat one measure of silence to establish a suitable tempo, then lead them in. You will be surprised and pleased to find they hit the key of Db major, and the cambiate, heretofore frequently rejected as nonsingers, are first to attack. Note also that the group never loses pitch, a phenomenon which will occur regularly in groups constituted on the basis of soprano, cambiata, and baritone. There appears to be no explanation for this phenomenon.

Vocal classification and the teaching of the first song should be accomplished as expeditiously as possible; the objective of the first lesson is for the class to realize a four-part choral achievement.

If feasible it is of considerable advantage to you if voice classification can be accomplished in all your general music classes prior to your first meeting with the school elective chorus. Thus most of the chorus will be classified before its first full meeting. If enrollment in the school chorus is still open after all your separate classes have experienced their first successful lesson, registration will increase substantially.

Observations Arising Out of the First Lesson

Contrary to popular opinion, the boy's voice does not *break*. This thought may not occur to you at all during the business of the lesson, but when the school day is over you might want to consider it.

The theory that boys' voices break during maturation stems from a traditional practice of church musicians who, reluctant to lose experienced boy sopranos, held on to them tenaciously until the voice, unable to withstand the abuse any longer, rebelled and *cracked* on the high notes. This does not occur in the system of classification recently presented. Neither will it happen if, following this procedure, boys are given music to sing commensurate with their natural vocal ranges, as enumerated on page 15.

Sometimes one or more boys presently classified as cambiate are in reality sopranos who, in a desire to be "adult," have associated themselves with cambiate during the classification. These boys are easily discovered because they can only *grumble* when the cambiata part moves into the low register. Schedule a brief meeting with these boys and ask them to sing "America." Pitch this in the key of Ab, and within a couple of minutes you will know whether they are sopranos or cambiate. If they are sopranos they will not be able to sing in the low cambiata range, and true soprano quality will be heard.

A parallel situation sometimes develops in the baritone part to which cambiate may stray. To correct this follow the same procedure used on the suspected soprano, but this time use the key of D and include in the group one or two boys who you know for certain are baritones. It is only in comparison with known baritones that cambiate can be diagnosed; otherwise the octave hearing illusion has to be reckoned with. As a double check, ask the boys to sing a couple of lines of "Old Folks at Home," not the refrain, using the key of G, starting note B below middle C. This time the baritones will eliminate themselves because in this key the melody is out of range, whereas cambiate will negotiate the music with ease.

Another observation to consider is that the *sound* or the quality of the group is unique. Sonorities produced by these children bear no resemblance to those of elementary school children, senior high school, or adult choral groups. At first it is a rough sound, with the lusty cambiate sometimes overpowering the others, and it could be offensive to the supersensitive musical ear. This situation, however, is temporary, and during the course of a semester a beautiful choral sound can be developed without too much effort. The ways and means of achieving this will be presented in Chapter Six dealing with choral techniques.

Delay tone building until the class or chorus has learned several part songs and become conscious of its choral potential. An introduction to tone concepts at too early a stage may result in a loss of interest. First teach several songs. Then by means of fine choral recordings, such as "Deep River and Other Spirituals,"[1] "The Lord Is My Shepherd,"[2] draw attention to the beauty of the *sound* or the quality produced by these choirs, and thereby establish a standard of achievement which you wish to emulate with your own group, be it a classroom or school choir.

Probably the most disquieting observation will be that some boys, particularly baritones, do not focus well on a tone and have difficulty in matching pitch variations. These boys must not arbitrarily be called nonsingers, or tone deaf; through patient remedial work they can be brought into focus and perhaps become your better singers. Some remedies have proved successful in the past. Remedial work is best accomplished in a strictly individual situation, as boys tend to withdraw in the presence of other students.

Remedial Measures for Out-of-Tune Singers

Schedule a series of daily appointments with each boy needing help, each appointment lasting about ten minutes. This might occur

[1] Shaw, Robert, "Deep River and Other Spirituals" (R.C.A. Victor Co., New York).

[2] Mormon Tabernacle Choir, "The Lord Is My Shepherd" (Columbia Records, New York).

before school commences in the morning, during recess, lunch breaks, or after school. During the meetings the boy should not be made to feel that something is wrong with him but that he is worthy of your special help in meeting his group responsibilities. A canceled appointment can prove quite a set-back to his development.

First the boy must be shown that only through lack of use have his vocal cords ceased to function properly. The condition of his voice would be similar to that of the muscles in his pitching arm after a winter away from baseball, and the best cure is exercise. The cure is not haphazard, it must be planned, and progress records of every boy should be maintained. It is within the power of the teacher to guide these boys to new and interesting experiences in choral music.

Now to get the boy singing, ask him to sing "good morning,"

It is essential that exact pitches be used consistently as designated above in order to place the voice in its most comfortable register. A casual pitch guess is not recommended. The boy's first response will indicate to you immediately whether the remedy will be accomplished quickly or will take time. No matter what happens do not appear disturbed, but at all times display kind concern and optimism.

Should the boy not reach the desired upper register, tell him to cup both hands together about waist high, pretend the sounds you want are in the palms, and with the leap to the second note of the pattern lift both hands smartly to the forehead. Stand in front of the boy and go through the same motion yourself, providing a strong stimulus. In many instances you will find the boy overshoots the second note, but this is good. The voice has shown upward movement. It is surprising and interesting to note that abrupt physical motion evokes a parallel pitch response.

In the event the desired response is not forthcoming quickly, do not labor the process by constant futile repetition; try something else. It is necessary to shake the voice loose from its narrow range; when this has occurred once, the battle is half won.

Take your subject into your confidence, tell him what it is you want from him and why. Suggest that he is in the school playground and that his friend Tommy has stolen his lunch bag and is rapidly disappearing from sight. Ask him to call out "Tommy!" urge him on, "he'll never hear you; louder! He still won't hear you; higher! Higher!" The moment a breakthrough has been detected pin him down at once to the "good morning" pattern. You don't need to worry about his voice; he abuses it much more while making himself heard above the crowd in the school yard, on the street, or even at home when he yells, "Hey, Mom, is supper ready?"

Another technique which has been successful in resolving the focussing problem is the teacher's exerting firm pressure with the palm of his hand on the subject's diaphragm. Have the boy sing the "good morning" pattern and, simultaneously with articulation of the upper tone, press in with some vigor, holding the pressure for a few seconds to encourage sustaining the tone.

The final resort is the *siren* technique. Tell the boy to start as low as he is able and imitate a police car siren, going as high as he can. Urge him on during the process. Here again, the moment a significant range movement is detected, transfer to the "good morning" pattern.

Few boys fail to react to one or more of the preceding stimuli. This does not imply there are no monotones, but they are rare and should not be so diagnosed until all known devices to prove otherwise have been tried without success.

Although the remedial measures have succeeded, the cure is rarely permanent immediately following the first treatment. The next meeting with the patient will probably reveal that his voice has reverted to its original state. This is a time for patience. Repeat the procedure you followed in the first remedial session. The level of achievement reached at the conclusion of the first session will be reached earlier this time, and it will be possible to move ahead.

Your subject will probably be at least familiar by ear with the chorus of "Jingle Bells," both words and tune. Ask him to sing the "good morning" pattern in the key commensurate with his vocal classification three times, then break quickly into "Jingle Bells" for four measures only. Without pause repeat from the beginning of the "good morning" pattern.

BARITONE

Good   morn - ing, good morn - ing.

BARITONE

Jin - gle bells, jin - gle bells, jin - gle all   the   way,

CAMBIATA

Good   morn - ing, good morn - ing.

CAMBIATA

Jin - gle bells,   jin - gle bells,   jin - gle all   the   way,

Continue this procedure for a few minutes, then let your subject sing through to the end of the chorus. The reason governing the choice of "Jingle Bells" for this drill is fairly obvious; the melody of the chorus is contained within the interval of a perfect fifth, and inasmuch as the upper and lower limits of the "good morning" pattern contain a perfect fifth, the transfer from the short drill to the melody is relatively easy. This is sufficient for the second personal interview. Persuade the boy to find a secluded area in his home where he can practice for a few minutes each day.

At the third session with your subject he will probably still be tone-bound, and work done in Interviews One and Two must be reviewed. However, the improvement reached during those first interviews should reassure you that it is now only a question of time, concern, and patience on your part until you will free the boy from his vocal limitations.

During a review of previous work the boy's voice will come into focus a little more quickly, and it is time to extend the range by another tone. This can be done by means of another tune most children have learned in elementary school.

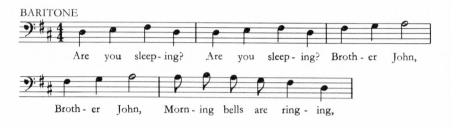

Here again precede the song with the "good morning" pattern. This may be sufficient for the third meeting, but if time permits and the subject appears eager, let him try "Oh! Susanna."

Urge him on to reach the highest note by beating time for him and raising your hands higher for a very strong beat on the higher note.

By this time the boy realizes that he can sing. He knows that he can sing "Jingle Bells," although he is not aware that this performance is confined to one key (D major for baritone or B♭ major for cambiata).

Without informing the boy of any change, pitch the key for "Jingle Bells" one tone higher, and ask him to sing again. You will find he negotiates the song comfortably. Should this obviously be successful, repeat the procedure, moving the key another step higher. Your subject is still quite confident he can sing "Jingle Bells," and he will not realize your objective until you tell him at the close of the procedure. If you ask him to sing it again in the higher key after you have revealed your innocent subterfuge, he will probably not do as well.

The fourth and probably final session with your special subject should begin with a leisurely review of all previous remedial work. Progress will be more rapid if you can orient the voice by chording on the piano while the boy sings.

Up to this point he has been confined to an interval of a major sixth; the objective for Lesson Four will be to extend the working range of the voice to an octave. Reach the octave span with the method used previously and with a tune your subject must have memorized aurally in elementary school, "Row, Row, Row Your Boat."

BARITONE

Row, row, row your boat, gent - ly down the stream,

Mer - ri - ly, mer- ri - ly, mer -

CAMBIATA

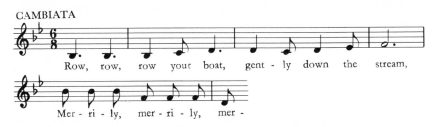

Row, row, row your boat, gent - ly down the stream,

Mer - ri - ly, mer - ri - ly, mer -

First, sing the tune, then play the appropriate tonic chord (D major for baritone, Bb major for cambiata), and lead in, using the "good morning" pattern as an introduction. Occasionally, for support, sing along with the boy.

It is often possible during this interview to add another note to the compass of his voice without letting your subject know what is happening.

Tell him you are first going to destroy the pitch, that you will then give him the pitch again, and this time you want more volume. Go to the piano, strike the keyboard with the palm of your hand several times moving from left to right; be careful not to play a chord as this could insinuate an unwanted tonality into the subject's subconscious ear. Place him with his back to the piano, quickly establish a new key, E major for baritone, Ab major for cambiata, and lead him in with the most recent song "Row, Row, Row Your Boat."

The subject, unaware that any new factor has been added, and with the confidence born of previous success, will negotiate the exercise without difficulty. Now let him see the piano keyboard and illustrate what he has done.

Impetus is given to any boy's vocal progress during these interviews if one or more boys without pitch problems can be persuaded to participate. Obviously they must be baritones to help a baritone, cambiate to help a cambiata.

Throughout this procedure it is important that you impress upon your subject the fact that he has a fine voice which you need urgently to improve the group sound.

From time to time refresher interviews may be advisable, but what has been prescribed above usually will prepare the boy to be a useful participant in your class or school choral group.

He must be seated in the group so that he is as far removed as possible from parts which he will not sing; he should be placed between boys who have secure pitch. The following disposition is advised.

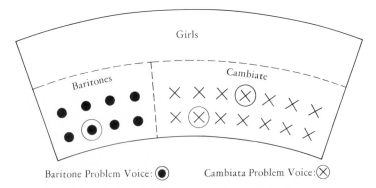

Baritone Problem Voice: ●   Cambiata Problem Voice: ⊗

Girls seldom have pitch focusing difficulties, but if any such become evident, the above procedure is effective, using the same keys applied to baritone voices, an octave higher.

Criteria for Selecting Appropriate Choral Music

Following the four-part choral achievement in the first lesson, suitable choral music which will be interesting to the singers and commensurate with their vocal resources must be found. To ensure this the following criteria for selecting music are proposed.

FIRST CRITERION

The most important criterion to apply is that of vocal range demanded for each part. If the music being considered is written for first soprano, second soprano, cambiata, and baritione there are no range problems. But if the voicing is for soprano, alto, tenor, and bass range, criteria must be applied strictly. Soprano and alto parts must be contained within

with a general tessitura lying between

The tenor part must lie between

printed pitch   actual pitch sung

with a general tessitura of

printed pitch   actual pitch sung

Remember the tenor actually sings an octave lower than the printed note when the G clef is being used.

The bass part must be contained within

and should observe the general tessitura

In melodic passages which build in intensity to a climactic peak, the upper limit of the soprano part may be exceeded for one or two beats without danger, but the part should descend quickly into the tessitura.

Music written for adults presents no problem insofar as the upper limit of boys' voices is concerned; the problem is to find adult music which does not descend below the lower limit, and which does not overuse the lower register of the tessitura.

For unison songs, or unison passages in part-songs, the range criterion will be

SOPRANO-CAMBIATA

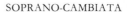

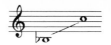

BARITONE

At first glance, the above would appear to eliminate a considerable number of unison songs found in the basic series books, the vocal mainstay of the general music program. Such, however, is not the case, for most unison songs appearing in these books are contained within an interval of a major ninth and are singable by pitching *doh* in such a key that the melodic range will conform to limitations imposed by the composite unison-octave range of junior high voices.

The above range criteria are submitted for the guidance of those who teach general music, to whom every girl and boy in the class is an active singer, or who organize their school chorus on a truly representative basis of students from Grades 7, 8, and 9. These criteria will not be operative for music teachers who direct a choral organization comprised solely of Grade 9 students selected for their ability to cope with the range demands of adult music. One of the drawbacks attendant on such an organization, however, is the one hundred percent personnel turnover each year, another being that cambiate (with the most beautiful tone quality found in junior high school) are rarely admitted. SAB music is *not* the answer. It is an escape from problems of boys' voices in the first change, and the bass part is too often and consistently low. In an organization operating on the SAB plan, any boy other than soprano must sing bass. Admittedly one or two boys who enter the first change with quasi-alto quality sometimes are acceptable in the alto part, but their further maturing makes the quality incompatible with that of alto girls.

Second Criterion

The second criterion to be applied in the selection of appropriate choral music for junior high school singers is that of having interesting supporting parts, particularly for boys. Girls do not seem to object to singing a part subservient to the main tune, even if it lacks interesting movement, but boys quickly lose interest in a monotonous part and frequently escape into the main melody at points within their range or, in the case of baritones, an octave lower.

Boys need parts to sing which move in a well-defined rhythm and line to a natural cadence, as for instance in the arrangement of "Santa Lucia" which was taught during the first lesson.

Third Criterion

A third criterion, and very important, is that of articulation speed of parts written for boys. The cambiata, having a deeper, thicker voice, is unable to articulate pitch changes as quickly as he could before the change set in; consequently parts intended for performance by cambiate should not move around very quickly. Young baritones need even more time in order to think a pitch and then articulate it. The baritone part should move steadily but quite slowly.

Another phase of articulation speed is worth consideration, namely, the nature of the intervallic movement of the parts being examined. Steps of diatonic major or minor thirds, perfect fourths or perfect fifths are easily negotiated. The leap of a major or minor sixth requires a little extra time to focus, whereas any leap of a seventh is disastrous. An octave leap is comparatively simple providing it is approached and quitted within the interval.

This is a particularly strong progression for baritones. Any augmented melodic interval is difficult to sing, and even the diminished fifth rarely works unless it is resolved in the same part.

Fourth Criterion

The final criterion concerns the text, or words to be sung. Do not use childish words. These young people have outgrown the cute little jingles so successful in elementary school; they can understand and interpret adult poetry with surprising sensitivity.

It is difficult at this time to discover choral music in quantity which while adhering to criteria presented above is at the same time commensurate with the choral ability of your group at the beginning of the school year; therefore, a number of suitable songs are presented in the following pages. In all probability the singers cannot read music at this stage, and the songs are arranged so that they can be taught as rote songs.

Do not introduce any unnecessary complexities such as words in starting a new song. Utilize the melodic patterns offered with each song, and let the class sing to *lah* until each part is sufficiently secure to add words.

While learning these songs students should be exposed to the progressive music reading program defined in Chapter Four so that transfer from rote to note will be smooth. If the music reading program is followed consistently for a few minutes each lesson, the singers will have acquired sufficient reading skill by the time rote songs presented here have been learned to make reasonable sense out of the printed page of music.

Invocation

Words and Music by Irvin Cooper

Oh! Susanna

Stephen Collins Foster
Arr. by Irvin Cooper

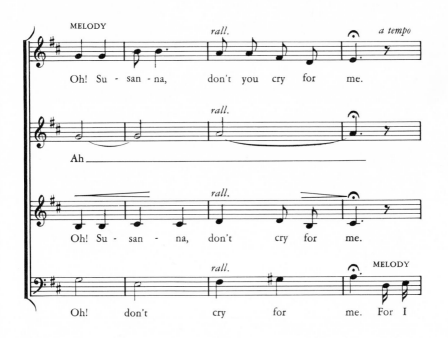

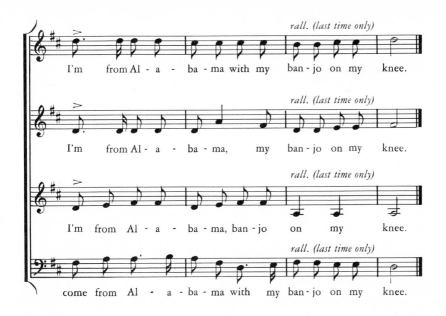

Oh! Susanna

CAMBIATA

Pattern 1. (sing twice)

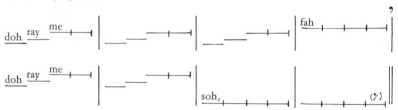

Pattern 2. (sing once)

*Return to
second half
of pattern 1.*

SOPRANO I

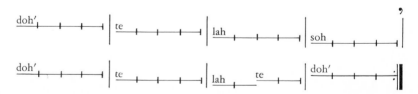

*Continue with
melody, "Oh!
Susanna . ."
then return to
second half of
pattern.*

SOPRANO II

Pattern 1.

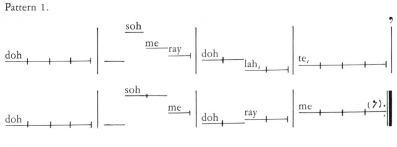

Pattern 2.

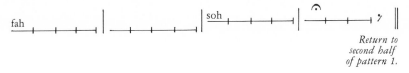

*Return to
second half
of pattern 1.*

BARITONE (middle section)

Polly Wolly Doodle

American Folk Song
Arr. by Irvin Cooper

Not too quickly

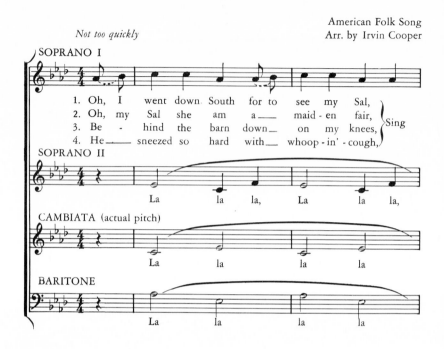

SOPRANO I

1. Oh, I went down South for to see my Sal,
2. Oh, my Sal she am a —— maid-en fair,
3. Be - hind the barn down — on my knees,
4. He —— sneezed so hard with — whoop-in' - cough, } Sing

SOPRANO II

La la la, La la la,

CAMBIATA (actual pitch)

La la la la

BARITONE

La la la la

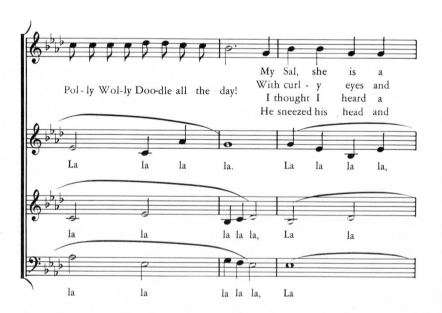

Pol - ly Wol-ly Doo-dle all the day!
My Sal, she is a
With curl - y eyes and
I thought I heard a
He sneezed his head and

La la la la. La la la la,

la la la la la, La la

la la la la la, La

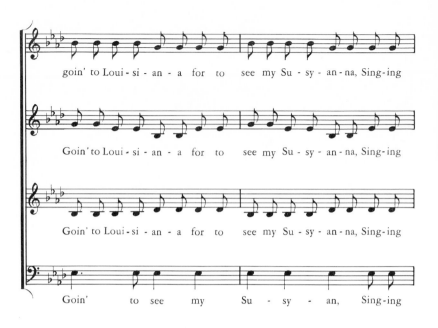

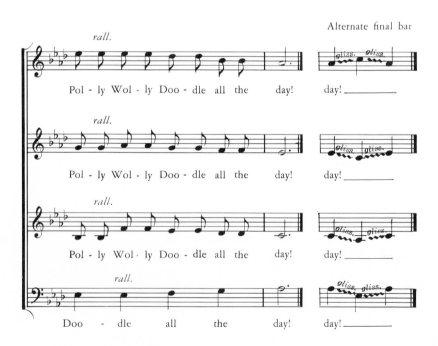

Polly Wolly Doodle

BARITONE

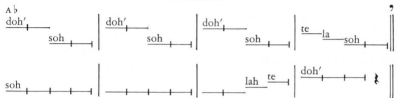

CAMBIATA

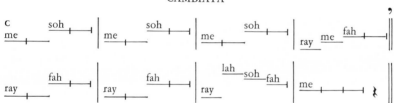

SOPRANO II

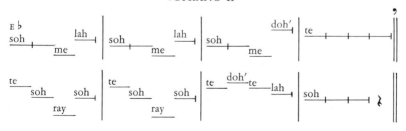

Good-bye, My Lover, Good-bye

American Folk Song
Arr. by Irvin Cooper

bye, my lov-er, good-bye! My heart will ev - er - more be true, Good-
Though far I roam a - cross the sea,

bye, my lov-er, good - bye!___ Good-

bye, my lov-er, good - bye!___ Good-

bye, good - bye!___ Good-

bye, my lov-er, good bye! ___ Though now we sad - ly say a-dieu, Good-
My ev -'ry thought shall be of thee,

bye, my lov-er, good bye! _____ Good-

bye, my lov-er, good-bye, good-bye! Good-

bye, my lov-er, good-bye, good-bye! Good-

Good-bye, My Lover, Good-bye

Pattern 1 will be used for verse responses one and three.
Pattern 2 will be used for verse responses two and four.
Pattern 3 will be used for the refrain only.

BARITONE

Pattern 1.

Pattern 2.

Pattern 3.

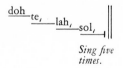

Sing five times.

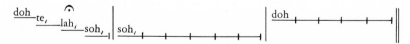

CAMBIATA

Pattern 1.

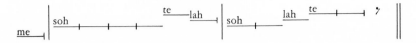

Pattern 2.

Pattern 3.

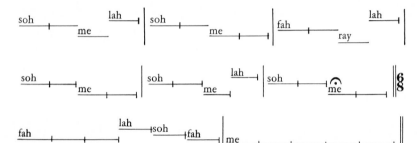

SOPRANO II

Pattern 1.

Pattern 2.

Pattern 3.

Sing melody

Sing twice.

The Old Gray Mare

American Folk Song
Arr. by Irvin Cooper

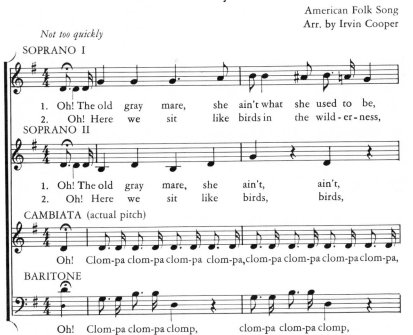

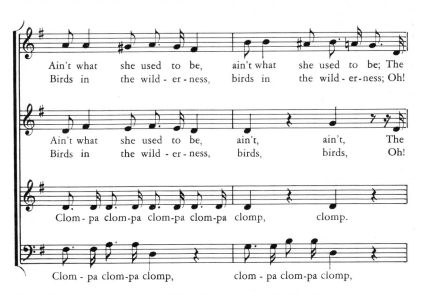

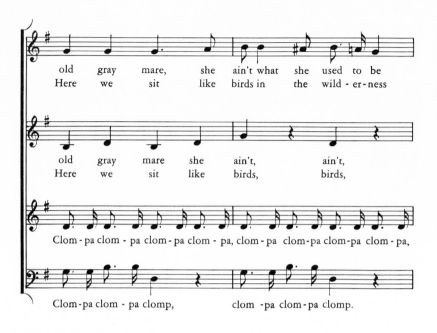

old   gray   mare,   she   ain't what   she   used to be
Here   we   sit   like birds in   the   wild - er - ness

old   gray   mare   she   ain't,   ain't,
Here   we   sit   like   birds,   birds,

Clom - pa clom - pa clom - pa clom - pa, clom - pa clom - pa clom - pa clom - pa,

Clom - pa clom - pa clomp,   clom - pa clom - pa clomp.

Man - y long years   a   -   go.   Man - y long years   a -
Wait - in' for the corn   to   grow.   Wait - in' for the corn   to

Man - y long years   a   -   go.   Man - y long years   a -
Wait - in' for the corn   to   grow.   Wait - in' for the corn   to

Man - y long years   a   -   go.
Wait - in' for the corn   to   grow.

Man - y long years   a   -   go.
Wait - in' for the corn   to   grow.

D.C. to verse 1. Go to
Fine, then to verse 2.
D.C.

go,———   Man-y long years a - go. ———
grow, ———   Wait-in' for the corn to   grow. ———

D.C.

go,———   Man-y long years a - go. ———
grow, ———   Wait-in' for the corn to   grow. ———

D.C.

Man - y long years a - go, ———   Man-y long years a - go.
Wait-in' for the corn to   grow, ———   Wait-in' for the corn to   grow.

D.C.

Man - y long years a - go, ———   Man-y long years a - go.
Wait-in' for the corn to   grow, ———   Wait-in' for the corn to   grow.

Old Gray Mare

BARITONE

Pattern 1.

Pattern 2.

CAMBIATA

SOPRANO II

The Blue Bell of Scotland

Annie McVicar

Old Scottish Tune
Arr. by Irvin Cooper

Not too quickly

SOPRANO I

1. O where, and O where is your— High-land lad-die gone?
2. O where, and O where does your— High-land lad-die dwell?
3. Sup-pose, and sup-pose that your— High-land lad should die?

SOPRANO II

1. O where, O where is your High-land lad-die gone?
2. O where, O where does your High-land lad-die dwell?
3. Sup-pose, sup-pose that your High-land lad should die?

CAMBIATA (actual pitch)

1. O where, O where is your lad - die gone?
2. O where, O where does your lad - die dwell?
3. Sup-pose, sup-pose that your lad should die?

BARITONE

O where, and O where is your— High-land lad-die gone?
O where, and O where does your— High-land lad-die dwell?
Sup-pose, and sup-pose that your— High-land lad should die?

O where, O where is your High-land lad-die gone?
O where, O where does your High-land lad-die dwell?
Sup-pose, sup-pose that your High-land lad should die?

O where, O where is your lad - die gone?
O where, O where does your lad - die dwell?
Sup-pose, sup-pose that your lad should die?

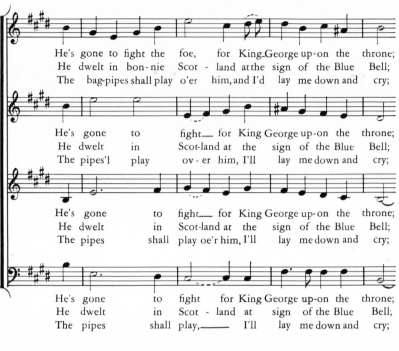

He's gone to fight the foe, for King George up-on the throne;
He dwelt in bon-nie Scot - land at the sign of the Blue Bell;
The bag-pipes shall play o'er him, and I'd lay me down and cry;

He's gone to fight— for King George up-on the throne;
He dwelt in Scot-land at the sign of the Blue Bell;
The pipes'l play ov - er him, I'll lay me down and cry;

He's gone to fight— for King George up-on the throne;
He dwelt in Scot-land at the sign of the Blue Bell;
The pipes shall play oe'r him, I'll lay me down and cry;

He's gone to fight for King George up-on the throne;
He dwelt in Scot - land at sign of the Blue Bell;
The pipes shall play,— I'll lay me down and cry;

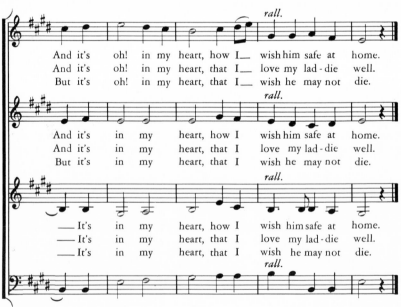

And it's oh! in my heart, how I— wish him safe at home.
And it's oh! in my heart, that I— love my lad - die well.
But it's oh! in my heart, that I— wish he may not die.

And it's in my heart, how I wish him safe at home.
And it's in my heart, that I love my lad - die well.
But it's in my heart, that I wish he may not die.

—It's in my heart, how I wish him safe at home.
—It's in my heart, that I love my lad - die well.
—It's in my heart, that I wish he may not die.

The Blue Bell of Scotland

BARITONE

Pattern 1 for first, second, and fourth phrases.
Pattern 2 for third phrase.

Pattern 1.

Pattern 2.

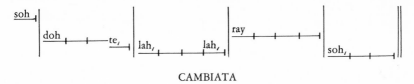

CAMBIATA

Pattern 1.

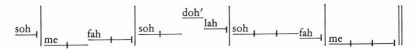

Pattern 2.

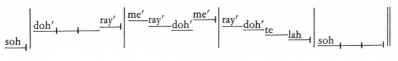

SOPRANO II

Pattern 1.

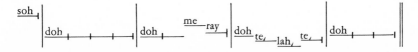

Pattern 2.

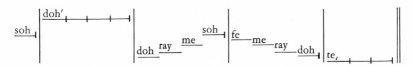

Old Folks at Home

There's where the old folks stay. All up and down the whole cre-a-tion
Man-y the songs I sung. When I was play-ing with my broth-er

Where the old folks stay. Ah
Man-y songs I sung. Ah

Where the old folks stay. All round cre-a-tion
Man-y songs I sung. When with my broth-er

old folks stay. All up and
songs I sung. When I played

Sad-ly I roam. 1. Still long ing for the old plan-ta-tion,
Hap-py was I; 2. Oh! take me to my kind old moth-er,
*Oh! how my heart is sad and wea-ry,

Sad-ly I roam. 1. Ah
Hap-py was I; 2. Ah

Sad-ly I roam, I roam. 1. Still long for
Hap-py was I, was I; 2. There let me
*My heart's wea-ry

down I roam, — 1. Still long for
hap - py was I; 2. There let me
*My heart's wea-ry

*words for D.S. after each chorus

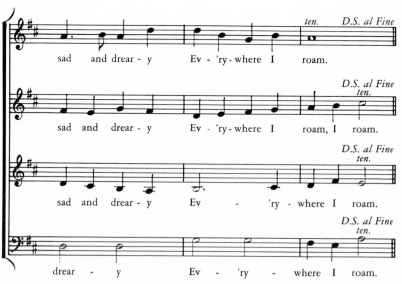

Old Folks at Home

Pattern 1 will be used for phrases one and three.
Pattern 2 will be used for phrases two, four, and six.

BARITONE

Pattern 1.

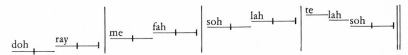

Pattern 2.

Pattern 3. (refrain)

CAMBIATA

Pattern 1.

Pattern 2.

Pattern 3. (refrain)

SOPRANO II

Pattern 1.

Pattern 2.

Pattern 3.

Old Aunt Jemima

Plantation Song
Arr. by Irvin Cooper

With vigor

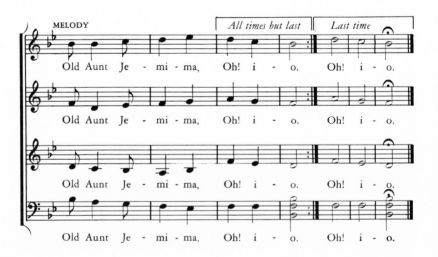

We Wish You a Merry Christmas

Cornish Folk Song
Arr. by Irvin Cooper

Jacob's Ladder

Spiritual
Arr. by Irvin Cooper

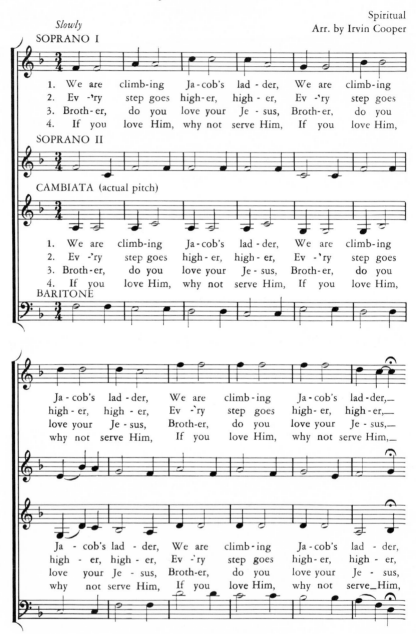

Sol - diers   of   the   Cross._____

Sol   -   diers   of____   the   Cross.

Early One Morning

English Traditional
Arr. by Irvin Cooper

NOTE: *For a sensitive interpretation sopranos should try for a light floating tone.*

ris - ing I heard a maid sing_in the val - ley be - low.
Mar - y, Re - mem - ber the vows_that you made_to be true."
wail - ing, Thus sang the poor maid_in the val - ley be - low.

sun was ris - ing I heard a maid in the val - ley be - low.
Mar - y, Re - mem - ber the vows that you made to be true."
wail - ing, Thus sang the poor maid in the val - ley be - low.

sun was ris - ing I heard a maid in the val - ley be - low.
Mar - y, Re - mem - ber the vows that you made to be true."
wail - ing, Thus sang the poor maid in the val - ley be - low.

"O don't de - ceive__ me, O nev - er leave__ me,

"Don't de - ceive me, Nev - er leave me,

"Don't de - ceive me, Nev - er leave me,

How__ could you use__ a__ poor__ maid-en so."

How could you use a maid - en so."

How could you use a maid - en so."

CHAPTER FOUR

THE MUSIC READING PROGRAM

Need for Music Reading

The objective of this program is to teach junior high school singers to understand music notation and to develop their skills in reproducing vocally what they see on the printed page. This kind of learning cannot be accelerated. No amount of desire on the part of teacher or singers can break through the learning speed. The teacher is therefore advised to set easy-to-reach goals for each lesson. It is sometimes advisable to spend several lessons on the learning and mastering of one technical difficulty.

One precept should be kept in mind at all times: this is a sight training program, not a sight testing program. Music reading, sometimes referred to as sight reading, frequently becomes nothing more than a continuous series of tests during which the singers are given new music to read which is in no sequence. Learning to read music through song singing is a completely unorganized process wherein specific technical reading difficulties appear by chance.

The youngsters will occasionally ask: "Why do we have to learn to read music, we are doing all right from the chalk board diagrams?" Point out to them that learning to read music will almost double their repertoire and that they are only using their ears at this time, but by adding to this the use of their eyes, songs are learned much more quickly and accurately, and there is not the same tendency to become bored with any song. Solicit their sympathy also for your own physical resources, draw attention to the unreasonable demands on your voice of literally pushing sounds into their ears.

This aspect of reading cannot be too highly recommended, for many fine teachers withdraw from school music, unable to cope with the physical demands involved in rote teaching. One cannot teach songs by rote, lesson after lesson, day after day. Teaching the youngsters to read music is essential to the welfare of the teacher's physical and nervous system; however, this is not the basic reason. By teaching the singers to read music the teacher is equipping them for self-directed music experiences in adult life. For many students, general music in junior high school is their terminal directed music experience, since the senior high school chorus or band engages a relatively small segment of the total school population. Therefore, unless the junior high school music teacher can equip his students to cope with music during their adult life, there seems little to be said in favor of a music offering at this level. Furthermore, the teacher may feel his avocation is without serious purpose.

Although an occasional boy or girl may be engaged in private instrumental instruction, it will be assumed that insofar as vocal music reading is concerned everyone's skill is negligible.

One other point needs stressing. The music reading program should not be regarded as an activity isolated from the song-singing program; as each new reading skill is acquired it should be applied wherever possible in facilitating the learning of a new song. It would be foolish to cover all the work in the music reading program, then tell the class "now we have learned to read music, let us put it to use."

COMPOSITE OCTAVE-UNISON VOCAL RANGE RESTRICTION

Before plunging into the techniques of teaching music reading, one problem must be considered seriously, that of the vocal ranges available. Obviously the singers cannot commence reading music requiring several parts. The introduction to vocal music reading must begin with everyone singing the same melody at unison-octave pitch.

This immediately imposes range restriction to the interval of a major ninth, a specific major ninth for the melodies to be used.

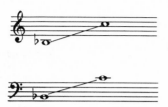

The first principle arising out of this problem is that careful attention must be given to establishing accurate pitch for the performance of each reading melody.

Here a method is presented for teaching vocal music reading through the medium of units of instruction. The length of time or number of partial periods devoted to each unit is the prerogative of the music teacher. Each unit will be referred to as a music reading lesson, but this division of the presentation of new learnings is by no means mandatory. With a group of quick learners it is quite possible to cover two such lessons in one music period. In any one music period the amount of time spent on reading instruction should not exceed ten minutes. Furthermore, if concentration lags before the ten-minute limit, it is best to move to some other phase of the music lesson. A psychological factor contributing to the success of a music reading program is the timing of the reading period with regard to other activities during the lesson. Best results are obtained if the lesson opens with the singing of a familiar song, followed immediately by the music reading activity.

At the start of the music reading program, singers should learn to relate a musical sound to a symbol. The series of symbols which have proven most effective, in the experience of the author, are the tonic sol-fa syllables derived from the Guidonian hexachord by John Curwen, an English clergyman, during the last decade of the nineteenth century.

Despite unresolved conflicts attendant to the use of numbers, letter names, solfège, general hand movement, and music syllables, the latter are most reliable in the early stages of sight training. This does not imply that other systems are not useful in other musical situations.

It is further proposed to use John Curwen's system of hand signs to ensure a more graphic presentation of tone relationship to the students.

INTRODUCTION TO MUSIC READING

It will be noticed that the spelling out of music syllables differs in some respects from that in general use. This is of slight consequence but is recommended to avoid confusion in pronunciation by the students, who find some difficulty in reconciling *do* with a "doh" sound, *re* with a "ray" sound, *mi* with a "me" sound, and so forth.[1]

After the first few lessons, spelling of the syllables will be discontinued, and thereafter only the first letter will be employed, *d* for *doh, r* for *ray,* etc.

Phase One: Introduction to Music Syllables

LESSON ONE

To start the first reading lesson explain briefly but concisely that all musical sounds have signs and names. Play the chord of B♭ major and sing the "good morning" pattern suggested on page 49 for remedial work with out-of-tune singers. Direct the class to sing the same pattern three times, using the hand signs for *doh, soh*

DOH   SOH

[1] A form of Anglicized spelling and pronunciation for the "sol-fa" syllables is preferred for use in this book. The pronunciation of doh, ray, fah, soh, lah, as here used, is self-explanatory. However, the letter "e" appearing in any music syllable will be pronounced "ee" as in "keel" or "feel." Thus, "fe" will be pronounced "fee," "se" will be pronounced "see," etc.

soh —	soh —	soh —
doh doh	doh doh	doh doh

as an instrument for stimulation and as a visual aid for focusing on the required pitch. Using hand signs for music syllables, the hand should move upwards or downwards to indicate pitch direction. A complete octave of signs should encompass a distance between the waist and high forehead.

Tell the class each of the hand signs used has a name: the lower one is *doh*, the upper is *soh*. Write these names on the board. Through the medium of hand signs present the following exercise to the class. Use a slow tempo.

soh —		soh —	soh soh soh soh	soh	
doh doh		doh doh		doh doh—	
1 2 3 4		1 2 3 4	1 2 3 4	1 2 3 4	

EXAMPLE I.

Draw attention to the fact that everyone keeps the same speed by means of a *beat*, that the music is divided into compartments each of which contains four beats, sometimes three beats. Further, if any note has a two-beat duration the extra beat is indicated by a dash. Be sure that syllables on the board are large and sufficiently bold to be seen from any point in the classroom.

Once again pitch the chord of B♭ major and direct the class in singing this exercise, pointing to each note a fraction of a second before you expect its vocal articulation. Repeat this process once or twice; remember this is sight *training* not sight *reading*.

The above procedure is quite sufficient for the first lesson and should not require more than five minutes to accomplish. Do not continue rehearsing the exercise to achieve perfection.

Some classes will achieve a reasonably adequate response more quickly than others. Despite the excellent educational precept that individual differences should be cared for and that appropriate higher goals and opportunities should be available for the quicker learners, at this stage music learning should be regarded as a slow growth process and easy-to-reach goals should be established for each lesson. Slower learning students may tend to lean on the others and be followers, but it is reasonable to assume that some learning is taking place.

LESSON TWO

The second music reading lesson should begin with a brief review of Lesson One, using some new tunes written on the chalk board, preferably prior to the lesson. Introduce the exercises first by using hand signs, then point to the syllables on the chalk board.

soh soh			soh soh soh		
doh doh	doh—doh —		doh	doh— — —	

EXAMPLE 2.

soh —		soh soh —	soh soh	
	dohdoh|doh		dohdoh	doh— doh —|

EXAMPLE 3.

Spend as little time as possible correcting errors, then proceed immediately to the introduction of a new sound, a new sign, a new name.

ME

Sing the following three times as a model for the class to imitate.

Good   morn - ing.

Be sure to establish the key of B♭ major for yourself and for the class. Do not write the above exercise on the chalk board.

Ask the class to sing the new "good morning" pattern three times; then draw attention to the new sound. Sing the pattern to syllables

soh		soh		
me		me		
doh doh		doh doh		doh — — —|

then illustrate with the appropriate hand signs, using a vigorous rhythmic motion and punching the hand forward for every note. The hand should also move vertically upwards or downwards to illustrate variation of pitch level.

Direct the class to respond by singing syllables as you present hand signs for the new "good morning" pattern. Follow through from this point by means of an exercise written (prior to the lesson) on the chalk board.

EXAMPLE 4.

Establish the key of B♭ major and point to each syllable as the class responds. Repeat once or twice as a familiarization procedure, not to learn the tune but to get the vocal feel of three sounds now incorporated into an organized scheme of learning. This is sufficient for the second music reading lesson.

LESSON THREE

The third music reading lesson should begin with a review of material presented in Lesson Two, using the following exercises or others of your invention. Write them on the chalk board, or better still, to conserve time, have them already written on the board before the class begins. Use the key of B♭ major.

EXAMPLE 5.

EXAMPLE 6.

Should there appear to be some loss of pitch orientation, revert to Lesson One, using only *doh, soh,* then review briefly the introduction of the sound *me.*

The next progressive step is to introduce the sound, the hand sign, and name of *ray*.

RAY

Explain to the class that this sound comes between *me* and *doh;* it is a *leaning* note and requires a little more volume. Illustrate the sound of this new note, incorporating the new hand sign through the medium of this melodic fragment, key of B♭.

	s				s							
d		m	ray	d		m	ray	d	—	—	—	‖

Note: at this stage *ray* will always appear between *doh* and *me;* in this way it is supported on either side by the nearest *doh* chord tone.

Following this illustration direct the class to sing the same fragment, responding to your hand signs. Repeat this until some vocal security is established. Move your hand with firm authority upward and downward as the signs indicate upward or downward pitch variation.

To incorporate the new note in a melodic expression, transfer the latest experience to Ex. 7, which should be written on the chalk board.

	s									s							
d		m	—	d	m ray	—	d	ray m		m	—	ray	—	d	d	d	— ‖

EXAMPLE 7.

Again, pitch the key of B♭ major and direct class singing by pointing to each note and dash to orient the eye movement.

When this has been done reasonably well tell the class it is possible to sing this melody using a different pitch sound for *doh*. Establish the key of C major and sing Ex. 7, but this time point only to syllables in the first two measures, beating time for the remainder of the melody.

At the close of this lesson the singers will have been exposed to three new aspects of reading: (1) a new note, *ray*, (2) change of key, and (3) removal of the beat from the chalk board. Tell this to your class and do not fail to compliment them on their achievement. Total time: 7 or 8 minutes.

LESSON FOUR

Lesson Four of the music reading program should begin with a brief review of Lesson Three, using the following melodies or melodies of your own devising, written on the chalk board, employing only syllables learned to date. The syllable *ray* should always be approached and quitted by step at this stage:

$$\text{d} \quad \text{ray}^{\text{m}} \; - \; \Big| \text{d} \; \text{ray} \; ^{\text{m}} \; - \; \Big|^{\text{m}} \; \text{ray} ^{\text{m}} \; \text{d} \; \Big| \text{ray} - \text{d} \; - \; \Big\|$$

EXAMPLE 8.

Use the key of B♭ major for a beginning, then change to C major or D♭ major; do not use any higher key yet.

$$\text{d} \quad ^{\text{s}} \; _{\text{m}} \; _{\text{r}} \Big| \text{d} \; ^{\text{m}} \; _{\text{r}} \; - \Big| \text{d} \; ^{\text{m}} \; ^{\text{s}} \; ^{\text{m}} \Big| _{\text{r}} \; - \; \text{d} \; - \Big\|$$

EXAMPLE 9.

The first time through point to syllables on the chalk board; the second time through use a beat only.

Use three beats for each division or measure.

$$^{\text{s}} _{\text{m}} \, _{\text{r}} \Big| \text{d} - - \Big| \text{d} - ^{\text{m}} \Big|^{\text{s}} - - \Big|^{\text{m}} - - \Big|_{\text{r}} - - \Big| \text{d} - ^{\text{m}} \Big| \text{d} - - \Big\|$$

EXAMPLE 10.

Explain to the class that in some kinds of music there are only three beats in each compartment (measure). A warning: when singing Ex. 10 boys will require extra stimulation to articulate the first syllable *soh*. Do not spend too much time perfecting these melodies or their reading function will be negated.

The next step is to introduce another new syllable, *fah*. Tell your singers there is a syllable between *soh* and *me*. To illustrate, sing this pattern, key of B♭ major.

d   m   ˢ   fah |m   —   —   —   ‖

Notice the new syllable is not introduced until the entire *doh* chord has first been established. Do not involve the class in any unnecessary complexities about a half tone between *me* and *fah;* sing the new melody, synchronizing hand signs as you sing. When you have finished draw attention to the hand sign for the new sound, which is *fah*.

Fᴀʜ

d   m   ˢ   m |d   m   ˢ   fah |m   fah   ˢ   fah |m   —   r   — |d   —   —   —   ‖

Eхᴀᴍᴘʟᴇ 11.

Pitch the key of B♭ major and direct the singers to respond to your hand signs as you sing the above melody. On the chalk board write syllables for the melody you have sung.

Follow the same procedure used in previous lessons with the boys and girls singing the syllable pitches as you point to them on the board. Should there be any roughness in the progression involving *fah* extract the pattern d   m   s   fah |m — — — ‖

and rehearse it two or three times, then return to the beginning of Ex. 11 and sing it through with the class. Spontaneous hand drill may be used if so desired, but care should be taken to avoid any intervallic leaps which involve *ray* or *fah*.

If time permits and if the youngsters are still interested repeat the melody of Ex. 11 using the key of C major.

LESSON FIVE

Lesson Five in the music reading program should be a consolidation of previous learnings, the sole objective being to attain more fluency with, and quicker articulation of, syllables learned to this point. Appropriate exercises for this purpose are presented here, for which keys of Bb major, C major, or D major may be used.

For chalk board use it is no longer necessary to spell out syllables, the initial letter will be sufficient.

d   m   d   s | d   m   s — | d   s   d   s |m m   d — ‖

EXAMPLE 12.

s —   d |m — — |m   r   d |s — — |s   m   d |r   m   r |d — m |d — — ‖

EXAMPLE 13.

m   m   s | f   m   r — |m   s   f   m |r   d   r — |d   m   s   m |d   r   d — ‖

EXAMPLE 14.

Toward the end of this reading session suggest that your class might want to take a very easy step forward by learning high *doh* (*doh'*). There is no need to explain that the sound is eight notes or an octave higher than the *doh* sound they have already learned; merely sing this melody, using appropriate hand signs.

d'
s   s   s   d' −
m   m   m   s   m
d   d   d − d −   d − − −

EXAMPLE 15.

This exercise *must* be used in the key of B♭ major in order to remain within the composite unison vocal range presented on page 16.

Following procedure already established for introducing a new sound, instruct your class to react to your hand signs, then write Ex. 15 on the chalk board and continue the routine.

LESSON SIX

Lesson Six begins with the usual review of previously learned syllabic progressions. Suggested exercises to write on the chalk board are presented below.

d' −   d' −
s   f s −   s − − − s f   s f
m   m   r m   m r   m r
d   d   d −   d − − −

EXAMPLE 16.

d'
m   m   f − −   f − −   f   f   s − −   s
r   r   r m   r m   m
d   d   d − −

EXAMPLE 17.

Note that owing to the use of *doh'* you are limited to the key of B♭ major in order to conform with the restrictions of the composite unison vocal range illustrated earlier. Do not rehearse the above exercises time and time again. There is a new syllable to be taught in this lesson, and the total time allotted to sight training should not exceed seven minutes.

The new syllable to be added in this lesson is *lah*. Illustrate the new sound for the class by reverting to the "good morning" pattern.

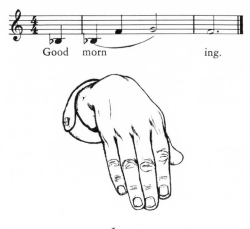

Lah

Ask the class to sing this twice or three times until it sounds secure, then give hand signs for

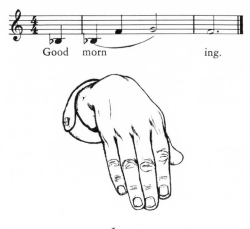

and let the group react to your signs, repeating until the reaction is satisfactory. Incorporate this pattern into a new exercise on the chalk board and continue with the usual routine from this point.

Example 18.

Keys of B♭ major or C major may be used for this melody. When learning new musical sounds and symbols it is wise to keep the vocal range within the cambiata tessitura. While cambiate will sing well-known songs which occasionally emerge to their higher range, it is difficult to stimulate them to do so when reading unfamiliar music. * (Note that this is the first time secondary tones have been approached or quitted by leap. Do not discuss this with the class.)

LESSON SEVEN

Music Reading Lesson Seven begins with the usual review, melodies for which are suggested below.

EXAMPLE 19.

$$\text{m} \; -- \; \Big| \; \text{f} \; \text{m} \; \text{r} \; \Big| \; \text{d} \; - \; \Big| \; \text{d}' \; \Big| \; \text{s} \; -- \; \Big| \; \text{s} \; - \; \text{l} \; \Big| \; \text{s} \; - \; \text{m} \; \Big| \; \text{f} \; \text{m} \; \text{r} \; \Big| \; \text{d} \; -- \; \Big\|$$

EXAMPLE 20.

Only one more step remains to complete the octave of the major scale. Sing the following vocalization to the class, using the key of B♭ major:

Loo loo loo loo   loo   loo

Sing it once more, this time using syllables and hand signs. Stress the new note *te*.

TE

```
                          d'        |te    —    d'    —      ‖
               s                    |
        m                           |
  d                                 |
```

Direct the class to sing the above pattern, responding to your hand signs, and follow this brief drill by incorporating the new sound into a melody previously written on the chalk board:

```
      d' — |te  l      | l  te  d'   | l         | s —      |          ‖
            |     s —  |        s    |   s  f    |   m      |          ‖
  d —       |          |             |      m    |     r    | d – – – ‖
```

EXAMPLE 21.

Point to each note while the class sings this melody the first time. For any subsequent performances pitch the key of B♭ major and beat time.

For the following two or three scheduled general music periods the music reading portion of each lesson should be of about five minutes' duration, objectives being: (1) to consolidate reading skills already acquired; (2) to eliminate all preliminary steps and read directly from the chalk board; (3) to accelerate gradually the articulation tempo; and (4) to introduce notes below *doh,*

```
                                          f   s
                            d   r   m
                 l,   t,
           s,
```

preparing the singers for *plagal* melodies which lie between lower and upper dominants such as "Home on the Range," "Auld Lang Syne," etc.

Draw attention to the addition of the number 1 at the lower right of syllables appearing below *home doh.* Explain that in order to show the difference between *home doh* and *doh'* an octave higher, a prime sign is placed at the upper right of high *doh* (*d'*) and that syllables progressing yet higher will be treated in like manner. Syllables appearing below *home doh* will be so indicated by placing the number 1 at the lower right of the syllable.

The series of melodies offered below may be used during this consolidation period. They are cumulatively more difficult in character,

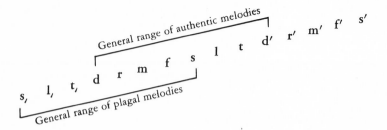

and, unsuspected by the students, they add such new difficulties as leaping to and from secondary tones *ray, fah, lah,* and *te.* Pitch the key for every melody and let the class establish the tonic chord from your hand signs.

Some of these melodies are actual song tunes which you can teach by means of hand signs or by reading from the chalk board, or a combination of both. Singers are now no longer solely dependent on your voice as the only medium through which they might learn a new song, because tonal memory is now reinforced by visual aids in the form of hand signs or syllables written on the chalk board.

Use keys of B ♭ or C major.

EXAMPLE 22.

Use key of C or D major.

EXAMPLE 23.

Use key of B ♭ major.

EXAMPLE 24.

Use key of C major.

EXAMPLE 25.

Use key of E♭ major.

EXAMPLE 26.

Use keys of C or D major.

EXAMPLE 27.

Introducing two quick notes to one beat (♩♩).

Use key of C major.

EXAMPLE 28.

Use key of C major.

EXAMPLE 29.

Use key of B ♭ major.

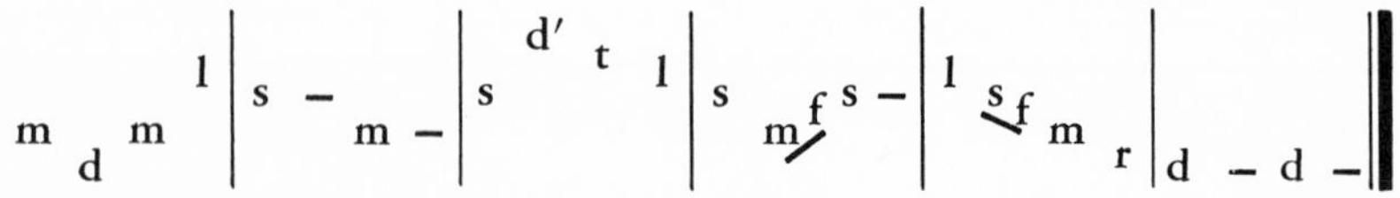

EXAMPLE 30.

Use key of E♭ major.

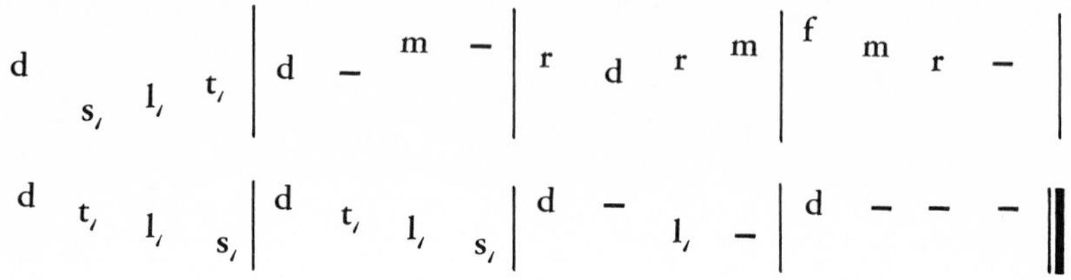

EXAMPLE 31.

Use key of C major.

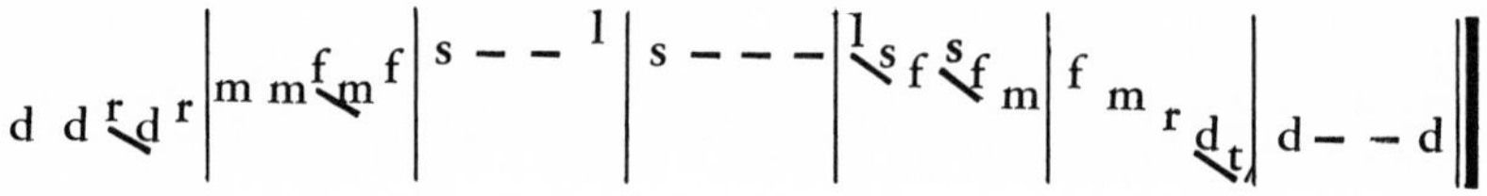

EXAMPLE 32.

Use key of E ♭ major.

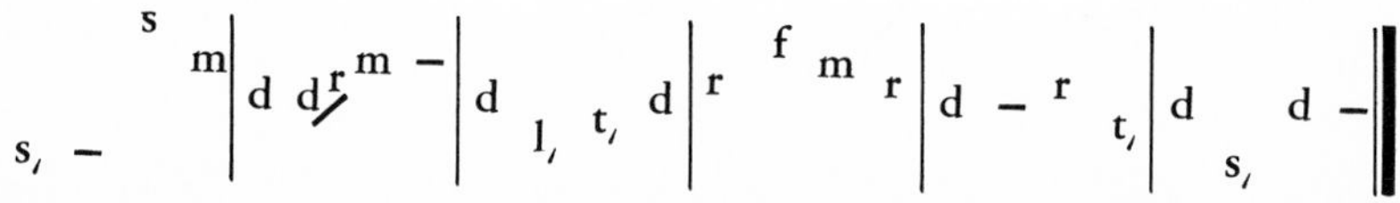

EXAMPLE 33.

A la claire fontaine

French Folk Song

Use key of D major.

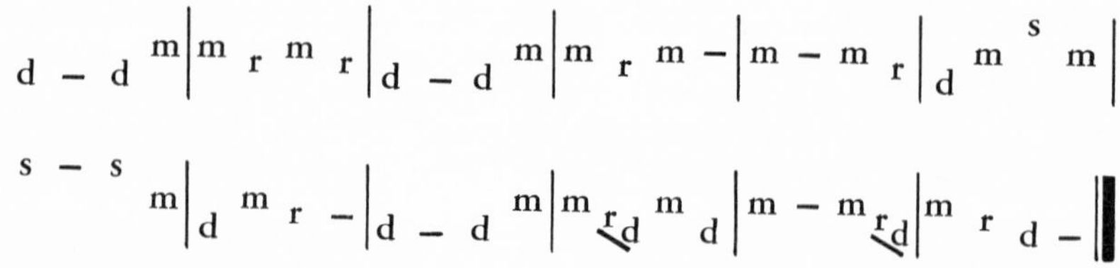

EXAMPLE 34.

Drink to Me Only

English

Use key of B♭ major.

m m m | f − f | ˢ f m | ᵣ m f | ˢ ᵈ f | m − ᵣ | d − − | − − ˢ ‖

ˢ ₘ s | ᵈ′ − | ₘ s s | ₘ s s | s − s | ¹ − s | s f ₘ | m − − | ᵣ − − |

m m m | f − f | ˢ f m | ᵣ m f | ˢ ᵈ f | m − ᵣ | d − − | − − − ‖

EXAMPLE 35.

LESSON EIGHT

Music Reading Lesson Eight should not be taught until the singers have demonstrated reasonably competent readings and performances of the foregoing melodies. When this point is reached draw attention to the fact that all previous melodies have begun with a note of the *doh* chord and have always ended on *doh. Doh* is the *home* tone.

Now tell the class that music such as this is said to be in the *major* style or mode, but there is also a good deal of music in which *lah* is the *home* tone. This kind of music is said to be in the *minor* style or mode.

Two new sounds are needed for music sung in the minor mode, and these sounds, their signs and names, will be taught in one reading lesson. To illustrate these new sounds sing for the students the following melodic pattern, using the neutral vowel *loo:*

Next sing the above pattern to syllables, using appropriate hand signs and stressing the new sounds.

Do not discuss the aspect of key center with the class. During your preparation for this lesson it will probably occur to you that the key

Use key of A minor (*doh* is C).

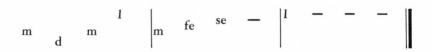

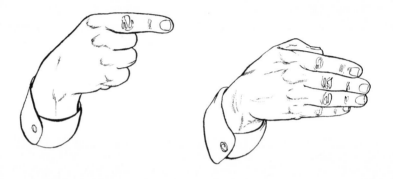

Fᴇ   Sᴇ

of A minor requires a key signature of no sharps or flats, and that *doh* falls on C. No sharps or flats is also the key signature required for the key of C major where *doh* also falls on C. This is one of the factors favoring the use of *syllables* as a medium for early instruction in music reading. Whatever is the staff position of *doh* in a major key it will remain in that position for the relative minor. The complexities surrounding relative tonalities of major and minor keys need not be mentioned to the youngsters if music syllables are used. The only aspect of music in the minor mode about which they need to be informed at present is that the home note is *lah*.

Proceed immediately in Music Reading Lesson Eight by incorporating the new sounds into a reading melody, following the teaching routine previously established for this procedure.

Use key of D minor (*doh* is F).

$$\text{l}_{/}\ \ \text{t}_{/}\ \ \text{d}\ \ \text{r}\ \Big|\ \text{m}\ -\ \ \text{d}\ \ \text{m}\ \Big|\ \text{l}\ \ \text{se}\ \ \text{fe}\ \ \text{se}\ \Big|\ \text{l}\ -\ \ \text{s}\ \ \text{f}\ \Big|\ \text{m}\ -\ \ \text{se}\ -\ \Big|\ \text{l}\ -\ \ \ \text{l}_{/}\ -\ \Big\|$$

EXAMPLE 36.

Should you wish to use music in the minor mode as a means of familiarizing the class with minor tonality during the song singing portion of the lesson, the following are recommended: "Go Down Moses" and "Miller of the Dee," both of which are to be found in *Songs for Pre-teentime*,[1] and "What Child Is This" from *Yuletime for Teentime*.[2]

LESSON NINE

Lesson Nine of the music reading program should start with a review of work accomplished in Lesson Eight, using melodies appearing below.

First orient the class to a key by playing the chord of B minor (D is *doh*) and directing them to respond to your hand signs using the pattern

$$\text{d}\ \ \ \ \text{l}_{/}\ \ \ \ \text{d}\ \ \ \ ^{\text{m}}\ \Big|\ \text{d}\ \ \ \ \text{t}_{/}\ \ \ \ \text{l}_{/}\ \ \ -\ \ \ \Big\|$$

This will be referred to hereafter as the *lah*₁ chord.

Use key of D minor (*doh* is F).

$$\text{d}\ ^{\text{m}}\ \text{d}\ \ \text{t}_{/}\ \Big|\ \text{l}_{/}\ -\ \ \text{d}\ -\ \Big|\ \text{r}\ ^{\text{m}}\ \text{r}\ -\ \Big|\ \text{d}\ \ \text{t}\ \ \text{l}_{/}\ -\ \Big|\ \text{l}_{/}\ \ \text{t}_{/}\ \ \text{d}\ \ \text{r}\ \Big|\ ^{\text{m}\ -}\ \ \text{d}\ -\ \Big|\ \text{l}_{/}\ -\ -\ -\ \Big\|$$

EXAMPLE 37.

[1] Irvin Cooper, *Songs for Pre-teentime* (New York: Carl Fischer, 1956).
[2] ———, *Yuletime for Teentime* (New York: Carl Fischer, 1954).

For each of the remaining melodies introduce the class to the *lah₁*, *doh, me* progression in whatever key is being employed.

Use key of B♭ minor (*doh* is D♭).

EXAMPLE 38.

Use key of F minor (*doh* is A♭).

EXAMPLE 39.

Use key of D minor (*doh* is F).

EXAMPLE 40.

This is sufficient for Lesson Nine. Do not spend too much time striving for total accuracy as more melodies in the minor mode will be used in the transfer from syllables to staff notation.

LESSON TEN

Lesson Ten of the music reading program should be devoted to a consolidation of all previous music reading skills. Reading melodies already used should be sung again; this time forsake the music syllables and sing the melodies to *loo*. Additional melodies may be found in

The Reading Singer.[1] In every instance the class should precede reading of the melody by responding vocally to your hand signs indicating the appropriate home tone chord—

                    s

      m   m | m

d | d   d   —   ‖

for major keys,

        d   m

l,   d |l,   d   l,   —   ‖

for minor keys,

d   m   d | d   d   —   ‖
               s, | s,

and for plagal melodies.

This lesson completes the first phase of the music reading program.

Appropriate keys are determined by the restricted unison octave range within which you must work.

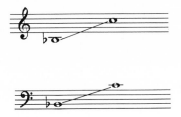

Phase Two: Introduction to Staff Notation

Before proceeding further it is necessary (1) that the general music class or choral group has acquired reasonable skill in reading melodies presented in music syllable form and (2) that concurrently with the vocal program the class or group has been exposed to a portion of the work presented in the music fundamentals program.

[1] Irvin Cooper, *The Reading Singer* (Boston: Allyn and Bacon, Inc., 1964).

This portion of the music reading program will serve two purposes: (1) it will transfer previous music syllable learnings to music staff situations, and (2) it will strengthen the students' concept of relationship between any diatonic tone and its home note or tonic.

The new series of music reading experiences will start at the level of Lesson Two in Phase One of this chapter.

LESSON ELEVEN

First tell the students you are about to teach them to read adult music, using lines, spaces, and shaped notes. Write the following melody on the chalk board. Reduce the vertical space to about half that which has been used previously.

EXAMPLE 41.

Follow established procedure by requiring your class to sing the above melody. In order not to waste time, erase all the *doh* signs, draw a horizontal line cutting through the area where these signs were first written, and replace all *doh* syllables with this symbol: ◦   A black square at the beginning of the music indicates the position of *doh*. Explain the *tie* in the final measure; the extra note with a *tie* gives *doh* two counts.

EXAMPLE 41a.

Ask the class to sing the melody again, still using *doh* as the word for the new signs. Once through is sufficient, then as quickly as possible erase all the *me* syllables, draw a horizontal line through the area where these signs were first written, and replace all *me* syllables with this symbol: ◦   Point out that in the first measure two tie notes will give *me* two counts.

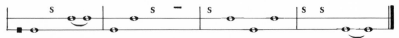

EXAMPLE 41b.

Once again ask the class to sing the melody, using syllables.

The next step is to erase all the *soh* syllables, draw a horizontal line and replace all *soh* syllables with this symbol: o

EXAMPLE 41*c*.

The class should sing the melody again, using music syllables, then sing it a final time to the neutral vowel *loo*. Do not point to the notes this time; lead in the class and continue by beating time. This entire procedure should not require more than seven minutes.

Should the school music budget be adequate it is desirable to have music reading books such as *The Reading Singer* for students. Without student books it is impossible to develop independent music reading proficiency, because work from the chalk board is directed by the teacher. Furthermore music on the printed page presents an entirely different visual aspect. Incidentally student books save a great deal of time otherwise spent by the teacher in chalk board copying.

LESSON TWELVE

Lesson Twelve of the music reading program should of course start with a review of Lesson Eleven. Inasmuch as the transfer to lines and spaces presents a more complex situation to the children, assimilation of the new medium takes place quite slowly, and there should not be any attempt to accelerate the learning process at this stage.

In using the exercises presented below, follow the complete procedure outlined in Lesson Eleven.

EXAMPLE 42.

When the class has concluded preliminary procedures and has sung the melody from the three-line staff, add extra lines to the staff at your discretion, showing that printed music uses the five-line staff, but no matter how many lines are added, if *doh* is placed on a line, *me* will always appear on the next line above, and *soh* will appear on the next line above *me*.

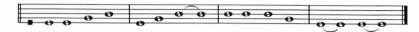

EXAMPLE 42*a*.

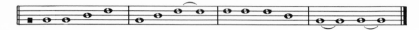

EXAMPLE 42*b*.

This is not as time-consuming as it may appear; the three lines on which notes appear remain constant while other lines are added or erased above and below. Assuming that your general music class has done a little work in the music fundamentals program, *doh* may also be placed on a ledger line below the staff.

EXAMPLE 42*c*.

It is important to note that, in spite of various staff location changes for *doh,* the performing key *must* remain C major for Ex. 39. Ideally this is not a good situation, but the exigencies of the composite unison-octave vocal range available for junior high school singers (boys and girls combined) leave no alternative. It is highly desirable from an aesthetic point of view for students to sing a melody in the written key. If this ideal were sustained, however, it would limit the number of different keys in which the singers might practice reading and would eliminate familiarization with the upper lines and spaces of the staff. To the music teacher who has perfect pitch this adjustment is far more difficult than it is for junior high school students who do not know enough to even sense a problem. Always pitch the *doh* chord in a key commensurate with the composite octave-unison vocal range. Junior high singers do not raise the issue that this is not the key in which the music is written. They are not aware of transposition at this stage, but it does ensure coverage of the visual aspects of music reading involving a wide range of keys.

There are two perfectly good reasons for not introducing clef signs at this time: (1) The use of clefs would automatically demand key signatures, and the students are not yet ready to absorb additional complexities. (2) When the time arrives to present clefs in the music reading program, it will be necessary to employ two clefs simultaneously, G clef for soprano and cambiata, and F clef for baritone. This would involve *doh* in two different staff locations for the same melody, another complexity which can be avoided by delaying the presentation of clefs.

Some music students at the graduate level find this procedure more difficult to assimilate than do undergraduate music education majors or classroom teachers. The absence of a key signature seems to disturb them, for it leaves the definition of major and minor thirds, perfect and diminished fifths without orientation. Junior high school children fortunately are unaware of such pitfalls.

Presented herewith are two additional exercises using only *doh, me, soh* to aid in familiarization with the staff.

EXAMPLE 43.

EXAMPLE 44.

Theoretically the singers could cope with Ex. 43 and 44 in the keys of E and F major, but this requires the cambiate to sing in the upper limits of their range at a time when they are not sufficiently confident of their new reading skills to sing with any authority. In any new music reading situation any notes which will have to be performed in an upper voice register should be avoided.

The purpose of Lesson Twelve has been to familiarize singers with staff lines and spaces, while extending the three-line staff to the five-line staff.

LESSON THIRTEEN

This lesson should begin with a brief review of previous music staff work, using only *doh, me,* and *soh.* Exercises for this activity are offered herewith. Sing through once to syllables, then to *loo.* If the class has not thoroughly absorbed the transfer from syllables to staff and

Use keys or of B♭, C, or D major.

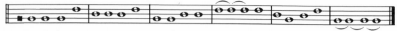

EXAMPLE 45.

Use keys or of B♭, C, or D major.

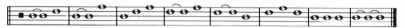

EXAMPLE 46.

fails to respond with any degree of musical accuracy, Lesson Eleven should be reviewed in its entirety. This should be done quickly, before returning to Ex. 45.

This lesson will parallel the music syllable development presented in Lesson Three, but now the note *ray* will appear in the *space* between *doh* and *me*. Reading from the staff is in itself a complex activity, and in order to absorb the mounting complexities slowly, *doh* will always appear on a line until all the syllables of the scale have been accounted for in this framework.

Established procedure should be followed in introducing the new factor. First set the key through the *doh* chord; then sing the melody to music syllables, followed immediately by the class singing, also to syllables.

Use keys of B♭, C, or D major.

EXAMPLE 47.

Let the class sing the melody again; once with music syllables as you point to the notes, once more using *loo* while you conduct.

LESSON FOURTEEN

Start with a review of previous *staff* learnings. The following melodies are recommended, and much time will be saved if they have been written on the chalk board in advance of the lesson.

The new learning for this lesson will consist of transferring the syllable *fah* to the staff and incorporating it with other staff members

Use keys of B♭, C, or D major.

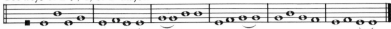

EXAMPLE 48.

Use keys of B♭, C, or D major.

EXAMPLE 49.

already so transferred. Do not complicate proceedings by discussing the incidence of a half tone between *me* and *fah*. To the singers this is a perfectly normal progression requiring no further enlightenment. Inasmuch as you are still placing *doh* on a line, *fah* will appear in the space between lines which support *me* and *soh*. Illustrate this by means of a brief drill. Pitching the key of C major, first use syllables,

Use keys of B♭ major.

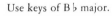
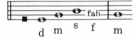

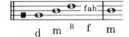

then sing to *loo*. Follow this immediately by incorporating the new note in a melody.

Use keys of B♭, C, or D major.

EXAMPLE 50.

Caution: do not over-rehearse. Try to keep the music reading portion of the period within a time span of seven minutes, otherwise concentration will break down.

LESSON FIFTEEN

This lesson commences with the usual review, for which purpose two melodies to be written on the chalk board appear below. Orient the class as to key by use of hand signs for the *doh* chord followed by *ray* and *fah*. Notice the skip from *ray* to *fah*.

Use keys of B♭, C, or D major.

EXAMPLE 51.

Use keys of B♭, C, or D major.

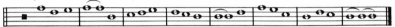

EXAMPLE 52.

Any weakly sung progressions should be given brief music syllable treatment and then sung again in the full context of the melody.

The new learning for this lesson will consist of the transfer of the syllable *lah* to the staff. As a consequence of the addition of *lah* to the vocal range encompassed in previous lessons there will be some restrictions in the number of keys available for music reading activity. Write the following pattern on the chalk board.

Use keys of B♭ or C major.

Using the key of B♭ or C major, pitch the *doh* chord; present the new pattern first by means of hand signs to which the class should respond by singing syllables. Transfer the action immediately to staff patterns, point to the notes on the board as the class sings, then incorporate the new symbol in a melody written on the chalk board prior to the lesson. Whatever key you have used in the preliminary steps should be retained for Ex. 53.

Use keys of B♭ major.

EXAMPLE 53.

LESSON SIXTEEN

This lesson begins again with the reading of new melodies incorporating previous staff learnings.

Use keys of B♭ or C major.

EXAMPLE 54.

Before singing Ex. 55 measures 4 and 5 should be taken out of context and presented by hand signs. The leap of a major sixth is new.

Use keys of B♭ or C major.

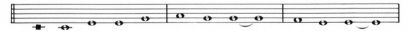

EXAMPLE 55.

The new learning for this lesson is a little more complex and takes more time and patience. It is concerned with the transfer of high *doh'* to the staff and offers some conflict because, whereas low *doh* appeared on a line, high *doh'* appears in a space. This seems most readily understood by students if the teacher refers to the syllable scale either through the modulator chart or by writing on the chalk board thus:

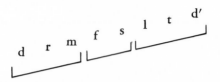

Demonstrate the *doh* chord and point out that between *doh* and *me* there is one note, *ray;* between *me* and *soh* there is one note, *fah;* but between *soh* and high *doh'* there are two notes, *lah* and *te,* which do not follow the comfortable pattern of *doh* on a line, *me* on the next line above *doh, soh* on the next line above *me.* If there were six or eight different notes in the scale it would have worked out nicely, but as there are seven different notes, when *doh* appears on a line *doh'* will appear in a space.

Following the general philosophy of this method, do not get involved in any unnecessary complexities here by referring to the situation arising if *doh* appears in a space. This will be dealt with in due course when the entire sequence of events is presented evolving from *doh* in a space. Again it should be noted that when the entire compass of the octave is used in an authentic melody *doh* to *doh',* the only singing key available is Bb major, due to the exigencies of the composite unison vocal range. Write these examples on the chalk board.

Establish the key of Bb major, let the class first respond to your hand signs, then respond again as you point to the chalk board. You may find it necessary to stimulate the cambiate to articulate confidently on

MUSIC MODULATOR CHART

doh' as it is rather close to their highest note. At this moment it is more than likely the tone quality will not please you, but just now tone quality is not the main objective, and overemphasis on quality might preclude a realization of your main objective.

Now incorporate the new learning in a melody.

Use key of B♭ major.

EXAMPLE 56.

Some resemblance to the "Star-Spangled Banner" will be noticed in the first two measures. This is an intentional aid; but the remainder of the national anthem is unsingable in unison at junior high school level because it does not conform to the composite vocal range defined on page 16.

Use key of B♭ major.

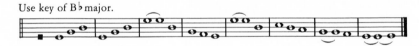

EXAMPLE 57.

The apparent transposition element involved in all these melodies will not trouble the singers. However, teachers who have perfect pitch might experience the same type of pitch confusion they undergo when reading an orchestral or band score.

LESSON SEVENTEEN

This lesson follows the regular review pattern, followed by a new step in the learning process. Below are two melodies incorporating past lessons acquired in transferring to the staff all syllables lying between *doh* and *doh'* with the exception of *te,* which will be the new factor

presented later in this lesson. These melodies increase in length and
sometimes skip to and from secondary tones.

Use key of B♭ major.

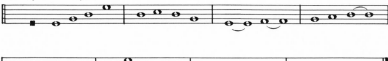

EXAMPLE 58.

In Melody 59 it might be advisable to employ a preliminary hand-
sign drill on the leaps from *ray* to *soh*, *fah* to *ray*, transferring these
immediately to measures 4, 5, and 9 of the melody written on the
chalk board. Note the *fermata* sign.

Use key of B♭ major.

EXAMPLE 59.

Only one note, *te*, is now required to complete the octave scale.
This is always an awkward sound to teach and for this reason has been
left until all the other notes have been thoroughly assimilated. To
accomplish more easily the transfer of *te* to the staff, an unusual key is
proposed in order to place the new note within the tessitura of the
cambiata voice. For this purpose the key of A major is recommended;
consequently, in order to remain within the composite octave-unison
range, eliminate *doh* and *ray* from the exercises written to negotiate
the initial transfer. Point out that *te* appears on the next line above
soh.

Use key of A major.

Follow established procedure in teaching this new factor, then proceed to incorporate *te* in the melody presented below. Make frequent use of hand signs to orient singers to the appropriate *doh* chord.

Use key of A major.

EXAMPLE 60.

Do not spend too much time mastering Ex. 60; be governed by the class attitude. The moment boredom or inattention becomes evident it is a waste of time and energy to continue. If, on the other hand, interest seems high, prolong the music reading activity, providing the class and you are in sight of an attainable goal.

Acquiring and retaining musical skills is a slow growth process which cannot be accelerated at the teacher's will. This fact must be accepted, and lessons planned accordingly. Although the human voice is an amazing instrument, it is a phenomenal accomplishment to teach junior high school students to observe a musical symbol, then from a given home note (*doh*) manipulate vocal chords in such a manner that they vibrate at will to the required frequency which will produce the sound illustrated by the symbol. Furthermore, the ability to change this frequency to other frequencies as the symbols progression indicates, sometimes necessitating rapid and violent frequency change, is little short of miraculous. This skill does not come quickly.

Therefore for the next few meetings with the class or group, be content to consolidate previous learnings. Do not rush into a new phase of reading. Melodies used previously might be reviewed; in addition some new melodies are offered below, which might be supplemented by others from *The Reading Singer*. Help the singers all you can, using hand signs to overcome difficult progressions and constantly reorienting the *doh* chord. Remember, this is sight training not sight testing.

Use key of A major.

EXAMPLE 61.

Use key of B ♭ major.

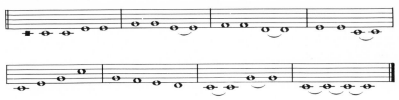

EXAMPLE 62.

Use key of D major.

EXAMPLE 63.

Use key of C major.

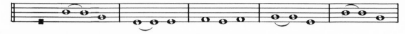

EXAMPLE 64.

Use key of B♭ major.

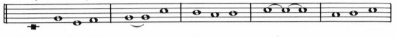

EXAMPLE 65.

At this stage of the music reading proceedings it is possible to transfer many of the lessons to the reading of a new song from a book or sheet of music.

LESSON EIGHTEEN

This lesson may be regarded as an extension of the consolidation work by using *plagal* melodies which lie between *soh*₁ and *soh,* thus requiring the use of *lah*₁ and *te*₁. In view of the fact that the past few music reading periods have been in the nature of review, there is little point in starting the present lesson with further review. Proceed immediately to the transfer of *soh*₁, *lah*₁ and *te*₁ to the staff.

Use key of E♭ major.

Use the same presentation techniques practiced in earlier transference to the staff.

Use key of E ♭ major.

EXAMPLE 66.

Use key of E ♭ major.

EXAMPLE 67.

Use key of E ♭ major.

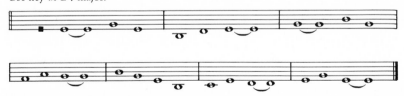

EXAMPLE 68.

There will be no presentation of melodies which combine authentic and plagal features because these are unusable in junior high school vocal work; the incidence of combination presupposes a vocal range of an eleventh, a third greater than the composite unison range available for mixed voice unison singing in junior high school.

Phase Three: Note-Length Values

LESSON NINETEEN

Phase Three of the music reading program is based on the assumption that classwork in the fundamentals program has progressed to the point where note duration values have been learned.

Explain to the class that all notes do not last the same length of time. For instance, *doh –* has two counts, *doh – –* has three counts, and so on. When these are presented in syllable form they are simpler to read, sing, and hold whatever number of counts is indicated. Now that students have started to use the staff in music reading, a simpler method of indicating long or short notes in staff notation must be found. The method of using ties for this purpose is very cumbersome.

Write the following rhythmic pattern on the chalk board. The

black notes are one-count notes, the open white notes are two-count notes. Two open white notes tied together will require one sound with a total of four counts.

Tell the class they are about to perform this *rhythm* exercise by using their hands in what is termed the *clap-shake* manner. A one-count note will be performed by clapping the right and left palms once, chest high. Thus the first bar of the rhythm exercise will require four claps, for which you should either beat time or point to the notes on the chalk board.

The half-note (open white) will be performed manually by clapping for the first count; then, without releasing the clap, grip the hands and shake firmly in about a six-inch arc for the holding beat. Two consecutive half-notes will require the following manual interpretation: *clap-shake, clap-shake;* and two half-notes tied will require *clap-shake-shake-shake.* Rehearse this once or twice with the class, then return to the chalk board and direct a *clap-shake* performance of the rhythm pattern proposed for this lesson.

Transfer this learning immediately to the staff, reverting once more to the simple melodic designs of Lessons Two and Eleven of the music reading series.

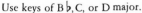
Use keys of B♭, C, or D major.

Example 69.

First have the class respond by *clap-shake* techniques only to the rhythmic aspects of the exercise. Establish a suitable *doh* chord, then instruct the class to monotone the rhythm of the exercise on *doh,* using the neutral syllable *loo* as you point to the notes.

Next, quickly draw a blank staff on the chalk board, with the *doh* marker inscribed, and drill on the *doh* chord formation as you point to the desired pitches on the blank staff. Class response should

first be in articulated music syllables, followed immediately by the same pattern using *loo.* Finally transfer the melody to the chalk board, combining rhythm and pitch sung to *loo.* It is recommended that Lesson Nineteen of the reading series be deferred a few general music periods to allow the new aspect of note time values to be absorbed thoroughly by the singers before adding new note value factors.

During these interim periods, one-beat and two-beat notes should appear in cumulatively more complex situations by adding progressively *ray, fah, lah,* and *te.* The terms *quarter-note* and *half-note* may now be introduced in the simplest possible context.

Tell the class that any merchandise in a store bears a label on the outside of the container to indicate type and quantity of goods contained inside. At the beginning of a song or piece of instrumental music, a label is imprinted to indicate the general content of each measure. Thus, if you beat four counts to every measure, each beat being of quarter-note duration, the label will be 4/4. Should the music require three beats to every measure, each beat having a quarter-note value, the label will be 3/4. These numbers are called the *timesign* or *time signature* and appear on the staff immediately preceding the first note.

SEVEN-STEP READING ROUTINE

Below is a step-by-step procedure to follow in the presentation of each melody for the purpose of reading. For some weeks it is advisable to follow this routine conscientiously without deviation until the singers have achieved a competence which justifies elimination of one or more steps of the routine. Keep in mind the routine here described is not sight *testing*, it is eye *training*.

To illustrate more clearly the various steps of the reading routine, the melody below will be used as a model.

Use keys of B♭, C, or D major.

EXAMPLE 70.

Step One

Extract different note values or significant rhythm figures from the exercise and write them in another place on the chalk board. Tell the class what you are doing.

Step Two

Ask the class to react by means of the *clap-shake* system as you point to various notes or groups of notes appearing in the extraction on the chalk board.

Step Three

Repeat the pointing process while the class reacts vocally, using the neutral vowel sound *loo* on the pitch of C.

Step Four

Transfer the pointing process to the complete melody written on the chalk board while the class again reacts vocally by monotone *loo* as in Step Three, expressing rhythm only on the pitch of C.

Step Five

Draw a blank staff on the chalk board, inserting no markings except the location of *doh*.

The melody appearing in the model, Ex. 70, is quite simple in character, requiring only the notes *doh, me, soh,* so that Step Five is relatively easy. Pitch the key of B♭, C, or D major, establish the fact that *doh* is on the second line, and instruct your class to respond by singing syllables as you point to the blank staff locations of *doh, me, soh.* Try to outline the curve of the melody in Ex. 70, but do not spend more than one minute on Step Five.

Step Six

Repeat the process advocated in Step Five, this time using the neutral syllable *loo*. Again, do not allow more than one minute for this step.

Step Seven

Transfer all this activity to the model, Ex. 70, on the chalk board, combining rhythmic and melodic aspects as you point to each note while the class sings.

The foregoing presentation is perfectly adequate for teaching music reading through the medium of melodies written on the chalk board. However, junior high school students must learn to apply these principles to the printed page of music in order to develop individual independence in music reading. If students have individual music books from which to read, there will, of course, be some slight modification of the seven-step routine defined above. The singers will be referred in Steps Four and Seven to the melody in the book rather than to the chalk board.

Students who sing from books can point with the index finger to each bar as it is being sung, tapping the appropriate count like a metronome for each bar. Thus a quarter-note will receive one finger tap, a half-note will receive two finger taps, two half-notes tied will receive four taps.

Below will be found a few melodies embodying music reading skills acquired up to this point. Follow the seven-step reading routine for each of these melodies.

Use keys of B♭, C, or D major.

EXAMPLE 71.

Adding ray.
Use keys of B♭, C, or D major.

EXAMPLE 72.

Adding fah.
Use keys of B♭, C, or D major.

EXAMPLE 73.

Adding lah, te, doh'.
Use key of B ♭major only.

EXAMPLE 74.

Adding soh,, lah, ray.
Use key of E ♭ major.

EXAMPLE 75.

LESSON TWENTY

No review work is needed if all melodies appearing at the end of Lesson Nineteen have been read and sung.

The new materials in this lesson are the whole-note symbol and the dotted half-note symbol. Little explanation is needed to describe the whole-note (four-count) symbol to students. ○ But the dotted half-note requires a little attention. Try this approach. Write on the chalk board  which receives a *clap-shake-shake* hand action. Point to the illustration, counting in threes as the class responds. Refer to the manner in which you eliminated the tie to make two tied half-notes into one whole-note. Illustrate this application to a three-count note by the following brief process: remove the stem from the quarter-note ♩ ● then remove the tie marks; conclude by reducing the head of the quarter note and moving it closer to the half-note. ♩. Follow the above presentation by a demonstration, applying this routine: (1) students *clap-shake* the rhythm as you point to the exercise; then (2) monotone the rhythm, using *loo* on a C pitch; and finally (3) sing the exercise to *loo* combining pitch and rhythm.

Here are two melodies to use as media for applying the new materials to practical situations. When presenting each of these melodies to be read and sung by your group, follow the seven-step routine prescribed in Lesson Nineteen.

Use key of C major.

EXAMPLE 76.

Use key of F major.

EXAMPLE 77.

LESSON TWENTY-ONE

Begin with a brief review of the previous lesson, for which the following melody is offered. Use the key of B♭ major and follow the seven-step reading routine.

Use key of B ♭ major.

EXAMPLE 78.

This lesson will be concerned with eighth-notes. To simplify the presentation of eighth-notes they will be used in pairs, thus avoiding premature complexities of the dotted quarter-note and compound duple time, which will come later.

First the new time values have to be incorporated into the *clap-shake* hand rhythm responses. The hand action involved in responding to ♪♪ or ♪ ♪ is accomplished by brushing the palms of the hands across each other in the same manner that a cymbal player manipulates his metal discs.

Tell the class about new note-length values and that the quarter-note splits into two eighth-notes. Write the following rhythmic pattern

on the chalk board. Clap the above rhythmic pattern as an illustration, speaking the words appearing under the notes.

Ask the class to use the appropriate *clap-shake* hand movements as you point to each *beat* of the rhythmic pattern on the board; then repeat the procedure with the class singing monotone *loo* on the pitch C.

Apply this to a melody which incorporates eighth-notes.

Use keys of B♭, C, or D major.

EXAMPLE 79.

Follow the seven-step music reading routine in presenting this new melody.

LESSON TWENTY-TWO

Begin with the usual review, for which the melodies are offered below. Follow the seven-step music reading routine in presenting these melodies. Should the class respond well to the reading activity abbreviate the procedure by eliminating Steps One and Five.

Use key of C major.

EXAMPLE 80.

Use key of B♭ major.

EXAMPLE 81.

The new material for Lesson Twenty-two is that *bête noire* of school music teachers, the dotted quarter-note, which is in fact a very simple rhythmic device to teach.

Tell the class that a new rhythm figure is to be illustrated. Write the following on the chalk board.

Refer to the dotted half-note (page 142) and apply the same principle used in teaching this note value to the above rhythm, thus:

The *clap-shake* action for the dotted quarter-note followed by an eighth-note is *clap sha-ky*, the right palm brushing upwards across the left palm for *-ky*.

Instruct the class to perform the above rhythm by using hand motions as you point through the exercise. Quickly incorporate this rhythm into a simple melody and complete the total reading performance by means of the seven-step music reading routine.

Use keys of B ♭, C, or D major.

EXAMPLE 82.

LESSON TWENTY-THREE

This lesson should follow the usual pattern, starting with a review incorporated in the following melodies.

Use keys of C or D major.

EXAMPLE 83.

Use key of E ♭ major only.

EXAMPLE 84.

This lesson is concerned with the use of a 6/8 time signature and the application thereto of previously acquired reading devices. It is assumed that the class has been following the fundamentals program presented in Chapter Seven, and that by now the students are familiar with the appearance of music written in 6/8 time. The transfer of theoretical understanding of compound duple time to its practical application in music reading is quite simple.

By now the students are thoroughly familiar with the *clap-shake* technique, which is so well established that liberties may be taken. Write the following rhythm on the chalk board.

Explain to the class that as long as each eighth-note has a syllable of a word to itself it will have a separate hook or flag.

If however two or more eighth-notes are sung to one syllable of a word, the flags of those notes are joined by a *beam,* and a *slur* mark joins the note heads.

This arrangement, however, does not affect the reading system. The important change in 6/8 time is that in the *clap-shake* routine each eighth-note receives a one-count clap, each quarter-note therefore receives a *clap-shake,* and each dotted quarter receives a *clap-shake-shake.*

Now, using these new values, demonstrate the rhythm on the chalk board by the *clap-shake* technique, asking a student to come to the board and point as you demonstrate. Employ a slow tempo.

Follow this immediately by directing the class to respond with appropriate *clap-shake* hand action as you point to the notes on the chalk board.

Transferring from hand action to vocalizing, direct the class to sing the rhythm to monotone *loo* on the pitch D as you point to the board.

Up to this point you have followed Steps One to Four in the regular reading procedure. Now complete the reading of the melody by continuing through Steps Five, Six, and Seven.

Use key of B♭ major only.

Come_with me and take_ a walk, o-ver the fields and o'er_ the hill.

EXAMPLE 85.

For the first time in this reading program you are advised to spend a few extra minutes eliminating rough places and developing the swinging rhythm of 6/8 time.

LESSON TWENTY-FOUR

Begin with the customary review, melodies for which are presented below. Draw attention to the tie in the final bar of Ex. 86.

Use key of B♭ major.

EXAMPLE 86.

Use key of C minor (*doh* is E ♭).

EXAMPLE 87.

This lesson will concern the use of the dotted eighth-note followed by a sixteenth-note. It is assumed that sufficient progress has been realized by the class in the fundamentals program to justify this new departure. The dotted half-note will also be introduced in a new situation.

Write the following rhythm on the chalk board:

First draw attention to the dotted half-note and refer to the procedure you used when the whole-note replaced two half-notes tied. The dotted half-note therefore in 6/8 time will receive *clap-shake-shake, shake-shake-shake*.

In order to present clearly the dotted eighth-note–sixteenth-note figure used in 6/8 time, revert to the dotted quarter-note–eighth-note figure used in 3/4 time, thus

Point out the *clap-sha-ky, clap* rhythm in Measures 3, 5, and 6, and transfer this action to this figure:

Now return to the original rhythm. Perform it yourself by *clap-shake* hand action while a student points to the chalk board rhythm. Follow

this by pointing to the rhythm yourself while the class responds with *clap-shake* hand action. Using the following melody, continue the various progressive steps of the music reading routine until the class sings the time and tune to *loo*.

Use key of C major.

EXAMPLE 88.

This is the final lesson in the formal presentation of note-length values in the music reading program. To cope with the many variants of note-value combinations encountered in choral literature is an impossible task. However, any class that has mastered the material in the foregoing section will be able to cope with most problems found in the literature they perform.

To emphasize a point made at the beginning of this chapter, do not isolate the music reading program from the song singing program. As various reading skills accumulate, apply them constantly to appropriate situations in the song learning process.

Four melodies appearing below may be used for consolidating music reading skills acquired to this point.

Use keys of C or D major.

EXAMPLE 89.

Use key of D ♭ major only.

EXAMPLE 90.

Use key of B ♭ major only.

EXAMPLE 91.

Use key of B minor (*doh* is D).

EXAMPLE 92.

LESSON TWENTY-FIVE

There is yet another aspect of time values which must be discovered by the singers. Occasions arise in music when a strategically placed silence is as effective as a continuation of the music sound. The teacher should explain that the composer has a system of signs for telling performers when these silences are to occur, and for how long the silences must be observed. To indicate a silence equal in length to a quarter-note the sign ⁀ is generally used, although some music dating from other centuries uses ⁀ for the same purpose. A silence equal in length to a half-note is indicated by the sign ═▬═ resting on a line of the music staff, usually the third. Two simple melodies which incorporate the new material are presented below for music reading.

Use keys of B ♭, C, or D major.

EXAMPLE 93.

Use keys of C or D major.

EXAMPLE 94.

A minor problem arises during the early stages of this work. The singers sometimes want to articulate something during the *rest* duration period. The problem can be eliminated before it becomes manifest by instructing the class to articulate the word "rest" for every beat which is thus involved. Apply this technique to Ex. 93. First use the exercise as a monotone expression on the tonic note (*doh*) of whatever key has been selected for eventual performance.

If the class is still using the *clap-shake* technique, both hands should be placed palms downward on the desk or lap during the vocal articulation of "rest."

This procedure is dubious because by articulating the word "rest," the silence is not secured; nevertheless, it is highly successful. The device may be discarded when students have developed a sense of *resting*.

The incidence of two quarter-rests in measures 2 and 4 of Ex. 94 may give rise to questions unless the subject has been covered in the music fundamentals section of the general music program.

LESSON TWENTY-SIX

Continue with the development of rest symbols. The following melody is offered as a review medium. Draw attention to the fact that a dot is rarely used to increase the duration of a rest by half its note value; thus a rest equal in duration to a dotted half-note would appear in the printed music as shown here, but this presents no problem.

Use keys of B ♭, C, or D major.

EXAMPLE 95.

This lesson is concerned with the printed symbols for indicating a rest equal in value to the time duration of a whole-note and a rest equal in value to the time duration of an eighth-note. The symbol indicating a rest or silence equal to time duration of a whole-note appears as shown, usually hanging from the fourth line. Incidentally a somewhat confusing factor to junior high singers or instrumental players is that this symbol is also used to indicate a complete bar of silence in any music, no matter what may be the time signature.

For indicating a silence equal to the time duration of an eighth-note, the following symbol is used.

Two melodies appearing herewith will provide media by which the singers may apply the new material to a choral situation. Do not as yet omit the rhythmic monotone *loo* procedure before attempting the melodic line.

Use key of B ♭ major.

Slowly

EXAMPLE 96.

Use key of B ♭ major.

EXAMPLE 97.

There is no point in proceeding to more complex aspects of rest symbols at this time. The purpose of the music reading program is to provide junior high school singers with techniques to apply to the printed choral music they will encounter. Only those facets of music learning are presented which further the development of the planned cumulative program of instruction.

Phase Four: Music Using Doh in a Staff Space

The music learning process is one of slow growth, and the music reading program has thus far dealt with one new aspect of music reading per lesson in an attempt to present a logical sequence of material to be mastered commensurate with the growth potential of the singing group or organization.

Singers with the most elementary level of competence, who have progressed in the general music class or choral group through the learning processes outlined so far in this chapter, should now be able to comprehend a printed unison melodic line. This will involve the simple elements of *time* and *pitch,* providing the home note *doh* appears on a line of the staff. (Thus far no clef signs have been used, and no music has been presented for reading purposes in which the home note *doh* has appeared in a staff space.)

DEFERMENT OF INSTRUCTION CONCERNING CLEFS

In order to present cumulatively yet simply the various stages of music reading, any complexities not vital to the progression of learning at any stage of development were delayed. For example, Phase Two of this chapter concerned the transfer of music syllables to appropriate positions on the music staff. To make this transfer as easy to negotiate as possible, *doh* always appeared on a line. This practice was maintained throughout the section.

Had music clefs been used at this stage, the teaching would have necessitated two staffs, one using the G clef for sopranos and cambiate, the other using the F clef for baritones. To complicate matters further, a definite pitch name would automatically be involved, and while the G clef singers were reading *doh* on a line, baritones would read an octave below, where *doh* would appear in a space.

In this section previous music staff learnings will be extended by introducing *doh* as a note in a space, and familiarizing the singers with new space relationships brought about by this new concept of the *doh* position.

Although your singers have become acquainted by now with the visual aspects of clefs in both the music fundamentals lesson and their song books, and in spite of the fact that learning a new song is a process involving a mixture of reading and rote teachings, it is not yet advisable to use a clef sign in the formal music-reading lesson. The use of only one set of staff lines is of great advantage until the presentation of clef signs has been completed.

LESSON TWENTY-SEVEN

Begin with a review of previous lessons by using any one of the exercises 89 through 92. The fact that your class has probably sung all these before is of no consequence; the students are not *sight singing,* they are learning to read.

This lesson will be concerned with music reading when *doh* appears in a space. It is not necessary to revert to the elementary routine outlined at the beginning of Phase Two of this chapter, wherein the staff evolved line by line. The singers are now familiar with the complete five-line staff.

It is sufficient to write Ex. 98 on the chalk board, drawing attention to the fact that in this melody *doh* appears in a space.

Use key of C major.

EXAMPLE 98.

Point out that, *doh* being in a space, *me* will appear in the next higher space, while *soh* will appear in the next space higher than that containing *me*. It should be noted that in presenting this new learning unnecessary rhythm complexities have been avoided to ensure undivided attention to and concentration on the new factor.

Sing this melody to syllables while a class member points to the melodic progression on the chalk board; then direct the singers to respond with pitch syllables while you point to the melody. Be careful to establish the key of C major for this performance. Conclude by having your class vocalize the melody to *loo* while you beat time.

LESSON TWENTY-EIGHT

Begin with the usual review, for which purpose two melodies are given below,

Use keys of C or D major.

EXAMPLE 99.

Use keys of C, or D major.

EXAMPLE 100.

This lesson consists of transferring syllables *ray* and *fah* to line positions on the staff. At this stage of music reading development the singers are capable of assimilating two factors in one lesson, thus considerably accelerating the learning process.

Illustrate the new positions of *ray* and *fah* by means of the following pitch patterns written on the chalk board.

In the key of C major sing these through for the class, using *hand signs* to illustrate your point more clearly, while one of the students points out the progression on the board. Next, direct the class to sing

by means of syllables while you point to the board progression, and follow this by the *loo* routine.

Transfer this immediately to the following melody, using the seven-step music reading pattern.* The leap to and from secondary tones is employed much earlier in Phase Four than it was in Phase Two.

Use keys of B♭, C, or D major.

EXAMPLE 101.

LESSON TWENTY-NINE

Begin with the usual review period, for which purpose Ex. 102 and Ex. 103 are presented.

Use keys of B♭, C, or D major.

EXAMPLE 102.

Use key of B♭, C, or D major.

EXAMPLE 103.

The new material for this lesson concerns the new look of *doh'* appearing on a staff line when *doh* appears in a space. This is the only lesson in Phase Four in which the new material will be confined to the addition of one note, consequently opportunity will be taken to incorporate more complex rhythmic aspects.

Write the following patterns on the chalk board.

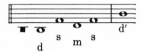

Use key of B♭ major.

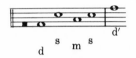

Sing these pitch patterns to syllables, using hand signs, while one of your class members points to notes on the chalk board. Next, direct the class to respond by singing syllables as you point to the board; follow this activity by using the *loo* routine.

Transfer this new material immediately to the singing of the melody appearing below, using the usual seven-step music reading routine.

Use key of B♭ major.

EXAMPLE 104.

LESSON THIRTY

Begin with a review of previous lessons as incorporated in the following melodies.

Use key of B♭ major.

EXAMPLE 105.

Use key of B♭ major.

EXAMPLE 106.

This lesson involves transferring the syllables *lah* and *te* to the staff, when *doh* appears in a space.

Write the following pitch patterns on the chalk board.

Use key of B♭ major.

Follow the usual procedure in teaching new locations for *lah* and *te*, then transfer the new material to a melodic situation, using the following exercise. For the sake of continuity and to ensure a reasonably successful reading, proceed through the seven-step routine.

Use key of B♭ major.

EXAMPLE 107.

LESSON THIRTY-ONE

Begin with the customary review, for which purpose two melodies appear below.

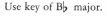

EXAMPLE 108.

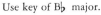

EXAMPLE 109.

In view of the leisurely manner in which this music reading series has developed, it may be assumed that on occasion the teaching of new material may be accelerated. This lesson will encompass transfer to the staff of three syllables, sor_1, lah_1, and te_1 in their relative positions below *doh*, when *doh* is a space note. The purpose of this step is to condition the class for reading and singing *plagal* melodies which lie between soh_1 and *soh*. The composite unison-octave vocal range found in junior high school restricts the key used to E♭ major.

Write the following pitch patterns on the chalk board and proceed to introduce the new lesson by means of the technique already established.

Use key of E♭ major.

Transfer this new material immediately to a situation which involves reading a melody line. Use the seven-step music reading routine.

Use key of E♭ major.

EXAMPLE 110.

LESSON THIRTY-TWO

Begin with a review of previous lessons, for which purpose two melodies are presented.

Use keys of E♭ or F major.

EXAMPLE 111.

Use key of D♭ major.

EXAMPLE 112.

This lesson concerns melodies in which *doh* appears in a space and the home note is *lah₁*. This, of course, involves minor tonality which, under normal circumstances, would also involve chromatic changes in notation. Such changes assume the presence of a key signature, and while it is reasonable to expect that students in the general music class will by this time have encountered key signatures in the music fundamentals program, it is not wise just yet to incorporate this learning in the music reading program.

In order to incorporate minor tonality into the music reading program yet avoid chromatically changed notes, the natural minor scale, which does not involve raised sixth or seventh degrees, will be used.

There is no necessity at this juncture to become involved in a discussion of the complexities arising in the use of the minor mode. Such technicalities as the raising or lowering of the sixth and seventh degrees or relativity between the major and minor keys should be postponed until the foregoing aspects of music reading have been thoroughly assimilated by the singers. As long as the position of *doh* is clearly indicated in each minor melody by the small black square, and the chord of *lah₁, doh, me* is established at the outset, minor tonality will evolve.

Use key of C minor (*doh* is E♭).

Write the above patterns on the chalk board and introduce them by means of the usual teaching technique. When the class appears to have assimilated this feeling, transfer the material to the following melody, which should be processed through the seven-step music reading routine.

Use key of B minor (*doh* is D).

EXAMPLE 113.

Phase Five: Introduction to Clefs and Part-Reading

LESSON THIRTY-THREE

Begin with a review session, for which two melodies are offered herewith.

Use key of B♭ minor (*doh* is D♭).

EXAMPLE 114.

Use key of C minor (*doh* is E♭).

EXAMPLE 115.

In Phases Two and Four of the music reading program (relating to transfer of syllables to staff notation), two syllables introduced in Phase One are apparently neglected. *Fe* and *se* used in the syllable presentation of the minor mode have been avoided in staff work, because the use of these syllables involves chromatic alteration against a key signature, and it has been expedient to avoid up to now the use of clefs or key signatures. It is not even possible to foreshadow the use of chromatic changes for minor music because signs for note alteration vary according to the use of sharps or flats in a key signature. For instance in the key of C major, which requires no key signature, *fe* would be indicated by the sign ♯ placed in front of the note *fah,*

When any specific note location on the staff has to be identified with a definite pitch, it is necessary to discard the blank staff and add clef signs. A two-staff system is now unavoidable because, as will be seen in the above illustration, sopranos and cambiate read *doh* on a line, whereas baritones read *doh* in a space.

It would have been possible to indicate *fe* and *se* by using sharp signs and explaining their significance in raising pitch. But in flat keys raising of the sixth and seventh degrees against the key signature requires the use of *natural* signs (♮):

For this reason *fe* and *se* were temporarily rejected. Our objective is to avoid complexities wherever possible in the interest of easy assimilation of new learnings.

It is now appropriate to transfer *fe* and *se* to staff notation and, as a result, to introduce clefs and key signatures.

It will be assumed at this point that students under general music instruction have been exposed to elementary aspects of the music fundamentals program, and that theoretically they are aware of the function of clefs, key signatures, and signs for *accidentals* (altered notes).

Lesson Thirty-three of the music reading series will concern the two staff system, employing the key of C major. So that the class may assimilate more quickly the visual aspects of the two staffs and two clefs system, *accidentals* will be deferred until Music Reading Lesson Thirty-four. Explain to the class that in the music they will sing, boys with voices in the second stage of the change will require a special staff of their own to accommodate low tones not sung by sopranos or cambiate. Draw the following pattern on the chalk board and draw attention to the fact that from here on, if *doh* is on a line in the G clef, it will appear in a space for baritones singing from the F clef.

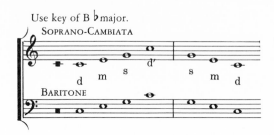

Pitch the key of Bb major, establish *doh* quite firmly, and ask the singers to respond as you point to the pattern written on the chalk board.

Transfer this learning to a melodic reading situation, using the following exercise.

EXAMPLE 116.

Follow the seven-step music reading routine throughout. Do not eliminate any of the steps on this occasion. Step Five, involving blank staff work, will require a two-staff system written on the chalk board.

Two points, previously referred to only briefly, now require some elaboration. First, if the singers are to be taught to read in many keys, the apparent discrepancy between the key of the printed music and the key of actual performance is an unavoidable expediency due to range limitations imposed by the composite unison range (page 16) available for mixed classes of boys and girls in junior high school grades. Not the slightest difficulty will rise if *you do not tell the singers they are engaged in transposition.* The moment three-part music reading becomes possible, explain the transposition to the singers.

The second point concerns the desirability of music reading books in the hands of the students, a matter which has been mentioned earlier but now becomes more urgent. Music written on the chalk board has completely different space dimensions than that printed and presents different visual aspects to the singer. Furthermore, the vocal teacher uses a great deal of valuable class time writing appropriate music reading material on the chalk board, material which often has to be erased and sometimes rewritten to meet the needs of consecutive classes at various levels of reading achievement.

LESSON THIRTY-FOUR

Begin with a brief review period, for which purpose Ex. 117 is recommended.

Use keys of B ♭, C, or D major.

EXAMPLE 117.

This lesson will involve the presentation of a chromatically altered note, which is occasioned by the transfer of the syllable *fe* to staff notation. Following established practice introduce the transfer by means of simple notational patterns written on the chalk board.

By means of the piano keyboard diagram illustrate the position of *fe* when a *sharp* sign (♯) is required in key of C major, then continue the illustration when a *natural* sign (♮) is indicated.

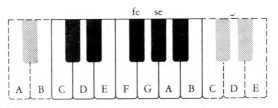

PIANO KEYBOARD SECTION

A simple principle may be taught here; in the key of C major and in all keys requiring sharps in the signature *fe* will be indicated by the use of a *sharp* sign, whereas in keys requiring flats in the signature *fe* will be indicated by the use of a *natural* sign.

Do not get involved in an exposé of the modulatory implications of *fe*. This would serve merely to confuse the singers.

In order to induce the tonal feeling of *fe,* sing the above pattern, using hand signs while a student points to the notes on the chalk board; then direct the class to sing as you point, accenting the sound of *fe.* Pitch the key of B♭ major. These patterns could be performed in other keys, but inasmuch as the melody which follows encompasses a greater range, necessitating the key of B♭ major, it is wiser to use this key in the preliminary exercises.

When the singers seem to know *fe* transfer it to a melodic situation, using Ex. 118 presented here. Explain the need for cancelling the sharp in Measure 5. Use key of B♭ major and observe all parts of the seven-step music reading routine.

Use key of B ♭ major.

EXAMPLE 118.

LESSON THIRTY-FIVE

Begin with the usual review, for which purpose the following melodies are presented. It should be pointed out to the singers that in music where the key signature is comprised of flats, *fah* will be a flatted note; thus to indicate *fe,* a natural sign will need to be placed just before the *fah.*

Use key of B♭ major.

EXAMPLE 119.

Use key of E♭ major.

EXAMPLE 120.

This lesson is concerned with the transfer of the syllable *se* to staff notation and its function in music written in the minor mode. Here are suggested note patterns to write on the chalk board.

The only means by which the singers can learn and assimilate a new musical sound is through hearing that sound played or sung for

Use key of B♭ minor (*doh* is D♭).

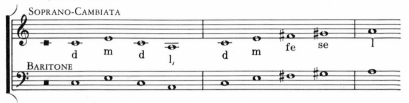

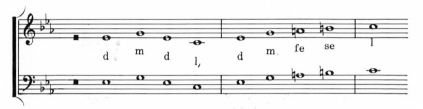

them in relation to sounds already heard and identified. *Se* is not an easy sound to establish in the singers' vocal competence, and this lesson may have to be used twice in order for the sound to become thoroughly familiar.

Using the above patterns follow the usual teaching routine in presenting the new sound and its *sign;* then transfer to a melodic situation using the following melody. Point out that the home note in this melody is *lah,* and that as the most frequently used notes in minor music are *lah,, doh, me,* this chord will be played to establish tonality.

Pitch the chord of B♭ minor (*doh* is D♭). Follow the seven-step music reading routine for Ex. 121 on page 170.

By this time students should have sufficient music reading competency to apply their skills to many unison songs found in any of the junior high school basic music series, *but* in some instances the keys in which the songs are printed will need to be changed in order to bring the melodic range within the composite unison junior high mixed voice vocal range.

Without being aware of theoretical implications involved, the singers have now been exposed to the most commonly used device for modulating to the dominant key by means of the raised subdominant (fourth). Modulation to the subdominant key is frequently encountered in vocal music, and it is desirable that general music students be exposed to the device by which this is accomplished, namely the lowered leading tone (seventh), presented in the following lesson.

Use key of B♭ minor (*doh* is D♭).

EXAMPLE 121.

LESSON THIRTY-SIX

Begin with a review session, for which two melodies are offered below.

Use key of B minor (*doh* is D).

EXAMPLE 122.

Use key of C major.

EXAMPLE 123.

This lesson involves a completely new sound, its syllable name and its function on the staff. This sound is produced by lowering *te* a half tone, and the syllable used for this sound is *taw*. Approach this new sound by reverting briefly to the syllable system, and writing this pattern on the chalk board.

$$\text{d}\quad^{\text{m}}\quad^{\text{s}}\quad_{\text{m}}\quad\Big|\quad_{\text{d}}\quad^{\text{m}}\quad^{\text{s}}\quad^{\text{d}'}\Big|\quad\text{t}\ -\ \text{taw}\ -\Big|\ \text{l}\ -\ -\ -\ \Big|\quad^{\text{s}}\quad_{\text{m}}\quad_{\text{d}}\ -\ \Big\|$$

TAW

Sing this pattern in the key of Bb major, using hand signs, while a student points to the syllables on the chalk board. Draw particular attention to the new hand sign, even though there may be little cause to use it in much of the future work.

Direct the class to sing syllables while you point to the board, then repeat the procedure to the neutral vowel *loo*.

Transfer the syllable pattern to a staff pattern. In the incidence of *fe,* the chromatic alteration was achieved by means of a *sharp* sign, ♯ or a natural sign ♮ in most keys using flats. To achieve chromatic alteration for *taw,* the seventh degree of the scale will be lowered by means of a *natural* sign in keys using sharps, and by means of a *flat* sign (♭) in all other keys.

Use key of Bb major.

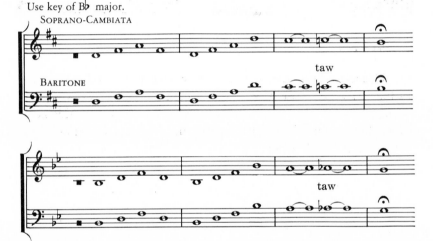

Repeat the procedure used in the music syllable presentation of this figure, first applying appropriate syllables, then *loo*. Do not spend too much time on this before turning to a melodic situation for which the following exercise is presented.

Should this type of progression prove troublesome in subsequent song singing, the class might return to this lesson for a brief drill session.

The general principle has now been well established that the prefix of a sharp sign raises the pitch of a note by a half tone, a flat sign lowers the pitch of a note by a half tone, and a natural sign may either raise or lower depending on the use of sharps or flats in a key signature, and it

Use key of B♭ major.

EXAMPLE 124.

will be assumed the singers have achieved some competency in responding vocally to these signs. Therefore, there will not be a detailed presentation of aspects evolving from chromatic alteration of other scale tones.

Singing groups which have followed the development of the music reading program thus far will find little trouble in solving chromatic problems when they are encountered in the song singing program. The final portion of the music reading program will be devoted to music in which all voices do not sing in unison or unison-octave.

One of the difficulties faced by vocal music teachers in junior high school is the tendency of boys to quit their own part if it is uninteresting and associate themselves with a more tuneful part. This is not a conscious operation on the part of the boys, but it often stems from an inability to read music. The easiest tune to assimilate is adopted therefore, and after this happens little can shake it loose in favor of the proper part. To avoid this situation, in the following music reading development every effort will be made to contrive singing parts which are totally different in character and melodically independent of each other. With this new complexity to challenge the singers the level of difficulty in other aspects will be the simpler one of earlier lessons in the music reading program.

Lesson Thirty-seven

Do not open with the usual review. There is not sufficient time in which to reach the desired goal of two-part music reading, unless the routine review is omitted. However, the nature of the new learning automatically involves some review procedure. Write Ex. 125 on the chalk board.

Use key of B♭ major.

Example 125.

Part one will be allocated to sopranos and cambiate, leaving part two for baritones. The fact that sopranos and cambiate are still singing together on part one of this melody imposes the composite unison range restriction, an interval of a ninth, on the scope of part one, which in turn dictates the key in which the exercise may be sung. Remember this is still *sight training,* not *sight testing,* consequently singers should be introduced to the above exercise by means of the established seven-step music reading routine. Although it may have been possible in previous exercises to eliminate one or more steps, it is better in the beginning of multiple-part singing to revert to the full routine for awhile. Steps one, two, three, and four may be taken simultaneously with the entire group, but you will need to point to every beat in each line during step four. Steps five, six, and seven, however, will have to be taken separately for each of the parts before combining them.

Should students be reading from books, instruct them to maintain
tempo by tapping each beat (not each note value) with the index finger
of the right hand, pointing to each measure as it is being sung. This
applies only to steps four and seven.

Before proceeding to music reading in three parts it is advisable
to continue in two-part singing for several reading periods in order to
develop some facility therein. The class will never attain perfection in
music reading, but the function of learning to read music is simply to
make the printed music intelligible to the singers. By diligent application they may learn to perform it and reduce to a minimum their de-
pendence on the music teacher's voice as a model for imitation. At this
age level there will always be need for a limited amount of rote singing
reference to negotiate difficult progressions in a part song. These
references will become less frequent, however, as reading skills improve. A few two-part singing exercises are offered below as media for
consolidating this development. Due to restrictions imposed by the
composite unison range, it is unlikely that appropriate two-part songs
will be found in much available song literature, even after transposition, particularly when tessitura is considered.

Notice in Ex. 126 through Ex. 129 that both parts are deliberately
contrasted as to rhythmic devices to reduce the chances of any voice
switching to the other part.

Use key of A♭ major.

EXAMPLE 126.

Use key of D♭ major.

EXAMPLE 127.

Use key of E♭ major.

EXAMPLE 128.

Throughout this music reading activity it is assumed the singers have applied their developing reading skills to facilitate the learning of new songs, and that the rote aspect of song teaching will be diminishing.

Use key of B minor (*doh* is D).

EXAMPLE 129.

LESSON THIRTY-EIGHT

Do not open with a review because the last few music reading periods have accomplished this. This lesson involves reading music written for three voice parts, for which purpose an exercise is presented on page 178 to be written on the chalk board. Note that each part is purposely contrasted with the others in matters of intervallic progression and rhythm.

Inasmuch as each of the three vocal parts—soprano, cambiata, and baritone—now has its own staff from which to read, plus an individual melody within the vocal range attributed to the voice, transposition by the teacher is no longer necessary. Music presented from here on is no longer restricted by the dictates of the composite unison range because no two vocal parts are singing in unison. It is possible to write for wider ranges and thus produce music much more interesting to read.

Unless you have an unusually fine class or group of singers, each part should be dealt with separately but quickly, beginning with baritone, followed by cambiata, then soprano, and finally combined as the total group.

It is no longer necessary to follow all the steps of the seven-step music reading routine. Students should now be fully aware of the

Use key of E♭ major.

EXAMPLE 130.

nature of their music reading lesson objective and have acquired considerable skill in reading new music, but they still need to cope with rhythmic elements of the exercise before proceeding to pitch elements.

A suggested routine follows for teaching music reading in multiple parts, providing of course the students have been exposed to the preparatory procedure outlined in this chapter. Three steps only are involved in this simplified routine.

Step one. Direct baritones to sing the rhythm of their part using the neutral syllable *loo* on one pitch only, preferably *doh,* responding as you point out each beat on the chalk board exercise. If the exercise is being read from a book, instruct the entire class to point with the index finger to each *beat* of the lowest staff in the system while baritones (only) monotone to *loo.*

Step two. Draw a blank staff on the board and engage baritones on a brief pitch orientation drill using *loo,* as you point first to the locations of notes forming the *doh* chord, then to the secondary tones incorporating any significant intervallic progressions found in the exercise to be performed.

Step three. Transfer this drill to the exercise, combining rhythm and pitch, as baritones, singing *loo*, respond to your board-pointing.

Some boys and some girls will appear during the weeks of work to be quicker learners and more musically reliable than the rest. Recognize this and ask for their assistance in helping the remainder, then place them strategically among the slower learners in order to instill confidence and a more secure pitch orientation.

Reading new song material is always of value, but there is still a need for music reading drill using graduated exercises which constantly progress in degree of difficulty and which combine the various problems in a variety of presentations.

EXAMPLE 131.

There is no time to create words for any music reading exercise, and if time *were* available there is little musical or literary value to such activity.

Use key of E♭ major.

EXAMPLE 132.

LESSON THIRTY-NINE

This final lesson in the music reading program extends the staff system to four staves. Although this is not strictly necessary, this chapter would be incomplete without attempting to realize the full music reading potential of junior high school choral singers. This particular lesson and subsequent development of music reading skills from this point are more appropriate for elective choral music groups than for the ordinary general music class situation.

Venturing into four-part music reading is quite a challenge to the singers. While presenting the first few exercises employ simple resources, reduce complexities to a minimum, and preserve the melodic line feature for all voices.

Three exercises offered herewith are written with these criteria in mind. The extra part will be allocated to soprano voices, and for this purpose that section of the class containing girls and boy sopranos should arbitrarily be divided into two numerically equal portions, designated as *Green* and *Blue* (see page 37). These parts should alternate; *Greens* singing the first soprano part in Ex. 133 and the second soprano line in Ex. 134.

The presentation of Ex. 133 and Ex. 134 to the class should follow the same teaching routine prescribed earlier for reading music written in three vocal parts, working with each part separately in this order: baritone, cambiata, second soprano, first soprano. One factor contributing to success in this endeavor is that of retaining the interest of the class. Do not spend time with any one part trying to attain perfection. When the cambiate are reasonably secure, combine them with baritones for a quick review. Similarly, when the second sopranos appear to have learned their part, combine them with cambiate and baritones before presenting the first soprano part. It may take a few more minutes to realize your total objective, but it involves the singers more frequently and limits restlessness.

Although this completes the instructions of the chapter, it should not be assumed that the singers have learned to read and that all further music reading activity may be transferred to song reading. Ex. 134 on page 183 is only the introduction to reading music in four parts. Continuation and extension of music reading activity is recommended, using *The Reading Singer,* in which new complexities such as modulation, chromatic alteration, rhythm patterns, and syncopation are approached progressively.

If the music reading program is followed for a few minutes in each music period, new songs will be learned quickly, and students and teacher will not be bored by the constant repetition inescapable in rote teaching. The most significant result, however, is that the boys and girls will become musically literate, and ready for musical enjoyment in senior high school and adult life.

A girl whose total music experience in junior high school has consisted solely of learning by rote second soprano or alto parts for choral numbers to be performed at district festivals or school concerts has been cheated. She has undoubtedly been *useful* to the choral director, but what has the choral director given *her* musically?

In addition to student benefits derived from music reading, there are benefits for the choral teacher. First, there is the elimination of the constant repetition and correction which is part of rote teaching.

Use key of F major.

EXAMPLE 133.

Secondly, the physical fatigue of rote teaching is greatly diminished. Thirdly, there is the great satisfaction of observing student skills develop.

The music reading program defined in the preceding pages of this chapter is correlated with another aspect of music learning, namely ear training. In the first phase of the program the introduction of every new note-sound was presented aurally, and its relationship to *doh* was stressed aurally as the teacher, by means of his voice, impressed it on the students. During these processes each new note-sound first had to be heard and identified by name before it was realized vocally by the singers.

It is absolutely essential in the development of student music reading skills that four or five minutes of every music period should be devoted to this activity.

Because scheduling for general music classes is not consistent throughout the country, or even within state or county school boundaries, no prediction can be made about the length of time it will take to cover the music reading program. Obviously the elective chorus

Use key of D major.

EXAMPLE 134.

which meets three or five periods a week will progress much more rapidly than a general music class which meets one period per week.

In developing this program, however, some basic time span should be envisioned during which these skills might be taught. The popular trend throughout the country is to schedule general music classes for one period of forty or fifty minutes per week for two semesters in either Grade 7 or Grade 8, rarely in both. This is not nearly a sufficient schedule apportionment. On the basis of one music period per week, the music reading program here proposed would require two semesters. It must be admitted ruefully that in a school where the general music class is limited to one period a week for half a semester, and there are many such schools, this music reading program could not be realized except in the elective chorus.

Coverage of the music reading program will vary from class to class. Some classes composed of slower learners will require a good deal of review work before proceeding to a new lesson, whereas a class of quicker learners may on occasion cover the material for two music reading lessons in one period. In this connection it is advisable to maintain a progress log of every class participating in the music reading program. By this means you may be aware of the class's current achievement level and prepared ahead of time with the appropriate chalk board work involved in the coming lesson.

A word of advice concerning the development of music reading: do not take the arbitrary position that each session *must* involve a new lesson. There will be occasions when the class has not absorbed new material sufficiently well. Remember, music learning is a slow growth and cannot be unduly accelerated. Generally speaking music reading is not an activity for which a home assignment can be allocated. Such growth takes place in the school music class during the few minutes of each lesson devoted to music reading.

Much has been said concerning the desirability of boys and girls learning pitch relationships in a wide variety of keys, and that due to the exigencies of the composite unison vocal range of junior high singers, it is necessary to pitch unison music reading exercises in keys commensurate with the total and tessitura limits imposed thereby. One of the desirable outcomes of this procedure is that boys and girls become accustomed to seeing notes on the upper part of the staff, and thus when they are confronted with this phenomenon in sheet music they do not try to avoid what appear to be high pitches. It cannot be stressed too often or too strongly that the key to full comprehension of his situation lies in a thorough understanding by the teacher of all vocal range and tessitura restrictions, particularly the composite unison range.

Constantly help singers through difficulties; don't continue letting them guess wrongly. Don't hesitate to sing with them; this is also an aspect of ear training. Remember, very rarely will singers of any age, unless they are in the professional class, read music accurately at first sight. It will always be *approximate* at first sight. If this were not so, first-rate choral organizations would require very little rehearsal time.

The music reading class will require constant stimulation, but, strange as it may seem, cambiate will respond more enthusiastically and accurately than any of the other voices.

Regarding use of syllables as a means of teaching pitch relationships in Phase One of this chapter, only those syllables have been presented which might be functional within the diatonic framework of major or minor tonality, or simple modulation to dominant and subdominant. From this it must not be deduced that chromatics are not available in solmization. To illustrate this point, the complete chromatic *syllable* system is portrayed below.

Descending

doh' te taw lah law soh se lah le te doh'
                fe   fe
       re me fah   fah me
doh de ray   maw ray raw doh

Ascending

The above is presented merely in order to supply more complete information regarding the music-syllable system. In Great Britain, where this system was first devised from the Guidonian hexachord and particularly in Wales, a great deal of music is published commercially in music-syllable form rather than in staff notation; thus singers (and instrumentalists) who perform from such printed symbols need to be familiar with all chromatic devices pertaining to syllable reading. Modulatory devices are available, but this text subscribes to the use of music-syllables solely as a medium for developing aural perception and vocal reproduction of simple pitch relationships and limits music syllable instruction to those aspects which are strictly functional to the music reading program herein prescribed.

As staff-line work develops and music reading skills improve, music-syllables are gradually discarded. They still remain a valuable reference, however, in solving stubborn pitch problems encountered in choral literature.

To realize more fully the music reading potential of junior high singers, teachers should expose them to fundamental theoretical instruction. A minimum coverage of scales, key signatures, diatonic intervals, note lengths, rests, and meter signatures is essential to understanding the choral score.

Any school music teacher, mindful of his responsibility to the full musical development of all students, will realize that there is a good deal more to his work than merely training performing groups to merit the well-deserved approval of concert audiences. While this is important for many reasons, it is equally important that non-public-performing music groups be exposed to the benefits of music participation and of understanding how to enjoy listening to music. The music literacy of all students is a most desirable goal in general music classes or elective performing groups, and in this respect understanding of the printed score is indispensable.

Administrators and parents have a right to expect that lasting music values will accrue to all children as a result of a strong school music program which has song singing and music reading as its core.

CHAPTER FIVE

THE EAR-TRAINING PROGRAM

Introduction

Ear training should be considered an integral part of the over-all school music program and should not be isolated from other aspects of music learning. The first phase of the music reading program was based on ear training, each new sound being committed to the ear prior to the visual presentation of its symbol.

The purpose of ear training in music is to teach students to listen attentively, interpret what they hear, and give their opinion of it. It is not an end in itself, but is a preparation for engaging with keener aural perception in music activities either as performers or consumers of music. It is also a means for developing discriminating taste in the choice of musical fare to be enjoyed.

As in other aspects of music learning, ear training is not a process to be approached haphazardly through vicarious, disconnected listening experiences accomplished by means of occasional record playing sessions. To be effective, ear training must be a cumulative process starting with the simplest of musical phenomena and leading gradually to the more complex. Student response must constantly be solicited to ensure total class participation.

The ear-training program should evolve from, and closely parallel, the music reading program. Organized ear-training activity should take place during every music period, immediately following the music reading activity. Each lesson should move quickly and should not exceed five or six minutes in duration.

The traditional concept of music dictation as a medium for ear training will not be adhered to in this program, as it is not a true criterion of hearing acuity. A student may perceive accurately what is being performed, but fall into error transcribing his response on music manuscript. Many school music teachers who experienced great difficulty in meeting college ear-training requirements are most adept with their own school music organizations in detecting error, refining tone, diction, phrasing, and other aspects of performance dependent on aural acuity of the teacher.

First, introduce the class to ear training. The athlete, no matter with what branch of sport he is concerned, engages in physical training to develop muscular strength and coordination; the radio or railroad telegrapher, in training, transmits and receives Morse code signals hour after hour to familiarize his ear with the sounds peculiar to each letter moving at high speed. The singer engages in vocal training, breathing, production, and so forth, in order to improve his singing. It is reasonable then to propose that the intelligent music listener should engage in ear training to sharpen perception, to develop concentration, and to understand thoroughly what is being heard.

Following the organizational plan adopted in the music reading program, the ear-training program will be presented in the form of a series of lessons, the first of which should immediately follow the first music reading lesson. A teaching routine will be established in the first lesson which will be used in all subsequent lessons.

Phase One: Introduction to Pitch Perception (Music Syllables)

Lesson One

Write the following on the chalk board:

GROUP 1

Use key of B♭ major for class singing.

1.

2.

3.*

4.

*Orient *doh* strongly using hand signs for music syllables.

Pitch the chord of B♭ major and direct the class to sing the exercises one after another as you point to the syllable letters on the board; then address yourself to the class, somewhat in this manner:

"On the board are four short exercises. I will sing one of these four, using *loo* instead of the syllable names; break for a moment to allow you to think; sing it a second time, break; then sing it a third time. I want you to look at the chalk board as I sing and pick the tune I am singing. *Do not* raise your hand or call out to let me know you have the answer, and *do not* tell anyone else.

"When I have sung the selected tune three times I shall tell you to close your eyes, *everyone,* while I call very slowly the numbers one through four. When I call the number of the tune you think belongs to the melody I sang raise your right hand very quietly. Don't make any fuss or noise which might give away your secret to someone who does not have the correct answer."

State once more the procedure to be followed, stressing again eyes closed and no calling aloud the discovered exercise number.

Select one of the exercises you are going to use (don't hint to the class in any manner which is the selected melody), pitch the key of Bb major, direct the class to sing the *doh* chord in response to your hand signs, then you (alone) vocalize to *loo.* Don't vocalize to *la,* otherwise you will contribute to confusion when you later reach the point where the music syllable *lah* is introduced. Pause for a few seconds, direct the class to sing the *doh* chord again; vocalize the exercise once more. Repeat this process to complete three vocalizations of the tune and address the class: "Close your eyes, *everyone.* If you think I sang tune number one raise your right hand quietly." Pause while you count any response. "If you think I sang tune number two raise your hand quietly." Continue this routine through the remaining numbers.

As a means of keeping the class alert, vary the rotation of your calling occasionally, 1-3-4-2, 2-4-3-1, using different combinations. Should you get 100 percent accurate response, which is often likely, there is no point in continuing the count. Just tell the youngsters how smart they are and leave it at that.

Should the correct response be poor in this or any similar activity in subsequent lessons, the following corrective procedure is recommended. Tell the class frankly that there were many wrong answers and that you will help them to find the correct one. In this particular instance it will be assumed you vocalized exercise number four.

Pitch the key of Bb major, then vocalize exercise four just as you did a few minutes ago. Follow immediately by directing the class to sing exercise number one as you point to the syllables on the chalk board. Address the class. "Close your eyes, everyone. If you think melody number one was the tune I sang raise your right hand." Should the response still be poor, which is most unlikely, direct the class again to sing exercise number one, while you sing exercise number four. This time it is obvious.

Using the same routine proceed to exercise number two, then

number three, following in due course with exercise number four. This time there is little doubt of obtaining 100 percent correct response. Simple? Assuredly so, but not too simple in the early stages of ear training. Remember, the objective of this program is ear *training,* not ear *testing,* although a periodic test is of value.

Do not confine the content of this or subsequent lessons to the identification of one melody only. Use two or sometimes even three from one group of chalk-board melodies prescribed for the lesson.

An odd psychological phenomenon is observed in this phase of music learning. The youngsters seem to regard the activity in the light of a game or contest. They enjoy it and often ask for more. Although this is not highly recommended, the contest-minded music teacher may occasionally inject a competitive element by dividing the class into two sections and operate a sort of *spelling bee* applied to music perception. It certainly develops hearing concentration.

Progress in ear-training activity should parallel closely that achieved in music reading. Keep a log indicating the achievement level of all classes following this program.

From this point, each lesson of the ear-training program will parallel the corresponding lesson of the music reading program. Thus, if a class is working on Music Reading Lesson Four the same class ought to be at Lesson Four in the ear-training program. In view of this and considering the detail with which each new learning of the music reading program was presented, it is unnecessary to labor the development of the ear-training program with repetitive detail. It will therefore be assumed the class is currently involved in music reading and that ear training is an extension thereof.

LESSON TWO

Introducing the music syllable *me*. Follow the teaching routine presented in Lesson One.

GROUP 2

1.

$$\text{d} \quad \overset{s}{\text{d}} \quad \overset{s}{} \; \Big| \; \text{m} \quad \text{d} \quad \text{d} \quad - \; \Big| \; \text{d} \quad \overset{m}{} \quad \overset{s}{} \quad \text{m} \; \Big| \; \text{d} \quad \text{m} \quad \text{d} \quad - \; \Big\|$$

2.

$$\text{d} \quad \overset{m}{} \quad \overset{s}{} \quad \text{m} \; \Big| \; \text{d} \quad \text{m} \quad \text{m} \quad - \; \Big| \; \text{d} \quad \overset{s}{} \quad \overset{s}{} \quad \text{m} \; \Big| \; \text{d} \quad - \quad \text{d} \quad - \; \Big\|$$

3. *

$$\text{m} \quad \text{d} \quad \text{d} \quad - \; \Big| \; \text{m} \quad \overset{s}{} \quad \overset{s}{} \quad - \; \Big| \; \text{m} \quad \text{d} \quad \text{m} \quad \text{d} \; \Big| \; \text{m} \quad \overset{s}{} \quad \text{d} \quad - \; \Big\|$$

4. *

$$\overset{s}{} \quad - \quad - \quad \text{d} \; \Big| \; \text{m} \quad - \quad - \quad - \; \Big| \; \text{m} \quad \text{d} \quad \text{d} \quad - \; \Big| \; \text{m} \quad \overset{s}{} \quad \overset{s}{} \quad - \; \Big\|$$

*Orient *doh* strongly.

LESSON THREE: MUSIC SYLLABLE *ray*

GROUP 3

1.

d m s – | m r d – | s s s d | r – d – ‖

*2.**

s – d – | s – d – | m r d r | d – – – ‖

3.

d – – – | r – – – | m s m r | d r m – ‖

4.

m r d r | m d s – | s – d – | m r d – ‖

*Orient *doh* strongly.

Lesson Four: Music Syllable *fah*

Group 4

1.

d − − − | m − f − | s − − f | m − d − ‖

2.

d r m f | s f m r | d r m f | s − − − ‖

3.*

s − m − | f s m − | m − f − | m r d − ‖

4.

d − − s | d r m f | s − d r | m − − − ‖

*Orient *doh* strongly.

Do not omit to direct the class to sing the appropriate *doh* chord, responding to your hand signs immediately before you sing *each* exercise.

Lesson Five: Music Syllable High *doh* (*doh'*)

Group 5

1.

2.

3.*

4.

*Orient *doh* strongly.

Lesson Six: Music Syllable *lah*

Group 6

1.

d –   s s | l – s – | l – s – | s d   s f m | r – r – | d – – – ‖

2.*

s l s f | m r d – | d m   s – | s l s – | d m s d' | d – d – ‖

3.

d – – – | d' – – – | s l s l s – – – | d' – s m | d r d – ‖

4.*

m f m r | d – m – | s l s f | m – r – | d – – – ‖

*Orient *doh* strongly.

Lesson Seven: Music Syllable *te*

Group 7

1.

```
        d'  t  | l  -      s  -  | l    t   d'        |              ||
                                               s                     ||
                                                         m   r       ||
  d  -         |                 |                  s        d  -     ||
```

2.

```
              |      | s  d' t |d' - - | l  t  l |         |        |          ||
  d  m  r |d - - |                               | s  -    |        |          ||
                                                        d |r - - |d - -     ||
```

3.*

```
            |       s  -  | l  - -  t |d'        |        |         |          ||
  m - -  |d  m  f                     |       s  |        |         |          ||
                                                | m  -  |d - d - |d - - -    ||
```

4.

```
          |d'  t  l.  s |d'  t  l  s |d'  t  l  s |              |    d' - ||
  s  -    |                                      |              |         ||
  d  -    |            |            |            | m  -  r  - |d  -     ||
```

*Orient *doh* stongly.

Note: It is not presumed that the students are identifying each and every aspect of these tunes, but they are undoubtedly learning to concentrate and to listen with a discriminating ear.

   The constant use of the key Bb major is not particularly desirable, but it is mandatory so long as the class is key-oriented by singing the

GROUP 8

1.

2.*

3.

4.

*Orient *doh* stongly.

various melodies. When the time comes that listening perception skills are sufficiently advanced to discard preliminary vocal orientation, any key may be selected for vocal presentation of the exercises by the teacher. However, the key selected should remain constant throughout the lesson.

Following Lesson Seven of the music reading program a period of consolidation was recommended before proceeding to Lesson Eight, but during this period a new use for some prior lesson was presented. The plagal scale was introduced which involved the use of syllables *soh*₁,

lah_1, and te_1 below low *doh*. To parallel this development in the ear-training program a set of appropriate exercises is offered on page 198. Use the key of E♭ major for class singing.

LESSON EIGHT: *Lah₁, doh, me* CHORD, WITH *lah₁* AS THE HOME NOTE

GROUP 9

1.*

$$l_{/} \quad - \quad d \quad - \quad \begin{vmatrix} m \\ \end{vmatrix} \quad r \quad d \quad - \quad \begin{vmatrix} t_{/} \quad - \quad l_{/} \quad _{se_{/}} \end{vmatrix} \quad l_{/} \quad - \quad - \quad - \quad \parallel$$

Use key of D major.

2.

$$d \quad d \quad ^{m\ m} \begin{vmatrix} s \quad s \\ m \quad - \end{vmatrix} \begin{vmatrix} f \quad f \\ r \quad r \end{vmatrix} t_{/} \quad t_{/} \quad l_{/} \quad t_{/} \begin{vmatrix} d \quad - \quad d \quad ^{m} \end{vmatrix} r \quad - \quad d \quad - \parallel$$

3.*

$$m \quad ^{l \ se} \begin{vmatrix} l \quad - \\ \end{vmatrix} m \begin{vmatrix} f \\ m \quad _{r} \end{vmatrix} m \quad - \quad - \begin{vmatrix} m \quad ^{fe \ se} \begin{vmatrix} l \\ m \end{vmatrix} d \end{vmatrix} l_{/} \quad - \quad d \begin{vmatrix} l_{/} \quad - \quad - \end{vmatrix} \parallel$$

4.

$$d \quad - \quad - \quad - \begin{vmatrix} l_{/} - \quad - \quad - \end{vmatrix} d - \quad - \quad - \begin{vmatrix} m \quad - \quad - \quad - \end{vmatrix} fe \quad ^{se} \quad ^{l} \quad m \begin{vmatrix} fe - \quad ^{se} \quad - \end{vmatrix} ^{l \ - \ - \ -} \parallel$$

*Orient *doh* strongly.

Lessons Nine and Ten

These lessons should be consolidation periods to develop aural discrimination skills through syllables so that this work may be transferred to the music staff. New challenges to aural perception may be presented by introducing intervallic leaps to and from secondary tones, also the interval of a sixth. Two sets of exercises are offered herewith as media for consolidation.

Group 10

1.

d – m – | d r f m | d – s – | d m l s | d′ – d′ – | d – – – ||

2.

d r m f | s l t d′ | d r m f | s l t d′ | s f m r | m – m – ||

Use key of G minor (*doh* is B♭).

3.

d – m – | d m l – | se fe se – | l se l – | s f m r | d m l – ||

4.

d – r – | d – m – | d – f – | d – s – | d – l – | d r d – ||

GROUP 11

1.

| d | | d | | s – f – | m r d – | s s | d m d – ‖
| | s, s, s, | | s, s, s, | | | s, s, | |

2.

| d – – – | s – – m r | t, t, | d – – – | f – – – | t, – – – | d – – – ‖
| | | s, | | | | |

3.

| d | t, | d – r | m | d | m – f | s – f | r – | t, | d r | d – – ‖
| s, | | | t, | | | | l, | | |

Use key of C minor (*doh* is E♭).

4.

| l, | d | l, l, | se, – – l, | t, – t, – | d | t, l, – | l, | d | l, se, | l, – l, – ‖

Phase Two: Introduction of Staff Notation, Doh on a Line

LESSON ELEVEN

This lesson of the ear-training program parallels Lesson Eleven of the music reading program by transferring syllables to music staff notation, reverting to the simplest melodic patterns involving only the sounds of the *doh* chord. In keeping with the three-line staff employed in Lesson Eleven of the music reading program the same type three-line staff will be used here.

GROUP 12

1.

2.*

3.

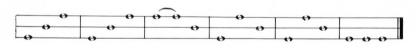

4.

*Orient *doh* strongly.

In the preliminary vocal familiarization of the above melodies music syllables may be used, or the neutral syllable *loo,* depending on music reading ability of the class. For tune recognition activity they should be sung slowly.

LESSON TWELVE: EXTENSION OF THE THREE-LINE STAFF TO FIVE LINES

GROUP 13
Use keys of B♭, C, or D major for class vocalization.

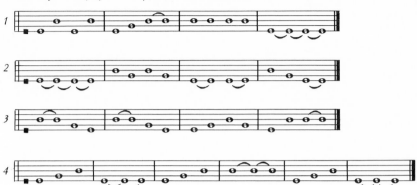

LESSON THIRTEEN: TRANSFER *ray* TO STAFF NOTATION

GROUP 14
Use keys of B♭, C, or D major for class vocalization.

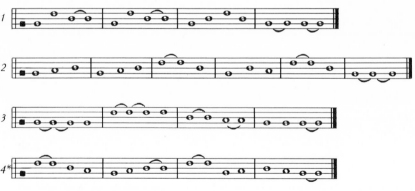

* Orient *doh* strongly.

Lesson Fourteen: Transfer *fah* to Staff Notation

Group 15
Use keys of B♭, C, or D major for class vocalization.

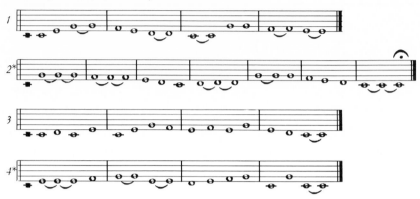

Lesson Fifteen: Transfer *lah* to Staff Notation

Group 16
Use keys of B♭, or C major for class vocalization.

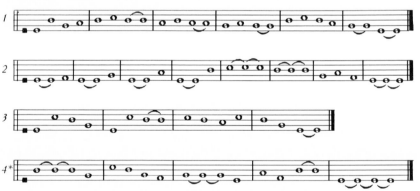

It is not important to know by what specific aspects students are identifying the melody performed. The main objective lies in training them to listen attentively and to analyze in their own way that which is heard.

* Orient *doh* strongly.

LESSON SIXTEEN: TRANSFER OF *doh'* TO STAFF NOTATION

The inclusion of *doh'*, further extending the range to an octave now limits usable keys to that of B♭ major unless: (1) only the upper part of the range is used, or (2) preliminary class vocalizing is discontinued. The latter is not recommended as a general practice, but it is not harmful on occasion to break away from the key of C major.

GROUP 17
Use key of B♭ major for class vocalization.

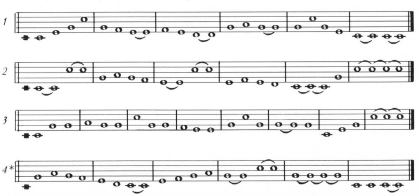

It will be noticed that in any group of ear-training melodies, similarity of construction in two or more melodies has been avoided. There is no educational or musical objective to be gained by confusing or tricking students into a false response. The slow growth nature of musical development referred to in the music reading program is equally operative in the ear-training program. Complexities unnecessary to a specific phase of aural perception are avoided until they are vital to the learning process.

* Orient *doh* strongly.

Lesson Seventeen: Transfer *te* to Staff Notation

Group 18
Use key of B♭ major for class vocalization.

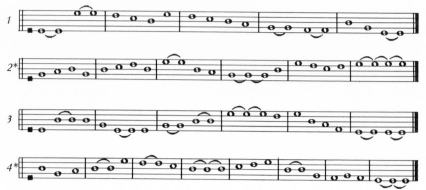

Lesson Eighteen: Plagal Melodies Lying Between *soh₁* and *soh*

Owing to the new orientation of *doh* in the melodic line, the key to be used by the class in the preliminary vocal familiarization activity will usually be E♭ major.

Group 19
Use key of E♭ major for class vocalization.

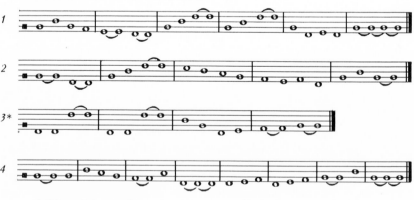

* Orient *doh* strongly.

Phase Three: Note-Length Values

LESSON NINETEEN

Presentation of note-length values, using quarter- and half-notes: to compensate for this new complexity, notes of the *doh* chord only will be used in this lesson. You may be able to dispense with the class singing routine at this stage; if so *you* should first sing the melodies through in sequence before selecting a melody for recognition, using the key in which written. At your own discretion this procedure may be followed from here on.

GROUP 20
Use keys of B♭, C, or D major for class vocalization.

GROUP 21
Use key of B♭ major for class vocalization.

* Orient *doh* strongly.

GROUP 22
Use E♭ as *doh* for class vocalization.

LESSON TWENTY: INCORPORATING DOTTED HALF-NOTE AND WHOLE-NOTE

Inasmuch as it is now desirable to combine some of the complexities involved in authentic, plagal, and minor melodies it will not be possible for the class to sing in one key all the melodies presented in one group. However, by the time students have reached this stage of the ear-training program and the parallel stage in the music reading program, the routine should be sufficiently established and aural acuity sufficiently advanced to permit elimination of preliminary vocal familiarization of the melodies to be heard.

GROUP 23

* Orient *doh* strongly.

LESSON TWENTY-ONE: INCORPORATING TWO EIGHTH-NOTES AS A BEAT

Should you desire the class to sing these melodies use the key of Bb major. If the class does not sing the melodies, prior to listening you should sing them 1 through 4, in that sequence, as a familiarization aid. This procedure is recommended for any melody group.

GROUP 24
Use key of Bb major for class vocalization.

LESSON TWENTY-TWO: THE DOTTED QUARTER RHYTHM

It will be noted that various complexities are now being incorporated in each group of melodies, minor mode, plagal melodies, etc., in addition to the new learning. This procedure is based on the assumption that after many weeks of cumulative hearing experience, students following this program are capable of perceiving some details of more complex melodies.

* Orient *doh* strongly.

GROUP 25

LESSON TWENTY-THREE: COMPOUND DUPLE 6/8 TIME

GROUP 26
Use key of B♭ major for class vocalization.

LESSON TWENTY-FOUR

Dotted half-note in 6/8 time; dotted eighth followed by sixteenth-note.

* Orient *doh* strongly.

GROUP 27

LESSON TWENTY-FIVE

Introducing two symbols for rests, one in the time duration of a half-note ▬ and another ⸘ in the time duration of a quarter-note.

GROUP 28
Use key of B♭ major for class vocalization.

LESSON TWENTY-SIX

Introducing symbols for rests in the time duration of a whole-note, ▬ and in the time duration of an eighth-note. ⸸

* Orient *doh* strongly.

As the aspect of the staff becomes more complex it is not possible
to deduce the exact process by which the listeners identify the
melody selected for performance by the teacher. In Lessons Twenty-
five and Twenty-six, for instance, one melody might be identified by
the rest symbols, while another might be identified by obvious characteristics of the melody line. The means by which the performed
melody is recognized is not important. The basic objective is training
students to listen attentively with considerable concentration. No two
people listen for similar things in any performance of music.

GROUP 29
Use key of B♭ major for class vocalization

Phase Four: Doh *Appears in a Space*

Up to this point the ear-training program has synchronized with
the music reading program. In Phase Four the ear-training program
will be accelerated.

Phase Four of the music reading program is concerned with vocal
realization of music wherein *doh* appears in a staff space. A parallel
concern will be seen in Phase Four of the ear-training program. It is
assumed by this time the students will have developed reasonable
competency in identifying, from a visual presentation of four melodies,
any one which is performed, providing *doh* appears on a staff line.

Inasmuch as it is a less difficult task to identify a melody than to
perform it, and in view of the fact that the class has acquired some

* Orient *doh* strongly.

visual and aural understanding of staff space relationships, the remaining portions of the ear-training program will not be limited to the presentation of one new symbol per lesson. Obviously then, future ear-training lessons will not synchronize with those of the music reading program.

Phase Four will start with the simplest presentation of *doh, me, soh* wherein *doh* appears in a staff space, but new complexities will appear quite early in the progression of learning.

LESSON TWENTY-SEVEN

Presenting the *doh* chord, when *doh* appears in a staff space.

GROUP 30
Use keys of B♭, C, or D major for class vocalization

LESSON TWENTY-EIGHT

Introducing music syllables *ray, fah* when *doh* appears in a staff space.

As was mentioned earlier it is not possible to determine by what precise aspects students identify melodies. In this particular group it is hoped that the incidence of *ray* and *fah* will present the basis of identification, but in the case of melody number three it is quite possible that identification might derive from the use of 3/4 time. The use of 6/8 time would undoubtedly be an obvious clue, having no relationship to the new learning involved in this lesson, or in some subsequent lessons, hence it is purposely omitted.

* Orient *doh* strongly.

The following melodies may be sung using keys of B♭, C, or D major. However if *ray* and *fah* (*doh* in a staff space) have not been presented in the music reading program, it is unwise to require the class to sing these melodies at this time.

GROUP 31

LESSON TWENTY-NINE

Introducing music syllables *lah, doh'* when *doh* appears in a staff space.

GROUP 32

* Orient *doh* strongly.

LESSON THIRTY

Introducing music syllables *te, te₁* when *doh* appears in a staff space.

GROUP 33

LESSON THIRTY-ONE

Introducing music syllable *lah₁* as the home note when *doh* is in a staff space.

GROUP 34
Use key of C minor (*doh* is E♭) for class vocalization

* Orient *doh* strongly.

Lesson Thirty-two

Presentation of plagal melodies lying between *soh₁* and *soh* (or *soh* and *soh′*) when *doh* is in a staff space.

Group 35
Use key of E♭ major for class vocalization.

Lesson Thirty-three

Introducing music syllable *fe* when *doh* appears in a staff space. To indicate *fe* a sharp sign (♯) will be placed immediately in front of *fah*. The use of the natural sign (♮) to indicate *fe* is explained in Lesson Thirty-four of the music reading program, and will be deferred to Lesson Thirty-four of the ear-training program.

Previous lessons are incorporated in each group of ear-training melodies, and as a result the students develop a keen sense of perception and discrimination in listening. There is no reason to believe or hope that the listeners will discriminate between melodies in Group 36 solely on the basis of the incidence of *fe*. However the sound of *fe* has a definite impact on the ear, and frequent exposure to this sound will impress it on the tonal memory of the students.

* Orient *doh* strongly.

GROUP 36

LESSON THIRTY-FOUR

This lesson is an extension of the work involved in previous aural experiences. The introduction of clef signs and key signatures is purely a visual development, and in no way affects the sound of the melody line, except when *fe* happens to require a natural sign in key signatures requiring flats. However, in minor mode music the use of *se* (the raised *soh*) merits some discussion. For all music in which the key signature demands sharps, *se* will be designated by the use of a sharp sign before *soh*. This is also true in the keys of D minor (key signature one flat) and G minor (key signature two flats). In all other keys where *flats* are employed *se* will be designated by a natural sign preceding *soh*. It must not be assumed that the listeners will identify the performed melody solely or in part by the incidence of *se,* but their attention is drawn to the nature of this sound, and it will become more firmly established in their total vocabulary.

This concludes the formal ear-training program insofar as it applies to general music at the junior high school level. Obviously this program could be greatly extended by dealing with chromatic sounds, and by the use and recognition of harmonic progressions, but these are experiences which belong in the senior high school general music program. There is not sufficient scheduled time in junior high school to go beyond what has been presented here. In many school situations

* Orient *doh* strongly.

GROUP 37 (mixed keys)

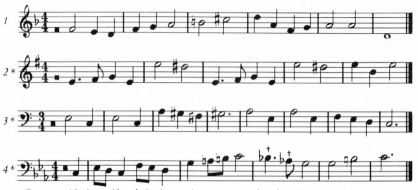

† Compare with the accidentals in the previous measure and explain this contradiction.

where only one period per week is allocated for general music, it is not possible even to complete the foregoing program in one year. However, completing at least a reasonable portion is possible. It is also possible and desirable to complete this program with the school chorus which meets several times each week. Five or six minutes in one lesson per week devoted to ear training will prove a very worthwhile medium for helping to develop musicianship in the school chorus.

In order to keep a record of the progress of each class and to orient the teacher on preparation for the next lesson, it is almost imperative that a log be kept. This could be in the same book used for recording music reading progress, a sample page for which is shown on page 219.

By the time this ear-training program has been completed, participating students will have been under instruction for almost one year. During this time they will have become accustomed to the idea that listening to music involves complete and undivided attention. They will have developed habits of aural perception through concentration, a closer acquaintance with the symbols of printed music, and a more adept interpretation of their meaning in performance. The habit of discrimination has also been fostered in the ear-training program, and this trait is most valuable in symphonic listening and in guiding students in the selection of worthwhile music experiences in adult life.

* Orient *doh* strongly.

Grade_____ Classroom_____ Semester_____

Subject	Lesson number (completed)																				Tests given						
Music Reading																												
Ear Training																												
Exciting Sounds of Music																												
Listening																												
History																												
Rudiments																												

Songs	Started Date	In Work	Completed	Date

MUSIC CLASS, OR CHORUS LOG

Phase Five: The Exciting Sounds of Music

The listening program proposed in Chapter Eight is based on the aesthetic responses of the students to the music; therefore, this present phase of the ear-training program will deal with the formal elements of music.

Although this phase of Chapter Five is an ear-training activity, it is not necessary to delay this learning until Phase Four of the ear-training program has been completed. As a matter of fact Phases One through Four are not even prerequisites for successful experience in Phase Five. It may be correlated with the listening program whenever the class is sufficiently ready to receive and absorb the information; consequently this portion of the chapter begins with Lesson One. Each lesson in Phase Five will consume a good deal more time than was the case with lessons in prior phrases of the ear-training program. Student interest and concentration will be prime factors in determining just how much time is allocated to this activity.

LESSON ONE

This lesson is concerned with elements essential for making music. An explanation follows which will illustrate the meaning of this to junior high students.

"When your mother makes a cake, or when commercial manufacturers prepare a cake mix there are several ingredients necessary, each of which is practically useless by itself. However, these elements when combined in the prescribed amounts, and heated in an oven produce a good tasting cake.

"The three necessary ingredients, or elements, to make music are *harmony, melody,* and *rhythm.* Alone they are usually unsatisfactory, but together they produce a pleasing musical experience for the listener. Quite often a composer emphasizes one of these elements strongly, while the others are not so important. Here is an illustration in which melody is emphasized."

For this illustration the teacher might play on the piano something like "Minuet in G" (Beethoven), "Nocturne in E♭" (Chopin), "Chanson Triste" (Tchaikovsky); or use a phonograph recording of "Morning" (*Peer Gynt Suite,* Grieg), "Caprice Viennoise" (Kreisler), "The Young Prince and the Young Princess" (*Scheherezade,* Rimsky-Korsakov), "Trumpeter's Lullaby" (Leroy Anderson).

The teacher can probably implement the above list and use melodic material commensurate with the assimilation level of the class being taught. It is clearly realized that direct reference to specific recording catalog numbers would be advantageous to the teacher, but, inasmuch as record manufacturers are constantly withdrawing items for which there is limited sale, such information may rapidly become obsolete and of little value.

LESSON TWO

The next element of music to present to the class is harmony. Tell your students that every single musical sound is part of a family of sounds, a nice family in which the members are in agreement. Proceed to the piano, hold down with the right hand the keys of middle C, E above, G above, and while you are holding these, strike forcibly with the left hand twice or three times on C three octaves below middle C, instructing the class to listen very quietly and attentively. The sounds of the right-hand chord will gradually materialize, this is the C major family or chord; do not become involved by going into detail about the word *major*.

Play a simple harmonic progression containing C-G-C-F-C chords. Avoid any melodic influence. This is harmony, families of sounds played in company with a melody.

Direct the class to sing *d, r, m, f, s, f, m, r, d*, while you accompany with major chords, C, G, C, F, C, F, C, F, C. The use of an autoharp is very illustrative for this demonstration. Do not discuss major, minor, diminished, or augmented chords. Be content with the general impression of harmony. Now we have two known elements, melody and harmony. Continue further illustration through recordings in which harmony is obvious. Suggested recordings: *Symphony in D minor,* second movement, opening section (César Franck); "On Hearing the First Cuckoo in Spring" (Delius); Overture to *Tannhauser,* opening section only (Wagner); a band composition, "The Storm King" (Finlayson); or a recording by choral organizations such as Mormon Tabernacle Choir, Roger Wagner Chorale, or Associated Glee Clubs of America, in which the music is sustained and moves in strong, sonorous progressions.

LESSON THREE

The third element, rhythm, is easily sensed but very difficult to explain. Rhythm is not merely tempo, nor is it simply meter, it is the life blood pulse, the swing which brings to vitality an otherwise dull, uninspired performance. Ask the class to illustrate your point by articulating a popular football yell, first without life or purpose, then as though a touchdown depended on their efforts. "Hold that line, hold that line," and "We want a touchdown," are apt illustrations.

Transfer this to a musical ear-training experience by using appropriate recordings featuring rhythm. Point out that rhythm is not a lone element, it permeates other elements. Suggested recordings: *Bolero* (Ravel), a very small portion; *Sorcerer's Apprentice* (Dukas); "Festival in Baghdad" (*Scheherezade*, Rimsky-Korsakov); "Sleigh Ride" (Leroy Anderson); "On the Trail" (*Grand Canyon Suite*, Grofé); *Pacific 231* (Honegger); "Rhythmic Suite" (Elmore).

At some time between Lessons Three and Four, at the music teacher's discretion, it is possible for grading purposes to administer a very brief test covering Lessons One through Three. Distribute to each student in the group to be tested a piece of paper approximately 7 in. x 5 in. and ask them the following question: "Portions of six phonograph recordings will be played. Each selection features one of the following elements of music: melody, harmony, or rhythm. In each selection identify the specific element featured."

The following general directions may be given to the students: "Write your name at the top right-hand corner of the paper, your grade, and classroom number in the top left-hand corner. Number your answers 1, 2, 3, and so on. Write only one word against each number; two words, even if one of them is correct, will be marked incorrect."

LESSON FOUR

Three elements necessary for the performance of any music are melody (the single line or tune), harmony (chords which accompany the melody), and rhythm (the heartbeat or swing). With these three elements present there is music of sorts, but there is one important ingredient which adds excitement and interest to all music; this is the *texture* of sound. Defining this elusive ingredient to students is not an easy matter; however, the following simile has often proved successful in meeting this difficulty.

"Cloth, cotton, wool, and silk are all materials which you might find clothing a well-dressed man. Each of these fabrics has its own particular texture, yet contributes to a total ensemble. However it is possible to have a complete garment fashioned from any one of these materials.

"There are two completely different kinds of sound texture in musical performance: the texture produced by voices and the texture produced by instruments. In music texture is known as *timbre*."

Demonstrate this by means of two recordings performing the same composition, for example, "Greensleeves" (orchestral) or "What Child Is This." The orchestral version might be a Mantovani recording, the choral version by the Norman Luboff Choir. If these are not available, any choral or orchestral recording will suffice providing tuneful music is used.

LESSON FIVE

There are four different kinds of sounds in adult vocal music, female high-voice, female low-voice, male high-voice, and male low-voice, known as soprano, contralto (alto), tenor, and bass. Illustrate the above by playing a portion (or all) from each of four recordings which feature the various voices. Some suggestions follow:

Soprano: "One Fine Day" (*Madame Butterfly*, Puccini); "Ich Liebe Dich" (Grieg); "Jewel Song" (*Faust*, Gounod); "None but the Lonely Heart" (Tchaikovsky); "The Moon and I" (*The Mikado*, Gilbert and Sullivan); "Summertime" (*Porgy and Bess*, Gershwin).

Contralto: "He Was Despised" (*The Messiah*, Handel); "Sapphic Ode" (Brahms); "Alone and Yet Alive" (*The Mikado*, Gilbert and Sullivan); "Bois Epais" (Edward Purcell); "My Heart at Thy Sweet Voice" (*Samson and Delilah*, Saint-Saëns).

Tenor: "Rudolph's Narrative" (*La Bohème*, Puccini); "All Hail Thy Dwelling" (*Faust*, Gounod); "Lo! 'Tis the Day" (Leoncavallo); "Every Valley Shall Be Exalted" (*The Messiah*, Handel); "A Wand'ring Minstrel I" (*The Mikado*, Gilbert and Sullivan).

Bass: "The Trumpet Shall Sound" (*The Messiah*, Handel); "The Two Grenadiers" (Schumann); "Song of Mephistopheles" (*Faust*, Gounod); "Old Man River" (*Show Boat*, Kern); "Song of the Flea" (Moussorgsky); "Toreador Song" (*Carmen*, Bizet); "Why do the Nations" (*The Messiah*, Handel).

As additional illustration, refer to recent or contemporary singers popular on recordings, radio, or television, such as:

Soprano: Joan Sutherland, Julie Andrews, Patrice Munsel, Helen Traubel
Contralto: Marian Anderson, Kate Smith, Roberta Peters, Rise Stevens
Tenor: Dennis Day, Jan Peerce
Bass: Lauritz Melchior, Ezio Pinza, Robert Goulet, Ernie Ford

There is a considerable amount of material to be covered in Lesson Five, and it may take portions of two or more music periods to present adequately the *sounds* of adult voices.

LESSON SIX

Extending the learning from Lesson Two, discuss the structure of a choir. Explain that almost every senior high school operates at least one organization which performs choral music, and that these large groups consist of students having soprano, alto, tenor, and bass voices. Just as you need a minimum of four wheels for the average automobile, a chorus requires a minimum of four different vocal parts to achieve good musical balance. True, some part songs are written for three or even two vocal parts, but such choral music requires the use of a piano accompaniment to produce a full sound.

Point out that voices have quite an advantage over mechanical instruments in producing various qualities of musical sounds. Further, the addition of words superimposed on these sounds contributes to a deeper understanding and appreciation of the intent of the composer when he wrote the music. The human voice has enormous potential for varied expression—love, tenderness, fear, anger, devotion, spiritual worship, tranquillity, happiness, grief—all are at the command of the sensitive singer. When a group of singers presents a joint expression of many of the above, the sound is most beautiful and moving.

This lesson deals with the presentation of the full choral *sound,* and it is a good idea to confine your presentation to this aspect of the compositions to be heard. Do not discuss the composer or the meaning of the words, merely draw attention to the quality of sound produced by choral singers. Aesthetic and historical aspects of music performed are dealt with in the listening program. Recordings for this lesson should be selected carefully. Quite simple, unaffected choral music is the most satisfactory, since the main objective of the lesson should not be overshadowed by a plethora of strange, exotic harmonies, or unusual rhythmic devices, or overwhelmed by large masses of tone or accompanying orchestral color. Unaccompanied choral music is best suited for this purpose and such recordings by any of the following choral groups are recommended. These choral organizations have become recognized nationally for consistently outstanding performance, and it may be assumed that some of their recordings will be available for many years to come: The Mormon Tabernacle Choir, The Robert Shaw Chorale, The Roger Wagner Chorale, The Norman Luboff Choir, and Fred Waring's Pennsylvanians, although the latter are usually accompanied orchestrally.

The amount of time allocated to this or future lessons dealing with the exciting sounds of music is contingent upon several factors: (1) teacher interest, (2) student concentration space, and (3) availability of time in terms of coverage of the total music program. It is far better to limit the time devoted to this phase of activity or music and leave the students wanting more, than it is to continue a lesson to the point of boredom. The moment concentration appears to lag, change to some other phase of music activity, preferably singing.

LESSON SEVEN

In this lesson the *sound* of choral music is again stressed; but here the *sound* of female voices is contrasted with the *sound* of male voices. For this purpose any recordings of female or male voice choruses may be used, providing the music is tuneful. Some recordings suitable for use as illustration are given:

For female voices: *Festival of Carols* (Britten), "Liebeslieder" (Brahms). For male voices: any recording by Associated Glee Clubs of America, Harvard University Glee Club, or the Fred Waring male voice chorus.

This lesson concludes the vocal-choral portion of this phase of the ear-training program, and it is possible that a simple test covering Lessons One through Four might be useful in order to interpret the effectiveness of your teaching or for grading purposes. The test might confine itself to one question: "Portions of five recordings will be played. Identify the performing medium used in each record (soprano, alto, tenor, or baritone solo voice), mixed voice chorus, female voice chorus, male voice chorus."

LESSON EIGHT

The remaining lessons in Phase Five of the ear-training program will be devoted to the *sound* of the orchestra, and the contrasting qualities or colors of its component instrumental groups.

Music learning is a slow growth; this is also true in ear training. The ear must perceive a musical sound many times in different contexts before its assimilation is complete, and the total orchestral sound is a combination of many contrasting tone qualities requiring a trained ear to appreciate fully all its exciting nuances.

The orchestra is comprised of four basic groups of instruments, each group having its own particular sound timbre.

1. Stringed instruments on which melody is performed by drawing a bow across strings stretched tightly along the length of the instrument. For some special effects the performer is instructed by means of the sign "*pizz.*" (*pizzicato*) to pluck strings with the fingers.
2. Woodwind instruments in the shape of a tube on which melody is performed by blowing into one end of the instrument. The tube is perforated by scientifically spaced holes and various musical pitches are obtained by closing or opening different combinations of holes by mechanical devices. More will be said about this in Lesson Nine.
3. Brass wind instruments, again tube-shaped but much wider in diameter than woodwinds, on which melody is performed by blowing into one end of the instrument. The method of blowing is somewhat different from that employed for woodwinds, and this will be described fully in Lesson Ten.
4. Percussion instruments on which sound is produced by striking the instrument with the hand, fingers, or a stick. To obtain sound from some percussion instruments, the contact point of the stick is covered with a ball of fibrous material to protect a fragile skin which stretches across the top of the instrument.

Stringed instruments of the orchestra come in four different sizes, violins being the smallest (23½″ long), viola a little larger (27″ long), violoncello (cello), much larger than the viola (48½″ long), and string bass, largest of all (72″ long).

Violin and viola are held by the neck of the instrument in the left hand of the performer and are tucked under the left side of the chin.

Violoncello (cello) is also held by the neck of the instrument, but because of its size it is placed in a semi-reclining position with the neck almost against the left shoulder, the lower body of the instrument between the player's knees, while a metal spike resting on the floor supports the lowest extremity of the instrument.

For performing, the string bass is held in a vertical position, but the instrument is so large that the performer has to stand, or sit on a very high stool.

If these instruments can be procured to show to the class, so much the better. If not, card illustrations should be obtained.

Basic tone color (timbre) groups of the orchestra—strings, woodwinds, brass winds—are often referred to as *choirs*. In the strings group, violins are likened to soprano voices (first violin part) and alto voices (second violin part), violas are likened to tenor voices, violoncellos are likened to bass voices, and the string bass (double bass), which plays much lower than the human voice, acts as a solid foundation for the entire string choir.

VIOLIN

VIOLA

Regarding the *sound* of the string choir, there are no words which can convey the timbre of tone color or quality. It must be heard and assimilated by the listener. One of the finest audio-visual aids for presenting the *sound* of stringed instruments is a sound movie distributed by Encyclopaedia Britannica entitled the *String Choir*. This is one of a series which includes the *Woodwind Choir,* the *Brass Wind Choir,* the *Percussion Group,* and the *Symphony Orchestra*. State departments of education have audio-visual materials centers which have these films available on loan. Space your showings two to three weeks apart.

Recordings of any of the following music for stringed instruments are recommended for class listening in order to establish *strings* sound. The main criterion for this selection is that they are sufficiently tuneful and rhythmic to retain the interest of junior high school listeners. "Fiddle Faddle" (Leroy Anderson); "Serenade for Strings" (Tchaikovsky); "Serenade for Strings" (Volkmann); "Celebrated Minuet" (Boccherini); "Andante Cantabile" (Tchaikovsky); "Valse Triste" (Sibelius); *Simple Symphony* (Britten).

VIOLONCELLO

Suggested recordings which feature pizzicato string playing are: "Playful Pizzicato" (*Simple Symphony*, Britten); *Symphony No. 4 in F minor*, third movement (Tchaikovsky); "Pizzicato Polka" (*Sylvia Ballet*, Delibes); *Symphony in D minor*, opening of second movement (César Franck); "Holiday for Strings" (David Rose).

Lesson Eight defined above may take several music class periods before it can be assumed that students have assimilated the *sound* of the string choir.

STRING BASS

LESSON NINE

The next orchestral sound to be brought to the class is that of the woodwind choir. The primary objective of this instruction is to familiarize the students with the sound of woodwinds, not to get involved in the physical aspects of the instruments or details pertaining to mechanical characteristics. It is, however, a good idea to obtain pictorial charts of woodwinds and display them on the music room bulletin board. If the music budget is too slim to purchase these, almost any edition of the *Music Educators Journal* contains advertisements using illustrations which can be cut out for bulletin board display.

The very name, woodwind, gives a simple clue to the nature of these instruments. They are made from wood, and musical sound is produced by blowing with the mouth. Some years ago certain instrument manufacturers produced a quantity of *wood*wind instruments fashioned in metal, but apart from the flute and piccolo they did not find lasting favor with performers.

The basic principle in obtaining sounds from woodwinds is similar to that used in producing sounds from a tin whistle or a flutophone. The human breath is directed into one end of a cylindrical (sometimes partially conical) perforated tube, and musical tones are produced by covering or uncovering various combinations of the perforations.

Modern instruments, however, contain so many perforations that the performer does not have a sufficient number of fingers or large enough hands to cover every perforation, and therefore mechanical devices (keys) have been built onto the instrument to cover its entire playing range.

It is so easy to digress from the *sound* aspect of woodwinds by presenting information concerning structure, mouthpieces, no reed, single reed, double reed, acoustical properties, and so on, but this is not advisable now. Should any students exhibit curiosity about such aspects of woodwinds, this material may be incorporated into a separate project study involving those interested. Suffice it to tell the class that there are three different qualities of *sound* issuing from woodwinds: (1) the flute sound, (2) the clarinet sound, and (3) the oboe-bassoon sound.

Recordings of the following compositions will serve to illustrate the above classifications:

1. *Flute sound:* "Dance of the Flutes" (*Nutcracker Suite,* Tchaikovsky); "Peter and the Wolf" (Prokofiev); "Flight of the Bumble Bee" (Rimsky-Korsakov); "Farandole" (*L'Arlesienne Suite,* Bizet).
2. *Clarinet sound: Rhapsody in Blue* (Gershwin); "Peter and the Wolf" (Prokofiev); "Clarinet Polka" (anon.). There are many examples obtainable from classical literature, probably highly desirable from a

FLUTE

musicological point of view, but they are neither attractive to the junior high school beginning listener, nor conducive to rapt attention. Appropriate records by Benny Goodman are very useable to illustrate clarinet sounds.

3. *Oboe-bassoon sound: Scheherezade,* second movement, beginning portion (Rimsky-Korsakov); *Sorcerer's Apprentice* (Dukas); "Peter and the Wolf" (Prokofiev); "Danse Arabe" (*Nutcracker Suite,* Tchaikovsky); *Violin Concerto,* second movement (Brahms).

In order to illustrate these sounds in combinations such as are usually found in orchestral music, the following resources are recom-

CLARINET

mended: *The Woodwind Choir* (sound movie distributed by Encyclopaedia Britannica); *Symphony No. 4 in F minor,* third movement, middle section (Tchaikovsky); *Divertimento in F major* (Mozart); *Sorcerer's Apprentice* (Dukas); "Scherzo for Wind Quintet," Op. 48 (Hindemith); *Symphony for Wind Band* (Berlioz); *Eine Kleine Kammermusik* (Hindemith).

Lesson Nine will require portions of several music periods. This will depend on the ability and attitude of students in your class. Some

Oboe

BASSOON

classes will respond readily to this type of work, and will absorb in-struction easily, whereas other classes will be sluggish, slow learners requiring shorter, more frequent doses of instruction.

LESSON TEN

Brass wind instruments are long metal tubes, narrow at one end, gradually becoming wider to the *bell* at the other end. If these instru-ments were formed in a straight tube the length would be so great that the performers could not hold them, so the manufacturers bend the tubes round and round to make them more compact for holding.

To produce musical sounds from these instruments a device called a mouthpiece is attached to the narrow end of the tube, and the performer blows into the mouthpiece through compressed lips, almost as though he had a fine hair on his lips and was trying to spit it off. Tones of different pitches are formed by pressing down the fingers on pistons (valves) which close off or open different sections of the tube.

Once again, the main objective is to present the *sound* of brass winds with as little diversion as possible. Therefore avoid any techni-cal discussion of the overtone system, valve fingering, or slide trombone positions. Pin a chart illustration on the classroom bulletin board. If the school budget cannot afford charts depicting instruments, ap-propriate illustrations may be cut out from advertisements in music journals, or from instrument manufacturers' catalogs, and displayed on the bulletin board.

There are two basically different *sounds* comprising the timbre of brass wind instruments, the French horn sound and the trumpet-trombone sound. The reason for this lies in the construction of the instruments; the French horn starts at the mouthpiece in cylindrical shape and remains cylindrical for approximately one-third of its length, then proceeds gradually to increase conically in bore for the remaining two-thirds. Trumpets and trombones start in cylindrical shape at the mouthpiece and remain cylindrical for approximately two-thirds the length of the instrument before becoming conical. As a result they produce a brilliant, more urgent sound than horns.

Neither words nor illustrations can convey the *sound*, however, and it is advisable to present the actual living sound as soon as the minimum necessary background can be disseminated. Recordings of the following compositions which feature brass wind sound are recommended for listening.

1. *French horn sound:* "Nocturne" (*Midsummer Night's Dream*, Mendelssohn); *Symphony No. 5 in E minor,* second movement (Tchaikovsky); "Peter and the Wolf" (Prokofiev); Overture to *Tannhauser* (Wagner).

FRENCH HORN

TRUMPET

2. *Trumpet sound:* "Trumpet Voluntary" (Purcell); "Trumpeter's Holiday" (Leroy Anderson); *Symphony No. 5 in E minor,* fourth movement (Tchaikovsky); or any recording featuring a current recording trumpeter.

3. *Trombone sound:* "Lassus Trombone" (Henry Filmore); Prelude to Act 3 (*Lohengrin,* Wagner); "Rakoczy March" (*Damnation of Faust,* Berlioz); *Scheherezade,* second movement, middle section (Rimsky-Korsakov).

A very fine visual-aid resource for rounding-off this instruction is the sound-movie *The Brass Choir,* distributed by Encyclopaedia Britannica, and referred to earlier in this phase of ear training.

Other compositions which feature the use of brass wind instruments are: Prelude to Act 1 (*Die Meistersinger,* Wagner); *Symphony No. 4 in F minor,* fourth movement (Tchaikovsky); or any recording by the Salvation Army Band.

TROMBONE

BB♭ Tuba

Lesson Eleven

The final group of sounds which completes the total orchestral sound is that produced by percussion instruments. Sound is produced in percussion instruments by striking or shaking them. They divide into two groups or types: (1) instruments which produce musical tones varying in pitch; and (2) instruments which merely create rhythmic noise.

There are so many varieties of rhythm instruments that to attempt to describe them would be a long tedious process. Therefore only those instruments will be discussed which are generally used in symphonic music.

TIMPANI

Rhythm instruments that are the most consistently used in orchestral music are timpani, sometimes called kettledrums. The reason for the latter title is fairly obvious because they appear to be huge copper kettle bowls minus spouts. Imagine a huge copper ball sliced into two halves. Each half would constitute the body of a kettledrum, across the top of which is a skin, tightly stretched. By means of adjustable screws placed around the rim of the bowl the skin may be tightened or slackened, thus changing the pitch. In modern instruments a mechanical device operated by the performer's foot can change the pitch one step at a time. The range of the instrument is quite short,

SNARE DRUM

an interval of a fifth, so it takes two of these instruments (one large, one small) to encompass all the sounds in our octave. The larger plays lower notes, the smaller plays higher notes.

BASS DRUM

CHIMES

CYMBALS

Timpani are usually tuned one to play *doh,* the other to play *soh* in whatever key the music is written. Some orchestral pieces require more than two timpani. While drums are rarely silent in the school marching band, they are used only for special rhythmic or dynamic effects in orchestral music.

There are far too many varieties of percussion instruments, particularly those associated with the modern dance band, to merit comprehensive presentation here. However, inasmuch as the bass drum, snare drum, triangle, and cymbal are frequently used in music written by composers of serious music, this portion of the ear-training program would be incomplete without their inclusion. The physical structure of these instruments, and the manner in which they are performed, are usually familiar to students. Some compositions which illustrate use of percussion instruments are: *Symphony No. 4 in F minor,* fourth movement (Tchaikovsky); *Musik für Kinder* (Carl Orff); "Melody, Mallets and Mayhem" (Saul Goodman); *Symphony in E♭ minor,* No. 103, "Drum Roll" (Haydn); *Sonata for Two Pianos and Percussion* (Bartók). An excellent audio-visual aid is available in the Encyclopaedia Britannica set of films entitled *The Percussion Group.*

Precise lesson plans offered previously for music reading and the earlier phases of ear training have been discarded in this particular phase of the ear-training program. The depth of presentation will be determined by the music teacher's personal interest in this phase of the program and by the concentration span of the students. Five or 10 minutes will usually exhaust the concentration span. Once concentration has lapsed, the teacher might change to some form of music learning where there is greater activity, possibly singing.

LESSON TWELVE

In previous lessons the characteristic sounds of various tone groups which comprise the orchestra have been presented; the next step is to combine them in illustrating the total orchestral sound.

Should the film series distributed by Encyclopaedia Britannica be available through the local materials center, or some central film library, *The Symphony Orchestra* provides the most dramatic presentation and illustration of the total orchestral sound. To use just any recording at this point would not achieve the desired objective. It is much more effective to employ compositions in which various instrumental tone groups or choirs may be easily distinguished. Two such

SYMPHONY ORCHESTRA (THE FLORIDA STATE UNIVERSITY,
SCHOOL OF MUSIC, ROBERT SEDORE CONDUCTING)

recordings are "Peter and the Wolf" (Prokofiev) and "The Young
Person's Guide to the Orchestra" (Britten).

One of the basic criteria in selecting listening music for junior
high school students is tunefulness; another is brevity. Recordings
which might be used to implement the above are: "Funeral March of
a Marionette" (Gounod); Overture to *Die Meistersinger* (Wagner);
"Flight of the Bumble Bee" (Rimsky-Korsakov); "Pomp and Circumstance March in D Major" (Elgar); *L'Arlesienne Suite No. 1* (Bizet).
There is no need for a supplementary list of appropriate recordings
to continue this phase of ear training; the learning is extended in
the listening program, Chapter Eight.

Phase Six: Design in Music

LESSON THIRTEEN

Lessons in this particular phase of the ear-training program are
concerned with teaching junior high school students to understand

and recognize elementary design or form in music by hearing recordings which illustrate some of the more basic musical forms.

Of all musical forms the three most easy to assimilate are *simple binary, simple ternary,* and *old rondo.* This particular lesson will present simple binary only, and it will be quite short because there is not much music available in this form. It is necessary to understand the structure of simple binary before proceeding to more complex forms. As the name implies, a piece of music in simple binary form has two sections. This is most easily illustrated by referring to the first song learned after voices have been classified, "Santa Lucia."

Let the class sing this song in parts, and point out the two formal divisions. Due to the range of this melody it will not sing well in unison, so use parts. Draw attention to the fact that the constant repetition at different pitches of the six-note melodic figure is known as a *sequence* and is a device used frequently by composers.

Another illustration of simple binary form may be found in the verse (A) and chorus (B) of "Jingle Bells." Use the key of D major for unison singing. Draw attention to the use of sequence in the verse. Simple binary form is illustrated by letters thus: A B ‖ or sometimes A :‖ ‖: B :‖. In both of these, A signifies first subject and B signifies the second subject.

LESSON FOURTEEN

The most popular form or design for a musical composition is simple ternary in which the first subject A is played or sung, followed by a second subject B, followed by a return of the first subject A. There are many songs written in this form in which the first subject is performed twice before the second subject appears: A :‖ B A ‖

To illustrate this, direct the class to sing "Oh! Susanna," one of the rote songs learned earlier. Encourage your class to find other songs in the same form. By this time, if not earlier, students will ask why these forms are being sung, not played on the phonograph. These simple forms are too short in themselves to be used in orchestral music, but they will shortly become a part of more complex music; for example, the main theme for the second movement of Haydn's *Surprise Symphony*.

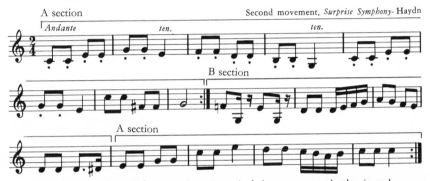

The range of this melody precludes its vocal use in a mixed class, no matter what key is used.

Should the class appear alert and receptive, play the entire movement on the record player to illustrate how a simple form may become complex by using variations. Caution the class to listen for one variation which strays away from the simple ternary design. Now introduce the term *theme with variations*, but do not continue with further illustrations at this time.

Lesson Fifteen

A simple attractive form which is often used by composers as a basis for more complex design is *old rondo* form, in which one main subject is used several times, each recurrence being separated by less important sounding music called *episodes*. A diagram illustrating this form would look like this: A e A e A, to which is added some appropriate closing music called a *coda*. The coda is very much like the conclusion of a letter: "Hoping to hear from you soon," "Sincerely yours," having no relationship to the communication in the letter, merely acting as a means of finishing off the letter.

Two excellent compositions for illustrating this form are "Serenade for Strings" by Volkmann and the Scherzo from *Midsummer Night's Dream* by Mendelssohn. Melodic extractions are presented here to aid in locating where the various formal divisions occur.

LESSON SIXTEEN

This lesson is concerned with an extension of simple ternary into *minuet and trio* form, a design used very frequently for the third movement of a symphony and sometimes in marches by Sousa. Though a little more complex than simple ternary, minuet and trio form is easily understood if the composition is presented as a composite of three separate pieces, each of which is in simple ternary form.

Minuet	Trio	Minuet
A :‖ ‖: B A :‖	C :‖ ‖: D C :‖	A ǀ B ǀ A ‖

It will be noticed that repeat signs are omitted in the last appearance of the minuet because it is customary to avoid repetition in the re-capitulation of the minuet.

Two very excellent illustrations of this formal design which are easy to comprehend and good ear-training materials are: the third movement of Haydn's *Surprise Symphony* and "Celebrated Minuet" by Boccherini. Notational extracts of subject matter from both these works are presented below and on page 252. The minuet is in 3/4 time.

This lesson might well extend through portions of two or three music periods if attention and interest of the class are maintained in presentation of the minuet and trio form. At the moment the goal is the students' perception of the formal structure of the music.

Other compositions which might be used to consolidate minuet and trio form are the third movements of these works: Beethoven, *Symphony No. 1 in C major, Symphony No. 2 in D major;* Mozart, *Symphony No. 40 in G minor,* and *Symphony No. 41 in C major.*

LESSON SEVENTEEN

Lesson Seventeen is concerned with the *theme with variations.*

One of the simplest illustrations of theme with variations form may be found in the second movement of Haydn's *Symphony in G Major* (Surprise), referred to in Lesson Fourteen. The *theme* to be used as subject for subsequent variations has its own simple ternary structural form A : ||| : B A : || which is maintained through all the variations except one, easily discernible in the minor mode. When Haydn's final variation is finished, a brief section of music is added (*coda*) to bring the composition to its natural conclusion.

A most interesting illustration of theme with variations is the fourth movement of Brahms' *Symphony No. 4 in E minor* in which the theme has no form, but consists simply of a melodic figure containing only eight notes.

As an introduction to hearing this composition teach the class (by rote) to sing the melody; then instruct the students to hum the air time after time while the record is playing. This procedure has quite an impact on the singers, because many times the melody is completely omitted by the orchestra and maintained in the listener's mind purely by vocalization. Prepare the class for the flute variation, because in this instance all notes of the *theme* will have to be sustained much longer. Employing the same compositional device used by Haydn in the second movement of the *Surprise Symphony,* Brahms adds a coda following the final variation. Notice how the sound of A♯ dominates every variation.

The Brahms composition under discussion is quite an extensive work and student concentration may start to wane. If this is noticeable, stop the record; explain why it has been stopped, and continue it another day.

Lesson Seventeen cannot be contained in one scheduled music period. The amount of time used in presenting the components of this lesson is purely up to the discretion of the music teacher, dictated of course by class ability to maintain concentration. Other compositions using the form are *Variations on a Nursery Tune* (Dohnanyi); *Enigma Variations* (Elgar); *Variations on a Theme by Haydn* (Brahms). Many other examples, perhaps not so readily understandable, are to be found in second movements of many symphonies.

LESSON EIGHTEEN

It is rare that junior high school general music classes proceed this far in ear training, but occasionally some groups do so. Without the two following lessons, information on the ultimate goal in ear training would be incomplete.

For the strongest and most important movements of symphonies, composers usually employ a structural design known by several names, *sonata form, symphony form, first movement form.* In this lesson the term *sonata form* will be used. A composition written in sonata form varies from other formal designs presented previously inasmuch as it contains two important subjects, each of considerable length. But perhaps the easiest way to illustrate the form is by means of a diagram or formula.

$$\text{Introduction} \quad \text{A } \mathit{link} \text{ B} \quad \overset{\mathit{codetta}}{:\|} \quad x \mid \text{A } \mathit{link} \text{ B} \quad \overset{\mathit{coda}}{\|}$$
$$\text{(optional)}$$

Not all music written in sonata form uses an introductory section, consequently in the above diagram it is designated as being optional.

Capital "A" in the formula represents a section of music in which the basic outline of the first theme or subject is stated then discussed briefly by different choirs of the orchestra so that it becomes established in the tonal memory of the listener. A eventually dissolves into a brief music passage whose purpose is to prepare the ear for the statement of a new subject in different key. This passage which leads the ear away from further discussion of A material is known as a *link* or *bridge* and is followed immediately by a statement of a second theme or subject, identified in the formula as B. Here again the basic outline of the subject is extended into a section by brief musical discussion, not usually so lengthy as the discussion involved with the presentation of A. The entire formal division defined above is called an *exposition,* and is brought to a conclusion by means of *closing* music, *codetta.*

In many symphonies the entire exposition (excluding the introduction) is repeated, apparently for the purpose of impinging thematic characteristics on the tonal memory of the listener. This being accomplished, the composition embarks on a leisurely, involved development of either one or both subjects, not at full length but in fragmentation, treating short motifs by sequence, extension, rhythmic alteration, harmonic alteration, and a great many varied devices at the disposition of the composer. The *development* or middle section, indicated by *x* in the formula, passes through a wide variety of keys and, avoiding the home key, varies in duration from very brief to quite long. When the composer decides enough has been said in the development the music moves unhurriedly toward the home key (tonic), and a modified recapitulation is begun by a restatement of A. "Modified" implies that this final statement of A *link* B is not an exact replica of the exposition inasmuch as the theme discussions are abbreviated, and furthermore B now appears in the home (tonic) key, necessitating considerable alteration of the link.

The movement is brought to a close by a section of music containing brief references to subject material reminiscent of the *codetta* in the exposition, but of proportions more in keeping with the conclusion of a movement rather than a section of a movement.

In introducing this form to the class aurally it is wise to select compositions in which the sectional divisions are easily discernible, and for this reason the first movements from two symphonies are recommended, namely *Symphony in G Major* (Surprise) by Haydn, and *Symphony No. 5 in C minor* by Beethoven. Basic thematic figures for first and second subjects of both compositions are presented below as a visual aid to tonal memory to foster a more intelligent understanding of the structural design.

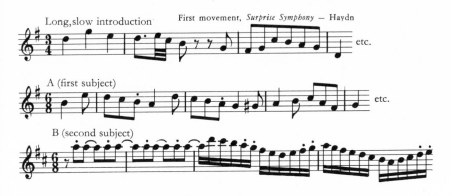

It will be more than obvious that the material presented in Lesson Eighteen will require many scheduled music class periods for adequate coverage. With this in mind thematic materials are offered herewith for two additional symphonies. Again, first movements are to be used, first from *Symphony No. 40 in G minor* by Mozart, and second from *Symphony No. 5 in E minor* by Tchaikovsky. The latter has been selected because of its tunefulness and appeal to young people.

As a matter of additional interest the introductory theme for the first movement appears in other movements, a device which serves to give unity to the entire symphony. However, the aesthetic value of such a technique is a little beyond the comprehension of most junior high listeners. Reference to this is pointless unless the entire symphony is to be played.

Other symphonies in which structural design of first movements agrees with the formula defined on page 253 are *Symphony No. 1 in C Major* by Beethoven; *Italian Symphony* by Mendelssohn, and *Symphony No. 8 in B minor* ("Unfinished") by Schubert. There are of course many others, but in the compositions suggested above, the formal structure is clear, without complex deviations from the basic plan, and they are also tuneful.

LESSON NINETEEN

This lesson presents two more aspects of sonata form, and represents the ultimate in music comprehension at the junior high school level. Admittedly, in order to reach this point in ear training, the music teacher must have high aspirations for his class, and an uncommon zeal to prepare his charges for subsequent self-motivated listening experiences of musical merit. Nevertheless, as mentioned in the previous chapter, without the inclusion of this information the topic would be incomplete.

The first additional aspect of sonata form to be offered in Lesson Nineteen concerns the use of more than one theme within one subject and presents a situation which is more easily described by means of a formula.

This figure is used powerfully in the development.

$$\text{Aa}'\ \textit{link}\ \text{Bb'}\ \overset{\textit{codetta}}{\ \Big\|} \ :\Big\|\quad x \quad\Big|\ \text{Aa}'\ \textit{link}\ \text{Bb'}\ \overset{\textit{coda}}{\ }\Big\|$$

The above is included here merely as a visual aid to clearer aural perception of form in performance. It must always be kept in mind that our present musical preoccupation is *ear training,* how the music sounds, not how it looks.

One of the finest, simplest expressions of this structure is found in the fourth movement of Beethoven's *Symphony No. 5 in C minor,* thematic material for which is illustrated on page 257.

The second and final aspect of sonata form for presentation in this lesson is that of *rondo sonata* form. Once again, definition of this form may be simplified by means of a formula.

$$\text{A}\ \textit{link}\ \text{B A}\ \overset{\textit{codetta}}{\ \Big\|}\ \overset{\text{C}}{\underset{x}{\Big\|\ \Big\|}}\ \text{A}\ \textit{link}\ \text{B A}\ \overset{\textit{coda}}{\ \Big\|}$$

It is undoubtedly sonata form since it contains two main subjects, while it also combines some aspects of old rondo form through the frequent return to A. C, which occurs during the development section, is rarely of sufficient length or strength to merit consideration as a major subject. An excellent music illustration of this form is the first movement of *Symphony No. 4 in E minor* by Brahms, thematic material for which appears below.

First movement, *Symphony No. 4 in E minor* — Brahms

Notice the interesting melodic fragments or motifs from which this theme is constructed. They are used separately and together in the development section. A at its second appearance in the exposition

Subject B

etc.

enters majestically by means of lengthening the time value of each of the first eight notes.

Conclusion

Most important in these lessons have been the ear-training practices and the listener's attention being drawn specifically to the recognition of certain musical phenomena and structures during performance. Aesthetic aspects of music in terms of student response are dealt with in "The Listening Program," Chapter Nine.

The students have acquired now a foundation for further exploration of the vast resources of musical composition. They have also been taught to concentrate, to sit still and listen, to derive meanings from music being heard. Not all junior high students thus exposed will carry these habits into adult life, but a number sufficient to justify the effort will do so.

While what has been presented in this chapter is more than adequate for the junior high school general music student, the college undergraduate music education major needs a much broader background of music literature if he is to prepare himself for an honest job teaching music literature. He needs to be on familiar terms with the great works of the masters. For teachers now in the field, and for potential teachers having no access to a good course in basic music literature, a "do it yourself" procedure is advocated, using books 1, 2, and 3 of *Essays in Symphonic Analysis*.[1] The author's delightful use of the English language and simple yet thorough explanations make interesting and informative reading.

[1] Donald F. Tovey, *Essays in Musical Analysis:* vol. 1, *Symphonies* (New York: Oxford University Press, 1935).

CHAPTER SIX

CHORAL TECHNIQUES

Function of Choral Techniques

Choral techniques are those devices and artifices employed by the music teacher to aid the class singing group or school chorus to reach its highest possible achievement level in understanding and performance of each and every choral work attempted. No junior high singing group will reach higher performing goals than those conceived by the music teacher because without his guidance and constant challenge for excellence they have not the remotest idea as to the nature of a sensitive, superior musical performance, or what it entails for them in the matter of work or aesthetic reward.

Excellence in application of choral technique is a very desirable goal, but attempting to emulate standards set by well-known professional choirs will prove a frustrating experience for the choral teacher at the junior high level. Over-refinement in any phase of early adolescent behavior is a most unnatural phenomenon. Excess time spent in achieving the ultimate in choral refinement is a debatable expenditure.

The wedding of fine words and beautiful sound, artistically performed, constitutes the most exquisitely satisfying of all musical experiences for both performers and listeners. Connubial bliss in such a wedding, however, is not achieved without a great deal of thought and diligence on the part of the singers. In the area of choral singing, responsibility for a supremely happy, compatible relationship is in the hands of the school chorus director or class music teacher.

Two attitudes are recommended: (1) Only music of good quality will be presented to the singers; and (2) nothing short of the finest possible interpretation will be tolerated as a final goal. How is this achieved? Such is the purpose of choral technique.

Before proceeding further, it must be emphasized that only basic choral techniques needed by the junior high school music teacher will be presented in this chapter. To discuss adequately all phases and subtleties of choral technique employed by the professional conductor would require a complete volume. Another point to consider is that due to the exigencies of schedule time available for general music, application of these choral techniques will have to be somewhat brief in general music singing. Too much concern for choral technique could conceivably defeat the main purpose of the general music program. The school chorus—elective, selective, or both—would, however, benefit considerably from a consistent application of these choral techniques.

WORDS AND MUSIC

The words of the song are an expression of the thoughts of the author, who feels that the ideas contained therein are worthy of passing on to posterity. Use of poetry enhances even commonplace thought, and the addition of fine music to poetry imbues the poetic line with even deeper, more subtle meaning. For instance, through poetry allied with music, love may be expressed in all imaginable gradations of fervor, from the wild outpouring of unbridled passion to the tender, hesitant murmurings. So it is in the depicting of all other aspects of human existence: through the application of music, words take on richer meaning.

Fine music, however, cannot often lift shallow thoughts or *little* words out of their innate mediocrity. Thus, in selecting songs for junior high school singers, word content should be an important criterion. However, it is the vocal propagation of the words with which the teacher should be most concerned. Every word of a song should receive its exact weight and dynamic treatment commensurate with its import in the over-all text.

PHRASING

Phrasing includes the combination of words into sentences, and the art of choral breathing at points which do not break the sense of the words. True, *staggered breathing* obviates the breaks being heard by an audience, but this is an expediency which encourages shallow breathing, and fosters broken phrasing habits in the individual singer.

An analysis of the words will show suitable breaks at which the chorus or class may take a breath and yet maintain the word sense, and often implement the dramatic feeling. Lack of attention to this important detail often minimizes the aural impact of an otherwise excellent chorus. As an example of phrasing carelessness of which so many choral directors are guilty, consider the performance of "Silent Night" from the point of view of words only.

> Silent night! holy night! all is calm,
> All is bright round yon virgin mother and Child,

How often is a breath made after the word "bright"? When this is done the line makes no sense whatsoever. Verse 3 poses a similar problem:

> Silent night! holy night! Son of God,
> Love's pure light radiant(ly) beams from Thy holy face,

Very few choral directors seem to notice a flagrant error in phrasing. A simple error may not be very important in itself but is most significant in its implications of phrasing carelessness in the remainder of the work. The national anthem of the United States of America, which always should be performed with dignity and pride, suffers most at the hands of careless phrasers, especially television-radio celebrities and football bands. Apparently not the slightest thought is given to sentence meanings and phrasing.

There is no general set of rules by which intelligent phrasing may be taught, however three basic suggestions will help: (1) Encourage singers to take deep breaths; (2) don't permit a breath break if there is no punctuation in the words; (3) study the text carefully before starting to teach the song. Mark breathing places on the conductor's score, instructing students to make similar markings on their own copies.

Thorough understand of all word meanings, coupled with desire and ability to articulate them with maximum effect, will lift any song out of a dull, mediocre performance, giving it new life and meaning.

Diction

Diction is the art of pronouncing words so that they can be understood easily and clearly by the listener and the sound will be pleasant to the ear.

Consonants

It seems elementary to remind the music teacher that words consist of vowel sounds separated from each other by consonants which, with the exception of *l, m, n, r, y, z,* cannot be sustained in speech or song. Generally speaking, consonants are merely syllable-dividers to be articulated with utmost precision.

One of the besetting sins of many choral groups is *lip-laziness.* It has a poor appearance and is conducive to solvenly articulation. Students need to be made aware of the necessity for lively lip movement when singing or talking. So often a consonant, inwardly sensed by the singer, is never propagated through the lips in performance. This is particularly noticeable in phrase endings. For instance, in words like "Lord, God," intent to pronounce the final consonant remains intent, and the final sharp impact of tongue against the back of the upper teeth never materializes. In good diction, sung or spoken, consonants should be crisp, clear, and confident. Tendency to over-hold on *m, n, ng* should be reserved for special occasions where the device has pertinent meaning, otherwise it becomes an overworked cliché.

Treatment of Letter *r*

Among the consonants mentioned above as having potential duration quality is one which requires special consideration, the letter *r.* It has duration potential but should never be used in this manner. By singing the word *far* and holding to the final consonant it will be obvious that in order to do this the tongue is holding a curved position at the back of the mouth which effectively blocks off the column of air from the lungs and vocal cords. The sensation of sound volume remains with the singer, but the listener perceives a disturbing reduction in volume.

In order to obviate this a few simple rules are offered which should be given to the class or chorus: (1) The letter *r* should not be articulated when it ends a word: "father," "mother," "cover," "matter," and so forth, *unless* the next word begins with a vowel sound in a word progression such as "father and mother." In this and similar instances the *r* in "father" is considered as a consonant separating two vowel sounds; it is articulated with a minimum of stress. (2) The letter *r* should not be articulated if it precedes another consonant: "word," "hard," "bird," "lord," "forward." In such instances the tongue should be low in the mouth until it must rise in order to articulate the consonant which the *r* precedes. (3) The letter *r* should be articulated when it separates two vowel *sounds*. In the following words *r* separates two vowels but not two vowel sounds: "care," "fare," "pure," "fire," "before." These and similar words belong to Rule 1 above. In words such as "carry," "Mary," "fury," "daring," the letter *r* should be articulated quickly as part of the second syllable, *Ma-ry,* not *Mar-y.* (4) The letter *r* should be articulated when it is the first letter of a word: "rough," "reason," "ride." (5) The letter *r* should be articulated when it follows immediately another consonant: "bright," "break," "cruel," "from," "great," "wrong."

Care in good use of the letter *r* can eliminate blocking of voice projection and in many cases heighten dramatic effect.

Vowels, of course, are the foundation of good choral sound, and require some careful consideration. Only essentials will be presented in this chapter.

TONE QUALITY

Diction becomes inexorably linked with the production of fine tone quality. Developing a round, robust, pleasing quality in voices of junior high singers is fairly simple, but instruction to the youngsters about the production of a good quality of musical sound must be reduced to its simplest terms. Some background information on the vocal production of musical sound is helpful in procuring good tone. The singers should be told about the basic physical process in creating vocal music: how air is compressed out of the lungs by action of the diaphragm and passes through the vocal cords which vibrate at the will of the singer, creating musical sounds. These are directed into the mouth cavities which amplify the sound before it is projected through the open lips in the form of singing. Formation of lips and position of the tongue determine the quality of singing sound. This may be an over-simplification, but it is adequate and reasonable enough to be accepted by junior high youngsters.

MOUTH FORMATION

Careless formation of the lips will result in poor, characterless tone; good lip formation will produce tone with firm, round, pleasing quality. To illustrate this more clearly, photographs appear below. Photograph No. 1 portrays a faulty but usual mouth formation from

No. 1

which unpleasant tones result, while any one of the other three (appropriate for the vowel sound required) will generally produce tones of pleasing quality. All needed vowel sounds can be accommodated by these three mouth formations.

No. 2

Photograph No. 2 illustrates good mouth formation for short vowel sounds as in "that," "sat," "hit," "with," "God," "not," "hot," "Lord," "cut," "but," also for the diphthong sound in words such as "fight," "might," "bright."

Mouth formation depicted in photograph No. 3 with *tongue low*

No. 3

in the mouth should be used for production of vowel sounds using *oo,* as in "cool," "moon," "soon;" and for vowel sounds using *ee* (tongue still low in the mouth), as in "peace," "steal," etc. The latter proposal may surprise some experienced choral directors, but this device automatically directs the air column into appropriate mouth cavities for the production of pleasing sound. The normal mouth position for spoken *ee* sound draws the back of the tongue to the roof of the mouth, effectively blocking off the air column, and results in a tightening of the neck muscles, producing an unpleasant sound.

Diphthongs are a form of pronunciation deriving from the juxtaposition of two different vowel sounds, not always involving the juxtaposition of two printed vowel letters. The most frequently occurring of these is the *i* sound in words such as "light," "white." Beautiful tone quality evolves in the singing pronunciation of this particular diphthong.

$$bright \; = \; brah\text{-}it$$

It is produced through mouth formation as illustrated in photograph No. 2.

Great care must be taken in this *and all other diphthong* pronunciation to ensure that the second half of the diphthong sound be articulated only when the syllable closes off. It must be considered as part of the following consonant. These would be wrong: *brah-i-t, brah-ee-t,* the latter being particularly offensive, and this rule applies to all similar sounding diphthongs, *right = rah-it; flight = flah-it,* etc.

Another diphthong which appears frequently and requires attention is that found in words involving the *ow* sound such as "crowned," "ground," "around." Securing good tone quality in the singing pronunciation of this particular diphthong involves a combination of two mouth positions:

$$crowned \; = \; crah\text{-}oond; \; ground \; = \; grah\text{-}oond$$

The first portion of the diphthong is sustained, and articulation of the second portion is delayed until the moment of completing the final consonant. Appropriate mouth formations are depicted in photo illustrations No. 2 and 3.

A further diphthong pronunciation is involved in the articulation of words with an *oh* sound, such as "rose," "bold," "cold," "moan." Production of this sound requires the round formation of the lips for the first portion of the diphthong (see photograph illustration No. 4), followed by a slight contraction into the *oo* formation for the second portion of the diphthong.

No. 4

rose = *roh-oos*   *bold* = *boh-oold*

Again it must be stressed, articulation of the second portion of the diphthong must be delayed until the final consonant closes off the word.

Before concluding this presentation of vowel articulation a word of caution is in order. Avoid diphthong treatment of words where it is not necessary, particularly in words using the *a* sound as in "Mary," "baby," "lady." Frequent misuse of these words results in *May-ee-ry, bay-ee-by, lay-ee-dy.*

Humming

The humming sound usually projected through closed lips has two disadvantages: it is not possible to vary the sound volume, and the sound thus produced lacks resonance. Resonance and variation of dynamic level can be achieved in humming sequences by forming *ng* with the tongue at the back of the mouth, and the lips open as in the *ah* formation. The breath should be ejected in a normal singing manner. The resulting sound is one of very pleasing string-like quality.

The choral teacher must decide what level of achievement he is willing to set as a reasonable goal for his group, commensurate with good taste and the concentration span of his singers. It is not unusual, after months of careful teaching, during a concert performance, for the chorus to become so stimulated by the applause of an audience that they forget all the niceties and simply "go to town" with all the energy they can muster.

The school chorus should be exposed to choral techniques compatible with its ability to employ them, but to strive for such vocal excellence in the singing portion of the general music class would be profitless. Members of the school chorus have usually elected to belong to the organization because they wanted to sing, because a friend was enrolled, or maybe just to get out of some other curricular chore. Inasmuch as they are present through their own choice, however, it can be assumed they will respond to musical challenges and accept the work involved more readily than members of a general music group who have been in many cases "drafted."

Intonation

A chorus which performs in such a manner that each singing part maintains accurate pitch is said to have good intonation. Junior high school singers (or even high school singers) need some training in the art of good intonation. Cambiate, when singing within their normal tessitura, seem to have a natural aptitude for singing with good intonation, and they will frequently anchor other parts which tend to stray.

FLATTING

Some causes of flatting, separately or in combination, are: lack of interest, lack of concentration, shallow breathing, poor posture, fatigue, hunger, poor room ventilation, and inability of the group to comprehend singing *over* rather than *under* a high note. Another cause, not readily recognized, is the frequent occurrence of the note B, particularly when it represents the third of the dominant chord in key of C major. Theorists in the medieval church system realized the strange impact of this sound and frequently avoided it by alternating B♭.

Popular opinion is that poor intonation refers only to flatting. This is not entirely true; poor intonation refers also to sharping.

Some remedies are fairly obvious, for instance retiring the song from the repertoire if there is lack of interest or concentration. Shallow breathing is not easy to rectify and is best overcome by teaching phrasing the very first time words of a song are introduced. This is most important, because if punctuation is allowed to slip the first time, the error becomes permanent and no amount of corrective effort can change it thereafter.

FATIGUE AND HUNGER FLATTING

Fatigue and hunger are among other causes of flatting during a singing class or chorus rehearsal. It is unwise to schedule chorus for the period preceding lunch, the final period of the day, or immediately following a physical education period. However, the school administration might not be able to schedule your groups at another time. In which case, extra stimulation is needed to evoke the best possible response from tired or hungry singers.

MUSIC LINE CONTRIBUTES TO FLATTING

Consistent flatting is usually confined to certain songs which appear to encourage a downward pitch drift. Factors contributing to this at junior high level are: long-sustained pitches, as in "Adoramus Te, Christe"; a tessitura which remains too high too long; difficult wide melodic intervals to negotiate; and, as was mentioned earlier, frequent appearance of the note B. Deep breathing and phrase understanding are recommended to combat persistent flatting, and if this does not help, the singing section which is drooping should rehearse the offending passage to the vocalise *lee,* lips formed to pronounce *ooh.* After the group has experienced correct pitch feeling in this manner, it is easier to do so with the words of the song.

Should the entire group appear to be sagging, raise the pitch of the song by a half tone. Do not ever scold them for going flat unless they are very obviously in a lazy mood. If the same song is losing pitch every rehearsal, the problem is not indolence. In some instances it is a single note that is never hit cleanly in the pitch center. To meet this problem, try to give the singers a concept of overshooting, then dropping into the required pitch. The following illustration may help in

describing an appropriate action. Spread the left hand, palm downward, level with the forehead. Spread the right hand, palm upward,
about chest level. Then bringing up the right hand smartly, overshoot
the left about six inches, dropping it with a slap, the right-hand palm

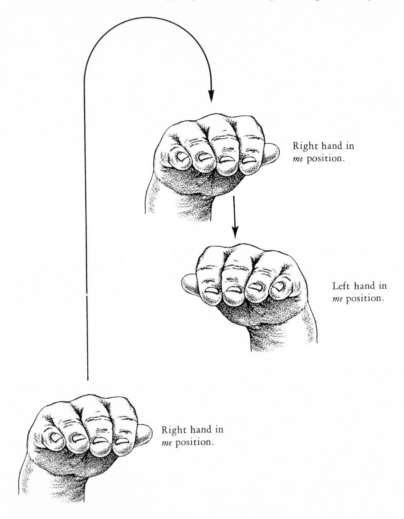

Right hand in
me position.

Left hand in
me position.

Right hand in
me position.

on back of the left hand. Instruct singers to emulate your action as they
sing the troublesome melodic leap, using *lee* as a vowel sound. This is
not a guaranteed solution, but it generally produces results.

Flatting in choral music with a piano accompaniment is not so frequent as in unaccompanied singing, but it does occur on occasion and

can usually be obviated by instructing the singers to listen to the piano as they are singing. However, one thing must be remembered: at the junior high level, instructions of this sort need repetition, lesson after lesson. Instant absorption is not one of the stronger qualities of young people in early adolescence. Let it be clearly understood, however, that frequent reference to the foibles of the junior high population should not be construed as derogatory or flippant criticism. The school music teacher will achieve greater success and enjoyment in teaching if he recognizes their idiosyncrasies, accepts them, and works with his subjects kindly but firmly.

SHARPING

Sharping is a less frequent offense than is flatting, but it does occur, sometimes in the excitement of a public performance, and particularly if the director has been over-stimulating in his concern for intonation on a high-pitched note or phrase. Exaggerated relaxation of the beat motions will usually bring down the pitch, or an overt hand motion pointing to the piano will signal the singers to listen to the piano.

It is of little use to tell singers during a rehearsal that they are singing sharp. They must be told how to bring it down. Two methods have proved quite successful in this kind of training: (1) Vocalize the offending passage to *loo,* keeping the jaw firm but not tight, and (2) pitch the song a half tone lower than written.

SINGING POSTURE

Posture, an important factor in intonation, requires constant checking in junior high choral work.

The position in photograph illustration No. 5 (page 274) is typical of junior high youngsters and should not be tolerated in either chorus rehearsal or general music singing. It promotes lazy, out-of-tune singing, and encourages slovenly breathing habits which in turn result in poor phrasing. The posture in photograph illustration No. 6 (page 275) places the body in a most advantageous position for full breathing and free projection; note the singer's back is not resting on the chair back and both feet are flat on the floor.

No. 5

Obviously singers cannot retain this posture throughout a lesson or rehearsal, and it is recommended the youngsters be taught to assume an "at ease" attitude during nonsinging intermissions. But the moment the teacher's handclap calls for resumption of singing, correct posture should be automatic.

Poor posture is prevalent when the singing group is seated, but a standing position does not solve the problem. Postures demonstrated in the photographic illustrations Nos. 7 and 8 (pages 276 and 277) are suggested as being conducive to free, open singing. They also produce a uniform stance which is pleasing to view from the audience.

During a public performance boys are never happy about their hands. Locking them behind the back becomes uncomfortable after a while, but placing them interlocked in front of the body is too feminine a stance to be accepted as a desirable male attitude. During a standing vocal performance boys might place thumbs downward inside the appropriate trouser pocket, palms turned in, fingers pointing downward, the index finger lining up approximately with the seam.

No. 6

Position of feet is also important for well-balanced standing vocal posture. A singer's heels should be approximately eight inches apart, toes approximately twelve inches apart; the foot nearest the stage wings being advanced about three inches. To the reader this may seem picayune, but it places the body in a well-balanced position, and uniformity in this adds much to steady tone, secure intonation, and good group appearance.

THE BEAT

The director's use of hand and arm gestures, plus appropriate facial expression, is the most important of all choral techniques to be acquired by the school music teacher. Unlike most group efforts, no individual in a singing group is ever *on his own;* each member must respond to the command of the conductor at the instant of command to achieve total unity of performance.

No. 7

By means of hand-arm motion and facial communication the director is responsible for the projection of every sound, word, nuance, and tempo of the chorus. In a public performance this is his sole avenue of communication with the singers. The technique of the beat therefore should not be treated casually or accepted as a natural aptitude of the college music education major, but should be developed thoughtfully and thoroughly.

In view of the fact that most college music education majors take at least one course in conducting, and since a treatise on conducting would require much more detail and space than is commensurate with the nature of this text, it will be assumed the reader is familiar with the basic techniques of conducting. Only certain aspects pertaining to the junior high situation will be treated here.

At the junior high level, in class or chorus, an easily recognizable beat should be maintained at all times by one hand, left or right. The use of the other hand should be reserved for interpretive gestures. Scope

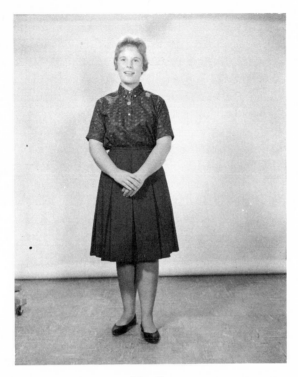

No. 8

of the beat indicates intensity or volume of sound desired: a wide strong beat calls for *forte,* while a narrow softer beat calls for *piano.* Care must be taken that the indication for soft singing is still firm and precise, otherwise the singers respond in such a manner as to give the impression that they are insecure.

The beat should be oriented in an area around the director's face, so that facial communication is possible, and elbows should be kept down. It is a common fault to allow elbows to rise to shoulder level, and this produces a quasi-comic attitude as though the director is about to take flight. Another common conducting fault is the director's call for power or sustained intonation by violent, nervous vibrations of outstretched hands. Apart from the fact that the visual aspect is ugly, the response elicited emerges with a very hard, strained, forced tone quality. This usually occurs at a phrase end or on a *fermata,* which can be realized easily by holding the interpretive hand forehead-high, while the beating hand maintains the required beat, slowing down to compensate for the duration of the fermata. Another favorable aspect of this technique is that the singers are not kept in doubt as to the exact moment when the cut-off will occur. Continuance of the beat in retardation enables the group to estimate duration of the fermata, and to conserve breath accordingly. The cut-off beat, particularly at the end of a song, should be executed smartly but with a minimum of arm motion. A grandiose closing gesture is to be avoided, even in a *fortissimo* ending.

The intent of the director should be easily identifiable by use of a specific gesture for a specific, desired response. To illustrate this point, the classroom music teacher or chorus director can establish a call for crescendo which merely involves widening the beat, using a narrowing beat to effect a decrescendo or diminuendo. The call for power should never involve exaggerated histrionics which tend to convey a sense of desperation to an audience and distract the listener.

Once this technique and the desired responses have been communicated to the singers, the same device should be used consistently thereafter to evoke the same type of response. Conducting style employed in the music classroom or chorus rehearsal should not be changed at a public performance: the tendency to overact in front of an audience should be curbed because it disturbs the youngsters.

Precision in attack derives from a precise, well-defined beat, and may be realized quite simply by hitting the first beat of a measure *at the top*, not at the bottom. In order to clarify discussion on this topic, diagrams familiar to all music education majors are presented below.

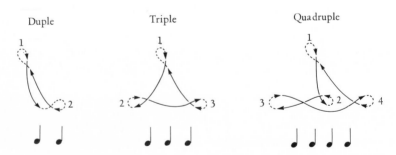

These diagrams are identical with those found in other texts, but trouble arises in their application to a practical situation. According to the above diagrams, and acceptable to most music directors, beat one is a *down* beat. Therefore it can be assumed that the downward stroke in each instance represents the duration of beat one. In general practice this is not so: the lower extremity of the downward stroke is often used as the attack on beat one. Thus, in performance beat one is actually an *up* beat, and, following this sequence to its logical conclusion, in quadruple time beat four becomes a *down* beat.

The college undergraduate music education major (also the teacher already in the field) is urged to try hitting beat one at the top of the beat. The technique has proved invaluable for obtaining precise attack and maintaining rhythm. There are no split-beat problems if beat one hits at the top, as the following diagrams will illustrate.

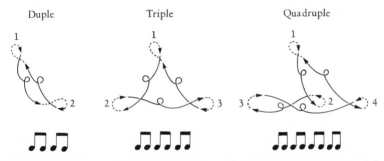

By using this system a split beat may be picked up at any point in the measure, without losing the direction of the routine.

Six-eight time is compound-duple and requires only two beats to the measure, unless split beats are called for in the interests of precision.

The above diagrams are capable of many combinations to accentuate such rhythms as:

$$\frac{6}{8} \; \text{♩} \; \text{♪♫♫} \; | \; \text{♪} \; \text{♩.} \; | \; \text{♫♫♩} \; \text{♪♩.} \; \text{♩.} \; \|$$

Six-eight time, using *top-of-the-beat* technique, offers unlimited possibilities for conveying rhythmic intent to the singing group.

When directing junior high music groups, beat a preliminary measure of silence before leading in the singers. The purpose of this is to establish tempo. Furthermore, if the song is accompanied, follow the same procedure with your accompanist. The accompanist should not make a rallentando in the measure before the singers enter; it breaks the rhythm and results in uncertain choral attack.

INTERPRETATION

Sensitive and imaginative interpretation of choral music, coupled with a confident beat, make all the difference between a good performance and a superlative one, not only for the delectation of an audience, but for the complete enjoyment of a song by the singers in a chorus or class.

The true secret of success in this endeavor is for the choral director to know every note of the music and to absorb the total meaning of the words. Every possible nuance should be explored, and the teacher's feelings about the selection should be discussed with the group. Do not become sidetracked by asking for group opinion.

The facial expression of the director mirroring the word meanings is absolutely essential to evoke sensitive treatment of a song by junior high youngsters. They are, by the way, capable of the most compelling interpretations when they understand what is wanted.

All choral music does not offer exciting opportunities for unusual interpretation, but variation of tempo and volume should constantly be sought and applied where appropriate. Variation, however, should not be injected merely for the sake of change, but rather to give fuller meaning and sensitivity to the unfolding of the text. Sensitivity to word meanings is the core of fine choral interpretation. Instruct each singing part of your group automatically to produce a slight crescendo when the line for that part rises, compensating with a decrescendo as the line descends again.

Another effective practice in achieving sensitive interpretation is to make a brief break where a period punctuates the text, and pause for a second or two before entering the next phrase. In public performance this allows the audience to assimilate thoroughly the message just completed before another chain of thought is started.

In order to obtain maximum sensitivity in song interpretation it is essential that the director be free of the printed score, and able to communicate facially with the singers. Words and music should be committed to memory, particularly during a performance. But extended choral works such as Brahms' *Requiem* and Handel's *Messiah,* performed by adult groups, could scarcely be memorized except by an extremely gifted director.

TONE QUALITY

Insistence on an over-refined tone quality can often interfere with reasonable interpretation in singing. Flour can be refined to such an extent that its ultimate product, bread, is devoid of nourishment; thus it can be with a singing group which specializes in the *loo-loo* style, where intensity is never permitted beyond the *mezzo-forte* level for fear of impure tone creeping in. There is little fear of this happening at the junior high level, except in the elective-selective chorus. The concept of pure tone is not easy to instill, though not impossible if the director has patience and the group can concentrate sufficiently. Good diction has a great deal to do with tone quality, and for this purpose the teacher is advised to follow precepts outlined earlier in the "Diction" portion of this chapter. Good vowel sounds are indispensable in good tone quality.

The outline of choral techniques defined in the foregoing pages of this chapter has been presented mainly for the guidance of the director of the junior high school elective chorus. Too much time should not be spent on this phase of choral singing in the general music class, yet such aspects as good tone and clear diction in song singing should be stressed constantly. No matter how simple a song might be, it is worthy of the best performance attainable by the group, chorus, or general music class. Overemphasis on choral technique results in less choral music being learned, and an encroachment on time which might be used for music reading, ear training, and other aspects of the general music program.

With the school chorus, however, it is an entirely different matter. Junior high school youngsters are capable of singing very difficult music, providing the ranges of the respective parts are commensurate with vocal ranges prescribed in Chapter Two. The scope of their emotional and dramatic choral interpretation is limited solely by the imagination, personality, and musicianship of the group director.

Junior high school choral directors should recognize the amazing choral potential of their students and challenge them to their finest musical expression in every lesson. They become very proud of fine choral achievement, but are quickly bored and disinterested with mediocrity.

CHAPTER SEVEN

FUNDAMENTALS OF MUSIC

Introduction

The fundamentals of music are the scientific side of music.

Boys and girls in a music class have the right to ask why they should study music fundamentals. Many people enjoy music without knowledge of fundamentals. Some people sing well and even play musical instruments without studying fundamentals. So why should the junior high school student study the fundamentals of music?

Sometimes the best way to answer a question is by asking one. Why study the reading and writing of words? Why not just listen to others talk and repeat what they have said? The answers to these questions are the same, whether the problem is one of music or of words:

1. We learn to read words or music in order to get our information first-hand.
2. We ourselves must read to be sure that our information is correct. (Sometimes we need to re-read words or music several times to be sure.)
3. We must be able to read if we wish to write.
4. We must be able to read if we want to carry on successfully the usual functions of life—to buy and sell things, to make a living, to protect ourselves, to be good citizens in a civilized society.

The average person interested in music as a pleasurable experience seldom cares to do more than to just enjoy it. This attitude does not warrant severe criticism, but if this person were told that his interest in

283]

music could yield more pleasure and satisfaction, he would doubtless be interested in knowing how.

Higher dividends of pleasure and satisfaction do come to those who have acquired a knowledge of music fundamentals. It teaches them to understand *how* music is written, *why* it sounds as it does, *where* it comes from, *how* it is put together, *why* it is performed in one way rather than another, *how* to improvise or "play by ear," *why* the listener reacts as he does, and it offers much other valuable information as well. A new world of meaning is available to those who *know*.

This chapter is divided into seventeen lessons. By holding one class weekly, it can be completed in one semester. When classes in fundamentals are alternated with another course, an entire school year would be devoted to this chapter. An additional semester would result in better assimilation of the course content.

At the first meeting of the class it must be arranged for each student to have a notebook for a written record of all lessons. The teacher must be painstaking in helping the students to collect accurate notes. All music examples and considerable other material should be put on the chalk board for inclusion in the notebooks of each student. Duplication for distribution of some of this material would be helpful. A notebook which contains pages of staffs for music manuscript as well as ordinary pages for class notes is necessary for best results.

Much of the text for Chapter Seven is enclosed in quotation marks. The purpose of this is to indicate to the teacher a way to present the various materials to the junior high school students. Such passages may be read directly to the class, but, for the sake of a more dynamic and personal presentation, the teacher should put the ideas in his own words.

Those parts of this chapter which are not enclosed in quotation marks are addressed directly to the teacher. The language employed suggests terminology appropriate to and understandable by the junior high school student. Through this procedure, adaptation of the material and terminology for the student is facilitated.

Division of this chapter into lessons suggests units of learning rather than a specific number of minutes in class. This is due to the fact that various classes absorb material in different lengths of time. For some groups one lesson might prove more valuable when spread over several lesson periods. For some classes portions of the chapters might be omitted.

The content included in this chapter is designed to be comprehensive in scope. Therefore, the junior high student should be able to complete all the lessons of each chapter, but this is not always possible.

Additional teaching aid and instructions for the teacher are indicated by enclosing other passages in brackets, i.e., [This rhythm may be clearly heard in the recording of the "Deer Dance" by Skilton.]

Assignments and definitions will be found at the conclusion of each lesson.

LESSON ONE: THE VALUE OF MUSIC FUNDAMENTALS

"When you listen to music you are aware that it makes you feel different. It may be exciting; it sometimes makes you feel happy, sad, quiet, disturbed—or like dancing, like marching, like being in church, in the army, at the fair, at the circus, and so on.

"Because of the spontaneous and natural feeling connected with hearing music, the general reaction is that it *just happens* like the song of birds, like the surf pounding on the beach, or like the blowing of a windstorm. Music does have a basis in nature (as explained in Lesson One of Chapter Nine), but it does not *just happen*. Music is created by men who understand the science as well as the art of music.

"An easy way to understand what is meant by the science of music is to realize that it means 'the Reading, Writing, and Arithmetic of Music.' By the time you have finished studying this chapter, you will recognize the fact that the science of music really includes more than just reading, writing, and arithmetic. For the time, however, let us be concerned only with the 'three R's' of music.

"Each of you in this class has the right to ask why you should study music fundamentals when you can enjoy listening to music without any knowledge of music fundamentals. You know, also, that people learn to sing very well and even to play musical instruments without studying fundamentals.

"Here are some reasons why you will profit from studying the fundamentals of music:

"First, it is a means to an end. That end is the increased understanding, appreciation, and pleasure in listening to music.

"Second, it will help you sing or play your part in chorus, band, orchestra, choir, etc. It will also be a great aid in harmonizing by ear, in improvising and in accompanying a song without a score from which to read.

"Third, a knowledge of fundamentals will help you in learning how to read music.

"In short, after each of you has learned the lessons in this chapter, you will be literate instead of illiterate in music. You will have many of the mysteries of music opened to your full view, and you will obtain considerable satisfaction from knowing 'what makes music tick.'"

Definitions

Music fundamentals—Reading and writing and arithmetic of music.
To be literate in music—The ability to read and write music.
To improvise music—To play music "by ear" without the help of notes. Also to compose and to perform music simultaneously.

Assignment

Write a paper comparing the benefits of knowing how to read words with the benefits of knowing how to read music.

LESSON TWO: RHYTHM

"Music is the combination of three elements: rhythm, melody, and harmony. The oldest of these is rhythm. Early man undoubtedly moved to rhythm before he sang melody or played harmony. (See Lesson 7 of Chapter Eight.)

"Rhythm has many forms. In architecture it is the framework of a building. In mathematics it is the recurring pattern of numbers. In poetry it is the emphasis on words to create meter. The natural world of stars, water, seasons, day, and night is filled with rhythmic patterns of all sorts. In music, rhythm is the system of beats and time values.

"Rhythm in music exists in time. Beats and time values are expressed in time. A beat may occur every second; a rhythmic pattern may be 15, 30, or perhaps even 60 seconds long. In architecture, time would not be a factor of rhythm; the rhythmic accent would be on space—inches, feet, and yards.

"Time makes the study of music unique. A note played a tenth of a second too early or too late is wrong, whereas a correct answer to a problem in arithmetic is not wrong just because it was produced a second or an hour late!

"A strong sense of rhythm is necessary for a music group to be able to perform together, and a melody is not satisfactory unless the time value of each note is correct. The beat of military music must be regular if men are to march to it.

"First of all, rhythm depends upon the *beat* which we feel in music. A beat is an accent in time—i.e., the *step* in a military march." [Play a military march or a grand march on the record player or perform a piece with a strong *beat* on the piano.]

"As you listen, tap your desk precisely (but not heavily) in time with the music." [Also ask for volunteers to do this singly with other music.]

"Tapping with the beat is the same as marching with the beat or dancing with the beat." [Play other music with faster or slower beats. Play a piece that has changes in time. Each student must learn to 'feel beats' in music and respond correctly, if he is to be successful in the study of any phase of music.]

[Have the class find the much more elusive beat while singing "My Old Kentucky Home" or "Carry Me Back to Old Virginny."]

"Here are the beats for the words of 'My Old Kentucky Home.' (See page 288.) The beat often falls on rests between the words while some words are several beats long. Sing the words and tap your desk lightly but precisely with a pencil every time a vertical line is crossed."

[In "Carry Me Back to Old Virginny," note that the second beat comes in the middle of the second syllable of the very first word, "Car-ry." This is called syncopation, a characteristic of the ragtime which is the predecessor of jazz. In this case, the syncopated rhythm occurs only in the first measure of the verse and the first measure of the chorus where the same word, "car-ry," is used the second time.]

"Rhythm also depends upon time values. Time values mean the varying length of notes. Sing 'Onward Christian Soldiers.' Every time another syllable or another note is sung, tap your pencil. Each *tap* is the *rhythm* of this piece. Here is a diagram to look at." (See page 289.)

[Allow the entire class to tap out the time values of the melody in "Onward Christian Soldiers," sometimes singing it and sometimes with silence. (Use key of B♭ major.) It will be a good sport to see whether the class can keep together without singing. A group of well-schooled musicians could do this, with or without singing. It will be found that, even while singing, the long notes are the most difficult to hold correctly.]

"Let us try another familiar song in which the rhythm is very difficult to perform accurately. You may use both hands in any order. Just

TABLE I

DIAGRAM OF BEATS FOR "MY OLD KENTUCKY HOME"
(*Keep the Beats Regular*)

(Beat)	1	2	3	4	1	2	3	4
(Sing)	The sun	shines	bright	in	the old	Ken-tuck-y	home,	—
	'Tis sum-mer	—	the dark-	ies	are gay;	—	—	—
	The corn	top's	ripe	and	the mead-ow's in	the	bloom,	While
	the birds	make	mu-sic	all	the day;	—	—	—
	The young	folks	roll	on	the lit-tle	cab-in	floor,	—
	All mer-ry	—	all hap-	py	and bright;	—	—	—
	By'n by	hard	times	comes	a knock-ing	at	the door,	Then
	my old Ken-tuck-y	home	—	good night!	—	—	—	—
	Weep	—	no more,	my	la -dy,	—	—	O
	weep	—	no more	to-	day!	—	—	We
	will sing	one	song	for	the old	Ken-tuck-y	home,	For
	the old Ken-tuck-y	home,	far	a-way.	—	—	—	—

Note: The symbol ⌢ over a note is called a *fermata* or *hold*. It means
that the note may be held as long as the performer wishes, but usually about
50% longer than the time-value of the note.

tap for every note, since this is the rhythm of the melody. Sing together."

[Use "Battle Hymn of the Republic," with its difficult rhythmic
patterns. If you wish, have someone count the beats out loud. Then let
several persons try it at a lively speed without singing or counting. It
will be a severe challenge for two or more persons to tap the note
values exactly at the same instant.]

"In analyzing rhythm in music, it should be remembered that
more than one rhythm will often be going on at the same time. The
melody will have one rhythm as determined by the length of each note.
The accompaniment may have another rhythm—slow, fast, regular or
irregular. Sometimes, as in the accompaniment of the drum for the
'Indian War Dance,' the rhythm of the accompaniment proceeds
through the entire piece with practically no change.

TABLE 2

RHYTHM

DIAGRAM OF BEATS AND TIME VALUES

FOR

"ONWARD CHRISTIAN SOLDIERS"

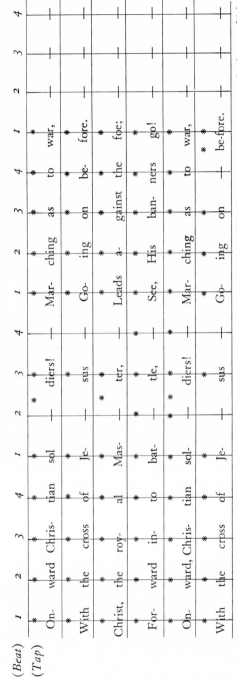

(Beat) (Tap)	1	2	3	4	1	2	3	4	1	2	3	4	1	2	3	4
	On-	ward	Chris-	tian	sol	*	diers!		Mar-	ching	as	to	war,			
	With	the	cross	of	Je-		sus		Go-	ing	on	be-	fore.			
	Christ,	the	roy-	al	Mas-	*	ter,		Leads	a-	gainst	the	foe;			
	For-	ward	in-	to	bat-	*	tle,		See,	His	ban-	ners	go!			
	On-	ward,	Chris-	tian	sol-	*	diers!		Mar-	ching	as	to	war,			
	With	the	cross	of	Je-		sus		Go-	ing	on		be-fore.			

Attention: Tap the *notes* not the *beats*. The notes (time values) are indicated by stars (*). The vertical lines are regular beats which measure the time value of each note.

289]

"When four persons sing together in barbershop quartet style, all four voices usually sing the same rhythm. The note values of each part are therefore the same."

[The following recordings from Chapter Nine will be particularly interesting from the standpoint of rhythm and may be used to make the class more aware of the contribution of rhythm to music: "Trepak" from *Nutcracker Suite,* by Tchaikovsky; "When Johnny Comes Marching Home (American Salute)," by Gould; fugue from *Schwanda,* by Weinberger; 'Saber Dance," by Kabalevsky; "Hallelujah" from *Messiah,* by Handel; "Country Gardens," by Grainger; "Stars and Stripes Forever," by Sousa, etc.]

Definitions

Beat—The pulsations at regular time intervals during music, i.e., the marching speed.
Rhythm—The note values in relation to the beat.

Assignment

1. Learn to tap the regular beats to "America" while you sing it. When you can do this, you have demonstrated its rhythm because beats are combined with the time values of the notes.
2. Practice doing this for other familiar songs.

LESSON THREE: MELODY

"After a concert or an opera, many persons can be heard humming or singing their favorite tunes. Melodies take hold of people. This is described by the popular phrase, 'haunted by a melody.' Some melodies, more than others, do just that.

"The best melodies are not necessarily the easiest to sing or to whistle. They are not always the ones which 'haunt' you. By definition, a melody is any succession of single tones. Therefore, it would seem that anyone could make up a melody. This is correct. But, while just any succession of tones would be a melody, it would not necessarily be a good melody. On the other hand, it could be a very good one. Children, as well as adults, sometimes find themselves humming or singing an original tune. Try it. If you know how to write it down, there would be no danger of forgetting it.

"Should you wish to make up a melody or tune you would be faced with the fact that its quality depends upon the choice of tones and rhythm. Thus the problem of creating a *fine* melody gets more complicated.

"What is your favorite melody? Hum or sing it to yourself. Does it influence your feelings? If it happens to be 'Home on the Range,' for instance, do you find yourself longing to go home—to a home built on the wide-open prairie far from the hustle and bustle of city life? 'Home on the Range' is a tune which men enjoy especially. This is true because most men are deeply involved in their business responsibilities and the necessities of adult life with the result that they enjoy dreaming or singing about the simple life.

"Home is always a favorite subject of people. Another home melody is the song named, 'Goin' Home.' This melody was taken from Dvořák's *New World Symphony*. (See Lesson Nineteen, Chapter Eight.) Sing the melody, and you will have the feeling of relaxing at home.

"Why do all people enjoy the melody of 'Way Down Upon the Swanee River' ('Old Folks at Home')? Doesn't the sound of the music make you feel that you would like to be there? The melody is supported by the pleasant harmony and words written by Stephen Foster. The rhythm of the melody is comfortable and inviting.

"Melody (with or without words) does these things. It speaks to the inner man. It stimulates his feelings.

"Melody, more than rhythm and harmony, speaks directly in musical terms to the soul of man. This is the reason the world has come to love Strauss' 'Blue Danube Waltzes,' 'Andante Cantabile' (Tchaikovsky), 'Minuet in G' (Beethoven), 'Humoresque' (Dvořák), 'Clair de Lune' (Debussy), 'The Swan' (Saint-Saëns), 'Pomp and Circumstance' (Elgar) and 'The Stars and Stripes Forever' (Sousa), just to mention a few from Chapter Eight. There are no words to any of these melodies. Yet all of them speak to the listener. Such melodies are truly songs that do not need words.

"On the other hand, words with melodies offer considerable help to the listener. The listener's response to the music is thereby spelled out, to a large extent, by the words. 'A Mighty Fortress Is Our God,' the 'Hallelujah Chorus,' 'Ave Maria,' 'Death and the Maiden,' and all the operatic arias—all of these have words, and the words make it possible for man to sing them.

"Yes, melodies have a habit of 'taking hold' of people."

Definitions

Melody—A tune or air which is formed by any succession of single tones.
A good melody—A choice selection of tones possessing a universal and lasting appeal to mankind.
Harmony—A system of combining tones in a progression of chords.

Assignment

Write a list of three favorite melodies. Tell why each one appeals to you.

Lesson Four: Harmony

"The world needs harmony. People need to live in harmony. People enjoy hearing harmony in music. The addition of harmony to a melody improves it.

"Man has created many musical instruments to provide harmony— the harp of ancient Greece, the dulcimer of Shakespeare's time, the guitar and banjo of the days of the Wild West, and the ukulele of today.

"Because the ukulele is a ready source of harmony for a singer, it is popular among young people on picnics, hay rides, around the campfire, in the home, and sometimes at school. Other harmony instruments popular with school children are the guitar and autoharp. Both the autoharp and the ukulele are easy instruments to play. The autoharp will automatically give you the needed chord when the proper bar is pushed. The only problem is to know which chord is needed! Even this problem is solved when the names of the proper chord are printed with the words of the song to be sung. (The use of the autoharp in school music is explained in Lesson Sixteen of this chapter.)

"When three or more tones are sounded simultaneously, a chord is produced. Harmony occurs when chords are connected in a system of tonal progressions.

"I want to demonstrate the part that harmony plays in music. Let us sing 'Love's Old Sweet Song' as a melody or solo without harmony. [Use key of Eb major.] Now let us sing it again with the harmony played on an autoharp, a guitar, a ukulele, or a piano.

"The difference between the two performances is harmony. It supports the melody. It adds tone color. Good harmony heightens the effect of the melody. The harmony part is called the *accompaniment*, since it accompanies the solo line.

"Still more pleasure will be added when the harmony of a piece is played with an interesting rhythm. Let us sing a song like 'Oh! Susanna' without accompaniment. [Use key of C major.] Now let us add not only harmony but rhythm by playing the harmony in various rhythmic patterns to fit the spirit of the music.

"Another way of adding harmony to a melody is to have two or more people sing (or play) other parts. When a number of persons sing each part, the group is called a *chorus*."

[Invite a group of singers who can perform three- or four-part harmony. A boys' or girls' trio or quartet or a chorus could demonstrate the function of harmony in music. The barbershop quartet style specializes in the light touch or in so-called "close harmony."]

[A performance of a vocal quartet or chorus would automatically demonstrate the three elements of music. In addition to *harmony,* it would incorporate *melody* and *rhythm.*]

"Yes, these three elements are the vital parts of all music: rhythm, melody, and harmony. When any one phase is weak or missing, the quality of the music suffers noticeably."

Assignment

Write a report comparing the harmony, melody and rhythm of "Love's Old Sweet Song" and "Oh! Susanna" and one other song.

LESSON FIVE: READING AND WRITING OF MUSIC

[This lesson concerns the staff and its relation to notes of the G clef.]

"The best plan developed by man to read and write music involves using a staff. There are several kinds of staffs, but the five-line staff is the one used today. On such a staff by including the space immediately above and below the staff, eleven different notes can be written. Any number of additional short lines can be added above or below a staff to provide for many additional notes.

These notes are on the:

first space above the staff,

second space of the staff,
first line of the staff.
first added line below the staff.

"What we need now are names for the notes. A simple system is used to name them. Notes are named after the ABC's from A through G. Here are their names when C is on the first added line below the staff:

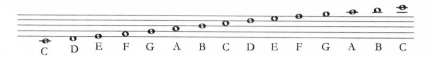

"Your attention should be called to two particularly important notes. The first note is C; it is on the first added line below the staff. Remember this C. It is called "middle C." Later you will discover that it really is in the middle of something.

"The other important note is number 5, which is on the second line, and its name is G. The reason attention is called to this G is that it has a clef sign called the G clef, or treble clef, named after it. And the reason this clef is called the G clef is because it locates G. You will notice that it looks something like a pretzel, but its ending spiral goes around the second line, which is the same line for the note G.

G Clef or Treble Clef

"Whenever a staff is used, it must be identified by a name. This clef is therefore called the G clef or treble clef. It is the most common clef. It is used for most vocal music, for all violin parts, and for the parts of many other instruments, including the right hand of piano music.

"It does not take long to learn the names of the notes in the treble clef. Practice drawing a treble clef sign at the beginning of a number of staffs (only one is necessary at the beginning of each line).

"Here is a method of writing a treble clef sign in two steps.

"Here is a method of writing notes so they can be easily read:

Step 1	Step 2	Completed notes

"Notes which are somewhat flat in shape and are made from two strokes of a pencil or pen can be read more easily than round, fat notes."

Definitions

Note—A musical symbol to specify a certain pitch or tone.
Staff—Five parallel lines and four spaces, used in music notation.
Clef—A musical symbol to identify a staff.
G Clef—A symbol which locates G above middle C.
Treble Clef—The same as the G clef.
Middle C—The note found on the first line below the treble clef staff.

Assignment

Write at least a page of notes with a treble clef at the beginning of each. Write the letter name of each note above or below it. Continue to do this until you know from memory the name of each note on the five lines and four spaces of the staff, plus the two lines and two spaces above and below the staff.

Lesson Six: Melody and Scales

"Everybody likes a tune. Few people like just a scale. Yet both are sometimes identical.

"Let us go back for a moment to Lesson Five. If the first five notes of the series of fifteen notes are sung with these words, you will hear an attractive melody."

[Have the class sing this several times; the tune is *doh-ray-me-fah-soh-soh-fah-me-ray-doh*.]

(rest)

Hop hop hop hop hop,   Nim- ble as a top.

"These same notes are also a scale. A scale is a stepwise progression of notes. An *ascending* scale is one that goes up, which means that each succeeding note is higher than the one before. A *descending* scale goes downward, and each successive note is lower than the one before. Our word 'scale' comes from the Latin word 'scala' meaning 'ladder.'

Ascending scale on C - Descending scale on C

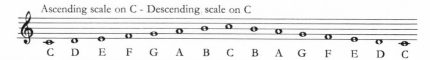

C   D   E   F   G   A   B   C   B   A   G   F   E   D   C

"This is the C scale. To play this scale on a piano, one must begin on C (the white key to the left of any pair of black keys) and strike one white key after another until the next C is reached. The descending C scale is simply the reverse."

[Have the class play and sing the C scale several times until the sound is established in the ear of each student, but for ease of singing, pitch the scale in B♭ major.]

"You will probably recognize the sound of the scale as the same ascending one sung with the syllables: *doh, ray, me, fah, soh, lah, te, doh'*, and (descending) *doh', te, lah, soh, fah, me, ray, doh.*

"This series of notes is called a major scale. It is the scale found in most of the music we hear today."

[Have the class sing the syllables a number of times until each student learns them.]

"In order to understand more about music, study the major scale. As you look at the series of notes from C to C, arranged in steps up and down the staff, it appears that each step would measure the same as the next one. However, this is not true. Perhaps if you sing the scale upward from *doh* to *doh'* you will recognize the fact that two steps are smaller than the others." [For aid in singing syllables, consult Chapter Four.] "To help the ear to hear these half steps, you should examine the white keys of a piano. You will note that some of the white keys have a black key between them and others do not.

"Pianos are tuned so that the black keys make half steps above or below the white keys. Thus the distance from a white key to the next white key with a black key between is two half steps, or one whole step.

"However, the distance from one white key to the next white key where there is no black key between is only a half step. Pictured as a ladder, the major scale looks like this diagram:

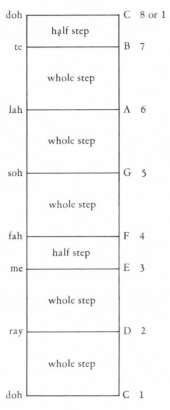

doh	half step	C 8 or 1
te		B 7
	whole step	
lah		A 6
	whole step	
soh		G 5
	whole step	
fah		F 4
	half step	
me		E 3
	whole step	
ray		D 2
	whole step	
doh		C 1

THE C MAJOR SCALE SHOWING THE DESIGN
COMMON TO ALL MAJOR SCALES

"From the above diagram it will be seen that all the steps are whole steps except from No. 3 to No. 4 (E to F) and from No. 7 to No. 8 (B to C).

"Learn to sing the major scale using the syllables. Listen for the half steps from *me* to *fah* and from *te* to *doh*." [Pitch the scale in B♭ major.]

"Learn to sing the same major scale by using the letter names C to C and also by singing the numbers, 1 to 8.

"Because scales are the foundation of music, you should be proud of learning to do the following:

1. Sing the major scale up and down by using syllables. [Consult Chapter Four on music reading for aid in singing syllables.]
2. Sing the major scale up and down by using letter names.
3. Sing the major scale up and down by using numbers.
4. Write the major scale up and down by placing the eight notes on the treble staff, C to C going up, and the eight notes, C to C, coming down.

"When you can do these four things and when you understand what has been told you in Lessons One, Two, and Three of this chapter, you will have a firm beginning for a knowledge of music fundamentals. Remember the proverb, 'Well begun, half done.' "

Definitions
Melody—A tune, a series of notes that seem to go well together.
Scale—A stepwise progression of notes; a ladder.
Major Scale—A stepwise progression of notes, each a whole step higher or lower than the one before except between the third and fourth steps and the seventh and eighth steps.
Over-learning—A degree of learning beyond the usual.

Assignment
1. Learn the four exercises listed above involving the singing and playing of the major scale.
2. Now, over-learn the four exercises so that you can do them automatically.

LESSON SEVEN: KEY SIGNATURES (SHARPS AND SHARP KEYS)

"We have already learned the name of one major scale. It is C major. By moving up the alphabet through B, you will find six more scales. They are D major, E major, F major, G major, A major and B major.

"The word *major* is a family name. It identifies the relationships between all notes of all major scales. The pattern of whole and half steps has already been explained in Lesson Six, where it was found that each step was a whole step except between steps 3 and 4 and between steps 7 and 8 of the scale.

"The only difference between all the various major scales is that they start on different notes, i.e., C, D, E, etc."

[Review the C major scale again by singing it with the syllables from *doh* to *doh'* and back again. Then do the same thing again, beginning on D, the next note higher. Sing from D to D and back again, and you will have sung the D major scale. The same progression of syllables should be used each time, beginning with *doh* and singing up to *doh'* and back again.

[In singing these scales through an octave, it will be noted that the cambiata voices may have some difficulty in singing the highest notes. Therefore, the tessitura of the class singing will be made more comfortable by pitching the C scale one step lower to B♭ and the D scale to C.

[Make it clear to the class that the *doh, ray, me* system of singing the major scale can be moved up or down according to any key such as C, D, G, A, or B, etc.]

"The major scale is nothing more than a musical ladder of sounds with whole steps and half steps always in the same places. Between what notes are the half steps to be found?

"The syllables *doh, ray, me,* etc., are sounds that are easy to sing. They help you remember the correct sound of the major scale with the half steps in the right places. Between what syllables are the half steps to be found?"

[Practice the class in singing the major scale up and down. Ask the class to identify by raising their hands each time a half step has been sung. Concentrate on recognizing the difference between half steps and whole steps. Do not become impatient, but demand concentration at all times. Ask some of the students to sing alone and to raise their hands when half steps are sung.]

"When a composer writes a melody he must decide which scale to use. Let us assume that he chooses a melody in a major key, which means the melody is built on a major scale.

"Now we shall return to the 'Nimble as a Top' melody of Lesson Six. A staff is needed, a treble clef at the beginning (to identify the staff), and notes and words as shown in Lesson Six.

"When this melody is sung in the key of C, the strongest sound will be C. When the singer arrives at the last note of 'Nimble as a Top,' it sounds as though he has reached a 'home base.' There are a number of names for this 'home base' sound. It is called the *tonic,* the *key,* or the *key note.* These names indicate an important function.

"Referring again to the 'Nimble as a Top' melody, it is said that it is written in the *key of C.* The *tonic* of this melody is C. It starts on C and ends on C.

"But if this same melody were written by starting and ending on D instead of C, it would be in the key of D, and the tonic of the melody would be D.

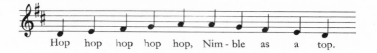

Hop   hop   hop   hop   hop,   Nim-ble   as   a   top.

"In the above example, the melody begins on D instead of C. This means that it begins one note higher. This means the scale is a D scale. This means that the key is D.

"Besides the change of beginning on D instead of C, another thing has been added to the music. Two small figures will be found immediately following the treble clef. They are called sharps. Examination of them will show that a box-like figure is formed in the middle of each; one of them surrounds the fifth line (the top line whose name is F), and the other one occupies the third space (whose name is C). Therefore the name of the first sharp is *F sharp* and the other one is *C sharp*.

"Sharps are convenient signs which are necessary for the proper writing of music. They have a very definite meaning. A *sharp* means to play or sing the note a *half step higher*. When sharps are placed at the beginning of the music, they form the key signature.

"In addition to using sharps for the signature of music, one may use them at any point throughout the music when it is desired to indicate a sound that is a half step higher. The sharp is placed in front of the note:

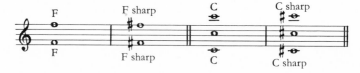

"How much higher is the note with a sharp than the same note without a sharp in front?

"Two sharps at the beginning of a piece of music mean that every F and every C must be played or sung a half step higher."

[The need for sharps in various keys can be illustrated at the piano by playing the white keys beginning on G. The class will easily recognize through the sound that some black notes are needed to establish the correct scale construction. It is suggested that a sequence be presented on the piano from the tonic C, up to G, to D, etc. This will demonstrate the circle of fifths, a basic principle of key relationships.]

"When sharps are used in a signature, they are always used in this order from left to right:

Sharps: 1   2   3   4   5   6   7

"Learn this rule for telling what major key is indicated by the number of sharps in the signature: *The major key is always a half step higher than the last sharp in the signature.*"

Definitions

♯—A sharp, meaning one half step higher.

Key signature—The sharps (sharp signs) at the beginning of a piece of music to show which notes must be raised a half step.

Music syllables—A progression of sounds applied to the various steps of the scale so that the proper pitch can be obtained for reading music.

Assignment

1. How many sharps would be necessary in the signature when the major scale has G as its tonic or home base? Give the order of sharps.
2. How many sharps are necessary for the key of A?
3. How many sharps indicate the key of E?
4. Give the rule for telling the major key of a piece of music when it has sharps in its signature. Practice using this rule.

Lesson Eight: More Key Signatures (Flats and Flat Keys)

"By this time, we have learned a good deal concerning the major scale and its relation to five different key signatures. All of these keys require one or more sharps in the signature in order to make the half steps fall at the right places in the major scale.

"Now we are going to study the same major scale in a new setting. The new setting will use a sign called *the flat*. A practical definition of a flat is 'one half step lower.' The flat looks somewhat like a half heart with a stem pointing upward: ♭. It may be placed on any line or space or added line or added space.

"In addition to using flats for the signature of music, they, like sharps, may be used also at any point throughout the music when it is desired to indicate a sound that is a half step lower. The flat is put in front of the individual note.

"Flats may be used in the key signature just as the sharps were used in Lesson Seven. When used in a signature, they are always used in this order from left to right:

"Flats and sharps are never used together in the same signature. Remember this rule: *The major key of a piece of music which has flats in its signature is the name of the next-to-last flat in the key signature.*

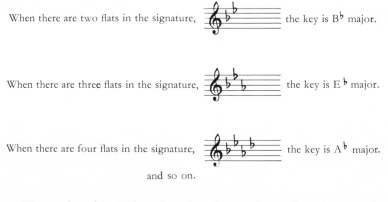

When there are two flats in the signature, the key is B♭ major.

When there are three flats in the signature, the key is E♭ major.

When there are four flats in the signature, the key is A♭ major.

and so on.

"Remember this: When there is only one flat in the signature, the key is F major.

"The meaning of the signature of the first examples above is that it requires two flats (B and E flat) to build a major scale beginning on B flat. The second flat (E) forms a half step between the third and fourth note of the scale, and the first flat (B) forms a half step between the seventh and eighth note (A to B flat).

"A third symbol with a function similar to sharps and flats is the *natural*. It is used when it is necessary to change a sharp or a flat back to its natural pitch. The natural is written ♮. The middle box either surrounds the line of the staff or occupies the space between any two lines."

F sharp   F natural   A flat   A natural

Definitions

♭—Flat, meaning one half step lower.
♮—Natural, meaning neither sharp nor flat, but as written.
These three symbols are all referred to as "accidentals" when found elsewhere than in the key signature.

Assignment

1. Write at the beginning of a staff the key signature for the key of B flat.
2. Now add the notes of the major scale to the staff.
3. Number the notes from 1 through 8, according to the progression from the tonic (1), stepwise to the octave higher (8).
4. Mark the half steps with a bracket.
5. Now do assignments 1, 2, 3, and 4 above for the key of A flat major and the key of F major.

Lesson Nine: Arithmetic of Music (Note Values)

"Man has been trying different systems of writing music for about two thousand years. It took him longer than that to perfect a system of writing words.

"There are a number of systems of music writing in the world today. The Western world employs a system which is characterized by accuracy of meaning and ease of understanding. Lessons Five, Six, Seven, and Eight have already revealed part of this system.

"Now we come to that part of the system of notation which deals with note values. This could be called the time-signature-arithmetic of music since it deals primarily with fractions and additions.

"Here is the basic explanation of all note values. Let us start with something which arouses pleasant feelings—a whole pie, which resembles a circle.

"A half a pie, therefore, would look like this:

"And small pieces would be as numbered:

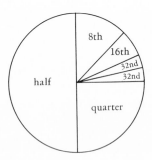

"This is simple arithmetic, isn't is? If you understand it, let us now return to the arithmetic of music. Remember that music exists in time. The pie above occupies space; music occupies time. A pie can be measured in inches and pounds; music is measured in seconds, minutes, and sometimes in hours.

"The best way to indicate time is by beats or pulsations. For instance, if you wish to show how long something lasts, you would say four seconds or three minutes, or you could count at the rate of one beat per second.

"Now let us build our system of time on the assumption that a whole-note ○ gets four beats. If a whole-note ○ gets four beats, how many beats would a half-note get? A half-note looks like a whole-note with a down or up stem added to it, ♀ or ♩

"If a whole-note ○ gets four beats, how many beats would a quarter-note ♩ get? This is like saying, 'If it takes four minutes to eat a whole pie, how long would it take to eat a quarter of a pie?' The answer to both questions is 'one,' isn't it?

"Here is a table of time values when a whole-note gets four beats:

Kind of note	Symbol	Number of beats
A whole-note	○	gets 4 beats
A half-note	♩	gets 2 beats
A quarter-note	♩	gets 1 beat
An eighth-note	♪	gets ½ beat
A sixteenth-note	♬	gets ¼ beat
A thirty-second note etc.	♬	gets ⅛ beat

"It will be noticed that every time a change is made in the symbols above, the note becomes only half as long (i.e., when a stem is added to the whole-note, or when the body of the quarter-note is filled in, or when a flag is added to the stem of the note).

"This explains most of the system of time values. The few remaining explanations will be given in the next lesson."

Assignment

Complete these statements when a whole-note gets 4 beats.

1. A whole-note is equal in length to _____ half-notes. (Answer is "2").
2. A half-note is equal in length to _____ quarter-notes.
3. A quarter-note is equal in length to _____ sixteenth-notes.
4. A half-note is equal in length to _____ eighth-notes.
5. A quarter-note is equal in length to _____ sixteenth-notes.

Illustrate each of the above five statements by writing the note referred to and the number of shorter notes which equals it.

LESSON TEN: ARITHMETIC OF MUSIC

"The symbol 4/4 is called the meter signature when placed on a staff. It means that there are four beats to a measure, and each quarter-note gets one beat.

"The vertical lines every four beats are called *bar lines* or just *bars*. The time between the bar lines is called a *measure*. In the example above, a measure lasts four beats. Bar lines are an aid to the eye in reading music."

[Have the class practice singing the above four measures with syllables and with attention to the time values. *Clap-shake* activity as used in Chapter Four, Phase Three is also recommended.]

"You will notice that the time values (or rhythm) have been altered in the second example above, but there are four beats in all eight measures of the two examples. You will also notice that the time signature used in the above example is a capital C, which means the same as 4/4."

[Have the class practice singing the above with due attention to syllables and rhythm. *Clap-shake* activity as used in Chapter Four, Phase Three is also recommended.]

"A *double bar* means the end of a composition or, in the instance of a very long piece, it indicates the end of a section.

"Other commonly used time signatures are 3/4, 6/8, and 2/4. The top number always indicates the number of beats per measure and the lower number indicates the kind of note which gets a beat. In other words, there are three beats to a measure, and a quarter-note gets a beat in 3/4 time.

"2/4 means there are 2 beats in a measure, and a quarter-note gets a beat. (It makes no difference whether the stems go up or down.)

"Two dots immediately in front of a double bar mean to repeat by returning to the preceding double bar with two dots on the right. If there is no preceding double bar with two dots, return to beginning."

[Have the class sing the above examples.]

"There remain only three more points of notation to learn at this time:

1. A dot (.) after a note is the same as writing '+ ½' meaning add one-half the value of the note which precedes it.

  Example: ♩ gets 2 beats.

  ♩. gets 2 beats + ½ the value of the half-note preceding it, making a total of 3 beats.

  ♩. gets 1 beat + ½ beat, making a total of 1½ beats.

  ♪. gets ½ beat + ½ of ½ for a total of ¾ of a beat.

2. A. A tie ⌒ has two meanings. When the two notes that are tied together have the same pitch, they are played or sung as a single note with the value being the sum of the two notes.

Example:

 means one note with a duration of two beats plus one-half of a beat, for a total of two and one-half beats.

 means four beats plus one, or five beats.

B. The second use of the tie symbol ⌒ is as a *slur* which may be placed over or under notes of different pitches to indicate that all the notes involved are to be slurred, i.e., played smoothly without a break between any of the notes.

Example:

[Practice singing the above four measures beginning with *doh* and using proper syllables and correct time values. Show the difference between the performance of the tied notes and the detached ones.]

3. A rest means silence.

A whole-rest means silence for the length of a whole-note, or four beats, or a whole measure, regardless of number of beats.

A half-rest means silence for the length of a half-note, or two beats:

Each quarter-rest means silence for one beat.

Other frequently used rests are:

Definitions

A dot after a note extends the length of a note ½ or 50%.

A tie ⌒ is a symbol to add any amount of time to a note by tying it to another note of the same pitch.

A slur ⌒ is a means of indicating that the *different* notes enclosed should be slurred together (i.e., performed in a smooth *legato* manner).

A rest in music means silence.

A whole-rest equals a whole-note in length.

A half-rest equals a half-note in length.

A quarter-rest equals a quarter-note in length.

An eighth-rest equals an eighth-note in length (thus 2 per beat when a quarter-note gets a beat).

A sixteenth-rest equals a sixteenth-note in length (thus four 16th notes to a beat, when a quarter-note gets a beat).

Assignment
1. Write 4 measures of 4/4 time using whole-, half- and quarter-notes.
2. Write 4 bars of 3/4 time using half- and quarter-notes and a dotted half-note.
3. Write 4 bars of 2/4 time using several quarter-rests.

LESSON ELEVEN: DYNAMICS

"A dynamic person is one who has a striking or strong personality. A dynamo is a machine which converts motion into electrical power. Dynamics in music indicate how much power is to be used in order to perform the notes at a loud or soft sound level.

"The effect of loudness and softness is well recognized. If a grand march is to be performed properly, it should be played loudly. A lullaby should be played or sung softly. If a grand march were played softly and the lullaby sung loudly, both would be failures.

"Therefore, proper dynamic levels are important in music. For this reason, composers usually write dynamic marks in the score of the music to help the performer sing or play the music properly.

"The system of dynamic marks is a simple one. It is based on two Italian terms:

f stands for *forte*—meaning loud.

p stands for *piano*—meaning soft.

"Here is the scale of dynamics from very soft to very loud:

Symbol	Italian	English Meaning
pp	Pianissimo	Very softly
p	Piano	Softly
mp	Mezzo piano	Medium softly
mf	Mezzo forte	Medium loudly
f	Forte	Loudly
ff	Fortissimo	Very loudly

"Occasionally this dynamic scale is expanded to include from three to six symbols (i.e., *ppp* or even *fffff*).

"Other symbols which indicate dynamics are:

Symbol	Italian Meaning	English Meaning
cresc.	*Crescendo*	Get louder gradually
descresc.	*Decrescendo*	Get softer gradually
dim.	*Diminuendo*	Get softer gradually
> or *fz*	*Forzando*	Accent
mor.	*Morendo*	Dying out and getting slower gradually

"The use of Italian words in music is sometimes questioned. This practice is the result of an age-old tradition. It should be remembered that music is, in many respects, an universal language, and, as such, it should use symbols that are recognizable in all lands."

Assignment
1. Make a copy of the first 25 dynamic marks from any piece of music. (Music for orchestra is the best source.)
2. Write the Italian meaning of each dynamic mark found in this music.
3. Write the English meaning of these Italian words.

LESSON TWELVE: MAJOR INTERVALS

"Examine the C major scale again. Here are the seven different letter names of the C major scale." [Practice singing them with the syllables and then with the numbers in correct rhythm, i.e., correct time values for each note. For a more comfortable tessitura pitch in the key of B♭.]

"All scale steps are named after the numbers 1 to 8. In the C major scale, the first note (C) is called the prime or tonic of C major, the second (D) is called the second, the next the third, on up to the eighth (C) which is called the octave. Number 8 is said to be an octave higher than number 1.

"Every scale is identified by its tonic. When the tonic of a major scale is C, it is known as the scale of C major.

"An interval is the difference in pitch between two notes. When the first note of a scale is sounded with the second note, the interval formed is called a *second*. Thus:

All the intervals above are major intervals except the fourth, fifth, and octave which are called perfect intervals. The most important interval is the major third. Notice that it is an interval of two whole steps."

Assignment

1. Determine the distance between the 2 notes for all the major and perfect intervals.
2. Learn to write all the major and perfect intervals on the staff for C major.
3. Learn to play all the major and perfect intervals on the piano for C major.
4. Learn to recognize them when played by someone else.
5. Learn to sing the syllables of these intervals as jumps from C up to all the steps of the C major scale.

   [In carrying through assignments 1, 2, 3, and 4, reference should be made to Chapter Four, Phase One where closely related material is presented.]

Lesson Thirteen: Triads of the Major Scale

"A *triad* is a combination of three important steps of a scale. The number three is important in many things. The Trinity is fundamental in Christianity. Geometry proves that three points make a plane, which is the reason that three-legged stools always sit firmly on any floor. For the same reason, the three wheels of a tricycle always touch the ground.

"Indeed, the triad is the foundation of the harmony of the Western world. Perhaps there is a reason. Strong evidence, if not proof, that the triad is the foundation of harmony will be seen by examining the notes of the harmonic series found in Lesson One of Chapter Nine. Partials 4, 5, and 6 form a triad. It is a major triad."

The major triad formed by partials 4, 5, and 6, when the fundamental or first partial is C.

"A glance at these three notes (C, E, G) shows that the triad is formed by notes 1, 3, and 5 of the C major scale. Another way to say this is that the major triad is formed by the tonic, the third, and the fifth. When these notes are sounded together, the result is pleasing, satisfying, and harmonious. Music abounds with major triads; most pieces begin and end with them.

"The C major triad is a triad with the root C, the third, E (a major third above or two whole steps), and the fifth, G (a perfect fifth above C or 3½ whole steps). You will understand this by recalling that all steps in a major scale are whole steps except between steps 3 and 4, and between 7 and 8.

"Thus, if the root is C, an E and G must be added to form a triad. If the root is D, the other two notes are F and A. If the root is on a line, the other two notes will be the next two lines above. If the root is on a space, the other two notes will be the next two spaces above."

Assignment

Learn to spell the triads on all the notes A to G. You will soon realize that you start with the root note and skip every other note. To help understand the "spelling" of all triads, write down a two-octave-long series of the notes: A B C D E F G A B C D E F G A. By skipping every other note, the triad on A is A C E, the triad on D is D F A, the triad on G is G B D, and so on.

Lesson Fourteen: Melodic Minor Scale

"Up to this point in our study of music fundamentals, all illustrations of melodies and scales have been in major keys. This was done because the major sound is the most natural one, and most of our great music is in the major mode. However, it is fortunate that there are other sources of harmony. The principal other source is the minor scale.

"In order to understand the character of the minor scale, let us refer to the major key melody of Lesson Three. But this time, instead of following the correct version of this little song, the third and fourth measures will be altered so that the melody keeps on going up. This gives an example of an ascending melody extending through a complete octave. Then, for the next four measures, the melody will descend over the same notes back down to the tonic C."

Melody in C Major

Hop hop hop hop hop, Nim-ble as a top.

Hop hop hop hop hop. Nim-ble as a top.

"Therefore, this new version is an ascending and descending major scale with several notes repeated."

[The class should practice singing the above version of the melody.]

"Now, let us contrast the major scale with a new and different kind of scale called the *melodic minor*. New words consistent with the feeling or mood of the minor scale are used with this:

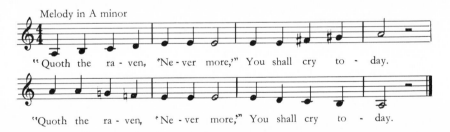

Melody in A minor

"Quoth the ra-ven, 'Ne-ver more,'" You shall cry to-day.

"Quoth the ra-ven, 'Ne-ver more,'" You shall cry to-day.

"A comparison of these two melodies shows that the major key begins on C, whereas the minor one begins on A. The major key is C major and the minor key is A minor.

"The note A is 1½ steps lower than C. This minor scale using A as the tonic is called the *melodic minor,* and it is referred to as the relative minor of the major scale. In other words, the A minor scale is related to the C major scale; both have the same signature, that is, no sharps and no flats.

"The sound of the major and minor scale is quite different. Play them, sing them, listen carefully; learn to recognize each, and study the way each is formed and note the differences. This diagram reveals the difference in the structure of each. In the diagram a half inch is equal to a whole step."

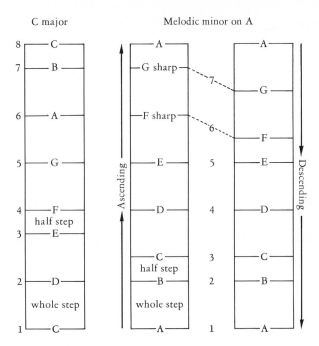

DIAGRAM OF MAJOR AND MINOR SCALES

"The only difference between these two *ascending* scales is the third note. However, attention should be called to the fact that two sharps have been used on steps 6 and 7. These two altered (or raised) notes make the minor scale more melodious, or easier to sing—at least when the scale is an *ascending* one. The situation is different when the scale descends.

"When the melodic minor scale descends, the F sharp and the G sharp (of the ascending scale) have been lowered to G natural and F natural. This gives an interesting variation in the sound for the *melodic minor* scale." [See diagram above.]

[Have every member of the class learn to write, play, and sing these two ascending and descending scales.]

Definitions

Ascending scale—The rising stepwise progression of notes.

Descending scale—The falling stepwise progression of notes.

Relative minor scale—The minor scale which has the same key signature as a major scale. (This means that the major and minor scales are *related* by signature. The tonic of the relative minor scale is always a step and a half lower than the tonic of the related major scale.)

Assignment

1. Write the melodic minor scale in the key of A, ascending and descending.
2. Learn to play the melodic minor scale in the key of A, ascending and descending.
3. Learn to sing the melodic minor scale in the key of A, ascending and descending.

Lesson Fifteen: More Scales and the Bass Clef

"Two varieties of minor scales occur in music. One is the *melodic minor* scale studied in Lesson Fourteen; the other is the *harmonic minor*. Here is a comparison of the harmonic minor and the melodic minor scales:

"For the first 5 steps, the two minor scales are identical; but the 6th step differs in going up, and the 6th and 7th differ in coming down.

"Ascending, the harmonic minor scale has one note (F natural) which differs from the melodic minor (F sharp). Descending, the harmonic minor scale has one note (G sharp) which differs from the melodic minor (G natural).

"Both minor scales have a definite *minor* sound, due to the all-important third step. In the A minor scale, C is only a minor third above the tonic C.

"Whereas the major third seems to cast sunshine over the music, the minor third seems considerably less "sunny" and contains a certain element of sadness:

Assignment

1. Play the major third C E on the white keys of the piano, followed by the minor third A C.
2. Play the major triad C E G followed by the minor triad A C E.
3. Play the minor triad A C E; then change one note to make it into the A major triad.
4. Play both minor scales beginning on A.
5. Sing both minor scales beginning on A, noticing that the melodic minor scale is rather easily sung whereas the harmonic scale is difficult. This is due to the jump of a step and a half from the 6th note to the 7th.
6. Interesting examples of the harmonic minor sound will be found in "March Slav" (Tchaikovsky), "Orientale" (Cui), and frequently in Jewish and oriental music.

"Another scale heard from time to time is the chromatic scale.

"The word *chromatic* means 'suited for color,' and the word *chromatics* means 'the science of color.' A chromatic scale is the progression of tones by half steps from any note to an octave higher. The use of chromatic scales or chromatic progressions makes the music colorful.

"Oriental music usually abounds in chromatic passages. This is to be expected, since the Orient is a part of the world where color dominates many things—clothing, art work, tapestries and rugs.

"The Oriental influence is evident in the work of the composer, Rimsky-Korsakov, who spent part of his life as a Russian naval officer. The color of the Orient is reflected in his writing. The opera, *The Golden Cockerel,* and his symphonic suite, *Scheherezade* (*Tales of a Thousand and One Nights*) are lengthy works full of chromatic passages. The 'Hymn to the Sun' (from *The Golden Cockerel,* by Rimsky-Korsakov) is a splendid example of chromatic writing."

[Play the "Hymn to the Sun," either in the original version for voice and orchestra, or as arranged for violin solo.]

"All steps in the chromatic scale are half steps. Because there are no differences in the size of steps of a chromatic scale, there is no indication of key. The chromatic scale just slips in and out at any part of the scale; it may flash its color like a will-o'-the-wisp and then suddenly disappear. Chromatic passages fit alike into major or minor harmonies.

"You may recall that, in Lesson Five, middle C was said to be in the middle of something. Here is an illustration:

Middle C

"Up to this point, you might have thought that only the five lines of the staff were needed. Now you see eleven lines used with middle C in the middle—five lines above and five lines below. The line for middle C is drawn only when middle C is used.

"The added staff is necessary for writing notes which represent sounds below middle C. The left hand of the piano needs these notes. So do the low orchestral instruments—the cello, bass viol, bassoon, trombone, tuba, and others.

"You will of course recognize the clef on the higher staff as the G clef. However, the clef on the lower staff is a new one. It is called either the F clef or bass clef. It is the F clef because the two dots locate the note F under middle C; it is referred to as the bass clef because the low or bass instruments usually are written on the lower staff."

Definitions
Chromatic scale—A scale that progresses by half steps.
F clef—A clef that locates F below middle C.
Bass clef—Another name for the F clef.

Assignment
1. Learn to sing the chromatic scale to the octave above, testing whether you arrive at a pitch exactly one octave higher when you sing the thirteenth note.
2. Place the F clef at the beginning of 5 or 6 staffs. Then draw in many notes at random on the various lines and spaces. Finally write the name of each of these notes when F is on the fourth line (bass clef).

LESSON SIXTEEN: HOW TO HAVE FUN PUTTING FUNDAMENTALS OF
MUSIC TO WORK

"Already some of the ways that fundamentals are useful have been demonstrated in this chapter. Yet one use of fundamentals has not been explained. This is the way to accompany songs on an instrument by using knowledge of music fundamentals.

"The quickest instrument to learn for accompanying songs is the autoharp. Regardless of whether the instrument used is the autoharp, the guitar, the piano, the organ, or the ukulele, the process is essentially the same: one must play the correct chord or harmony for the melody.

"It is surprising how many songs can be accompanied by the important I, IV, and V chords. Let us review these chords in the key of C major and assign the names of each chord including the introduction of a new chord, the dominant seventh chord.

"Note *1*. The IV chord is called the subdominant because it is below the dominant or V chord.
      2. The dominant seventh or V^7 chord may be used instead of the dominant chord. The addition of the seventh (F in C major) gives strength to the sound and makes a better resolution to the I chord which usually follows.

"Learn to play the progressions I-V-I or I-V^7-I on the autoharp. This will take only a few minutes.

"Then sing, or have someone else sing, the following songs while you accompany by pressing the bars of the autoharp and stroking the chords indicated. (In order to establish the key for each song, it is a good idea to play the I chord, the V^7 chord, and the I chord as an introduction before beginning to sing.)"

Assignment

1.   OLD FOLKS AT HOME   *Key of C*

Stephen Foster

C G^7 C   F   C G^7
'Way down upon the Swan-ee Riv-er, Far, far a-way,

C G^7 C   F
There's where my heart is turn-ing ev-er,

C G^7 C
There's where the old folks stay.

C G⁷   C   F   C   G⁷
All up and down the whole cre-a-tion Sad-ly I roam

C   G⁷   C   F
Still long-ing for the old plan-ta-tion,

C   G⁷   C
And for the old folks at home.

G⁷   C   F   C
All the world is sad and drear-y Ev-'rywhere I roam.

C G⁷   C   F
Oh, dark-ies, how my heart grows wear-y,

C   G⁷   C
Far from the old folks at home.

[One step lower than C major will serve as a more comfortable key for the cambiata voices. However, the V⁷ chord F A C E♭ is not on the autoharp; the V chord (F A C) may be used instead.]

2.   SILENT NIGHT   *Key of C*

(For soprano and boys unchanged voices)   Franz Gruber
                                              Joseph Mohr

C   G⁷   C
Si-lent night! Ho-ly night! All is calm, all is bright.

F   C   F   C
Round yon vir-gin Moth-er and child, Ho-ly in-fant, so ten-der and mild,

 G⁷   C   G⁷   C
Sleep in heav-en-ly peace, Sleep in heav-en-ly peace.

3.   DOWN IN THE VALLEY   *Key of F*

(For sopranos and baritones)   Kentucky Mountain Song

F   C⁷
Down in the val-ley, the val-ley so low

                               F
Hang your head o-ver, hear the wind blow.

F   C⁷
Hear the wind blow, dear, hear the wind blow,

                             F
Hang your head o-ver, hear the wind blow.

4.   CLEMENTINE   *Key of F*

(For sopranos and baritones)   Folk Song

F   C⁷

In a cav-ern, in a can-yon, Ex-ca-vat-ing for a mine,

                    F   C⁷   F

Dwelt a min-er, for-ty-nin-er, And his daugh-ter Clem-en-tine.

                                                C⁷

Oh, my dar-ling, Oh, my dar-ling, Oh, my dar-ling Clem-en-tine!

                    F   C⁷   F

You are lost and gone for-ev-er, Dreadful sor-ry, Clem-en-tine!

5.   POLLY WOLLY DOODLE   *Key of C*

                                                         Folk Song

C

Oh, I went down South for to see my Sal,

                            G⁷

Sing Pol-ly Wol-ly Doo-dle all the day!

My Sal she is a spun-ky gal,

                            C

Sing Pol-ly Wol-ly Doo-dle all the day!

Fare thee well! fare thee well!

                    G⁷

Fare thee well my fair-y fay.

I'm goin' to Loui-si-an-a

For to see my Su-sy-an-na,

                            C

Singing Pol-ly Wol-ly Doo-dle all the day.

6.   OH! SUSANNA   *Key of C*

                                                      Stephen Foster

C   G⁷

I came from Al-a-ba-ma with my ban-jo on my knee,

    C   G⁷   C

I'm g'wan to Lou'-si-an-a, My Susanna for to see.

C
It rained all day the night I left,

   G⁷
The weather was so dry,

 C
The sun so hot I froze myself,

  G⁷ C
Susanna, don't you cry.

 F   C   G⁷
Oh! Su-san-na, don't you cry for me.

  C   G⁷ C
For I come from Al-a-ba-ma with my ban-jo on my knee.

7.   JINGLE BELLS   *Key of F*

                       J. Pierpont

(For sopranos and baritones)

F   Bb
Dash-ing thru' the snow in a one horse o-pen sleigh,

    C⁷   F
O'er the fields we go, laugh-ing all the way;

         Bb
Bells on bob-tail ring, mak-ing spir-its bright,

   C₇   F
What fun it is to ride and sing a sleigh-ing song to-night!

(For all Junior high school voices)

Jin-gle, bells! Jin-gle, bells! Jin-gle all the way!

Bb   F   C₇
Oh, what fun it is to ride in a one-horse o-pen sleigh!

F
Jin-gle, bells! Jin-gle, bells! Jin-gle all the way!

Bb   F   C₇   F
Oh, what fun it is to ride in a one-horse o-pen sleigh!

8.   SHE'LL BE COMIN' 'ROUND THE MOUNTAIN *Key of G*

(For sopranos and baritones)   Southern Mountain Song

G
She'll be com-in' 'round the moun-tain when she comes, Toot, toot,

$$\text{D}^7$$
She'll be com-in' 'round the moun-tain when she comes, Toot, toot,

G   D^7
She'll be com-in' 'round the moun-tain,

C   G^7
She'll be com-in' 'round the moun-tain,

G   D^7 G
She'll be com-in' 'round the moun-tain when she comes. Toot, toot!

"Another way to play the harmony as an accompaniment to a song is to *improvise.* Another term for improvising is 'to play by ear,' or 'to fake.' All three terms mean that the person playing the accompaniment does not need the notes. Rather he relies on his ear (and knowledge of fundamentals) to tell him which harmony is correct.

"One must have a 'good ear' to improvise well. However, as in most things, 'Practice makes perfect'—or at least it helps!

"The person who improvises an accompaniment 'senses' which chord is correct. Being well acquainted with the sound of the various chords on his instrument and allowing the melody to suggest which chord is correct enable many people to play the proper harmony to all familiar songs. Learn to accompany all nine songs 'by ear.' Let your ear tell you when the chord changes and which chord to play.

"Now figure out 'by ear' the proper chords on the autoharp for the American folk song, 'Shoo Fly.' "

SHOO FLY

Shoo, fly, don't bo-ther me; shoo, fly, don't bo-ther me.
Shoo, fly, don't bo-ther me, for I be-long to some-bod-y.
I feel, I feel, I feel like a morn-ing star,
I feel, I feel, I feel like a morn-ing star.
Shoo, fly, don't bo-ther me; shoo, fly, don't bo-ther me.
Shoo, fly, don't bo-ther me, for I be-long to some-bod-y.

"Now do the same thing with any other familiar songs that you know. To play accompaniments is fun. To improvise, to 'play by ear,' to 'fake' music—all are fun. Get out your guitar, piano, or ukulele and try it. You will find that putting music fundamentals to work is fun indeed."

LESSON SEVENTEEN: SUMMARY

"Let us take a final look at some of the important things we have learned in this chapter:

"*Music* is a combination of rhythm, melody, and harmony. These are not the only elements of music, but they are the most important ones.

"*Rhythm* is a combination of beats and note values. It supplies a framework made of time. This rhythmic framework sometimes moves fast and sometimes slowly. It can be regular and strong or irregular and complicated. Rhythm has a great deal to do with our response to music.

"*Melody* is the theme, the *air,* the tune, or the musical narrative. It is the song we sing. It moves horizontally through the music. It seems to be the soul of music.

"*Harmony* is the system of chords. A chord results when three or more tones are sounded simultaneously. Harmony may be soothing, pleasant or "good" harmony; at other times, it is strident, harsh, and dissonant. The contrast between consonant and dissonant harmony gives a living and exciting character to music, not unlike life itself. Both consonant and dissonant harmony added to melody adds musical color and interest. Harmony adds perpendicular depth to music.

"*Reading and writing music* is like reading and writing words. Just like the spoken word, music cannot be seen; but notes and a staff, like printed words, are visible and convey meaning. Notes on a staff represent music. When read and performed, these notes turn into specific tones. The system of writing music is a simple one based on the first seven letters of the alphabet. A staff of five lines is used, but additional lines may be added below and above. *The treble or G clef locates G above middle C. The bass or F clef locates F below middle C.* Middle C is on the added line between the treble staff and the bass staff.

"*A scale* is a stepwise progression of notes. A scale could be called 'the stuff melodies are made of.' The major scale consists of 7 notes or tones. The next note above number 7 is the repetition of the first, only one octave higher. All scale steps in the major scale are whole steps except those between steps 3 and 4, and between 7 and 8.

"*Key signatures* at the beginning of a piece of music tell the reader that certain notes must be played a half step higher or a half step lower than usual. Sharps (♯) raise notes one-half step; flats (♭) lower them one-half step; a natural (♮) changes the sound from a sharp or flat back to the *natural* (original) sound.

"*Arithmetic* is the basis for the symbols which indicate the length of time a note is to be held, that is, how long or short it is. The *note value,* or time value, is the length of the note.

"*Arithmetic* is found, also, in *time signatures.* Time signatures are fractions. The numerator tells the number of beats per measure, and the denominator tells which kind of a note gets a beat. Bar lines divide the music into measures with the specified number of beats indicated by the numerator. Bar lines are a visual aid to facilitate reading.

"*Dynamics* is a simple system based on two Italian terms, *forte* (meaning loud) and *piano* (meaning soft). Dynamic marks indicate the degree of loudness or softness to be employed in a performance of music. This system of dynamics in music is universal, and can be understood by all musicians regardless of language or nationality.

"*Intervals* are the distance between two notes or tones. When the distance is from one note to the next above or below, it is called a second. When the interval is from one note to the second note above, it is called a third, etc.

"*The major triad* is the foundation of our harmonic system. A triad is three alternate notes—the root plus a third and a fifth above. In C major, C E G is the tonic triad. The interval from 1 to 3 is a major third (two whole steps) and from 1 to 5 it is a perfect fifth (3½ steps). In A minor, A C E is the tonic triad. The interval from 1 to 3 is a minor third (only 1½ steps), whereas from 1 to 5 is a perfect fifth. These statements regarding major and minor triads can be checked on the white keys of the piano, since neither sharps nor flats are involved in either triad.

"*The melodic minor scale and the harmonic minor scale* are more colorful than the major scale. The main reason for this difference is the minor third.

"*A chromatic scale* is the progression of tones by half steps from any note to an octave higher.

"*Fundamentals of music are put to work* in Lesson Sixteen through the performance of accompaniments on the autoharp. Nine familiar songs are demonstrated as examples of the use of the I, IV, V, and V⁷ chords."

The music fundamentals described in this chapter are incomplete. There remains much to learn about rhythm, melody and harmony, dynamics, tone color, phrasing, chords, scales, and musical form. One never learns everything about anything; every endeavor must have a beginning. If we are "well begun" perhaps we are "half done." Hold on to your knowledge of music fundamentals as a valuable personal possession which will help you read, write, and listen to music.

CHAPTER EIGHT

THE LISTENING PROGRAM

Introduction

The importance of *listening* is evident in the very nature of music itself, since music is an auditory communication. As such, it can be *heard* only. *Music cannot be seen.* You may think you are seeing music when one says, "Look at this music." However, what is meant is, "Look at these notes which represent music," or, "Sing these notes and listen to the music which they represent." Thus the basic response connected with music is *listening*. The performer must listen, the audience must listen, the composer must have listened to and recorded the notes of the music which he was creating. The key to music has always been, and shall always be, *listen*.

However, the physical act of hearing music is only part of the problem of good listening. A student may hear the teacher talk, but absorb little of what was said. A church-goer may hear the preacher, yet go to sleep. A person reading a book may "hear the words" of an author, yet absorb little or nothing of the significance of the written words. Likewise, when an important piece of music is performed for an audience, most of the value is lost unless those individuals project themselves into the music by listening *discriminatingly* and responding *cordially*. To listen *discriminatingly* means to use one's mental capacities in an active and vital way. To respond *cordially* implies that the hearer allows himself to respond without prejudice and without restraint.

To prepare the listener to hear music to the best advantage is the objective of Chapter Eight. Basic questions which need answering in an adequate program of listening are: "What does music mean?" "What is good music?" "How should I listen to music?" "What is a theme and variations?" "Can you hear more than one melody at a time?" etc. Such questions are the subjects of the twenty lessons which comprise this chapter. By sharing the listening experiences which make up these lessons, every boy and girl should obtain a background sufficient to assure each to become a mature and intelligent music lover.

Chapter Eight uses the same method of presentation as does Chapter Seven. It offers a minimum explanation of each lesson which could be read by the teacher to the class as each new phase of the listening program is presented. For convenience, these words of explanation are enclosed in quotation marks. Usually the teacher should paraphrase in his or her own words the ideas and explanations enclosed in quotes. This would remove any stilted effect of reading. As an added aid, instructions to the teacher are enclosed in square brackets [ ].

In substance, Chapter Eight is a cumulative series of lessons which will establish a firm and legitimate basis for listening to music. In Lessons One to Three, the three cornerstones of music listening are set in place. By the time the students arrive at Lessons Nineteen and Twenty, they should be prepared to listen with a worthy degree of discrimination and response to representative symphonic and chamber music.

The approach and explanation employed in this chapter are paced for junior high school boys and girls. The music selected has appeal for young and old alike, because it is "good music." All good music appeals to appreciative adults, and much of this same music appeals to youngsters. For the purpose of this chapter, only that part of good music which does appeal to the junior high school student is included.

The twenty lessons are planned for periods of 20 to 25 minutes each. They could be used in connection with a course in music appreciation, but are presented herewith as a series of listening periods in a program of general music. By using one every two weeks, the course will be completed in one school year.

It is expected that the best record player available and a fine sounding recording will be properly placed before class begins. Every student must be expected to keep complete notes on each lesson. It is hoped that the teacher will not have to take the time necessary to call the roll. Instead, he should be prepared to begin immediately, as follows.

LESSON ONE: WHAT DOES MUSIC MEAN?

"I look forward very much to this class with you. Both you and I should certainly enjoy it. The first thing I want to do is to play a recording for you. Your part will be to write your reaction to the music. Write what the music means to you, or what is suggests to you as you listen to it. Don't worry about what I or anyone else thinks about what you write. I am not going to tell you anything about the music, or even the name of the selection. What I want you to do is to tell me what the music makes *you* think about. The music will last three minutes. Shortly after it stops, you should be finished with your comments. Here goes. Listen closely."

[Play one of the following or similar recording, the music of which should be unfamiliar to the class: "Arab Dance" from *Nut-cracker Suite* by Tchaikovsky, or "Valse Triste" (Waltz of Sadness) by Sibelius. Collect the signed papers. Without identifying the writer, read six or eight of them to the class. These comments will vary, of course.]

"From the comments of your classmates, it is apparent that the same music usually means different things to each of you. Is this the way music should affect you? Is this to be expected? 'Yes.' Music (particularly what we call good music) is expected to mean different things to different people. Music is for people. It is for you, the listener, to think about in your own way. Music lets you be free to think and react as an individual. Since there are differences in all of us, we can expect different results.

"Actually, were I to play the same piece over again even now, some of you would doubtless hear new and different things in it, and therefore you would feel differently toward it.

"Here is one of the most important things about listening to music: *When you listen to music, you, the listener, are the most important person. It is up to you to decide what any particular piece of music means to you.* With just this amount of information about music, you are already well on the road to know how to listen and, later, how to understand and appreciate music. By the time you finish this course, I will expect you to be capable of great enjoyment in music."

LESSON TWO: WHAT IS "GOOD MUSIC?"

"So often we hear people refer to certain music as 'good' whereas other music is considered 'not good.' The difference between the two is interesting. Good music usually continues to be performed from generation to generation. This means that it often is old music, which in turn usually means that it does not wear out easily. Some of our best music today is music which has given more and more people pleasure over hundreds of years. Today it sounds as fresh and in-teresting as it did when it was composed. Usually, good music means more to the listener after many hearings than it did the first time he heard it.

"In a few minutes I am going to play a selection for you which each of you probably has heard many times. It is popular particularly at Christmas time, since the words are about Christianity. The more one hears it, the more one enjoys it. It never seems to wear out. It affords increased pleasure to the listener each time he hears it. This means that this music 'wears well'; it means that this music is 'good music.'

"The test of time (Does it last?) applies to almost all things: friendships, investments, real estate, shoes, clothing, etc. A dress that looks nice for only one wearing would not be considered satisfactory because it lasts for only one wearing. Likewise, a stock certificate that yielded only one or two dividends would not be a good investment. However, a friend whom one loves and appreciates more and more as the years go by is a friend indeed. A good friend passes the same test as good music, because they both last well. The music you will hear now was written over two hundred years ago. It is the 'Ave Maria' by Bach."

[Have the record ready to go; play it through without comment.]

"Let's listen to another selection. Relatively speaking, this piece is a new piece, since it was composed only about a hundred years ago. Most of you will probably recognize it as the 'Blue Danube Waltzes' of Johann Strauss. Even after a hundred years, it is probably the most popular waltz of today."

[Play "Blue Danube Waltzes" for orchestra, by Johann Strauss.]

"Now, how about trying an experiment? I would like to find out how you respond to a repeat performance of the first number, 'Ave Maria.' It is true that selections are hardly ever repeated immediately, but let's try it."

[Repeat "Ave Maria" (Bach). The teacher should discuss the meaning of the second performance of "Ave Maria." Did it sound somewhat different when heard the second time? Did anyone hear anything new the second time? How many recognized and remembered various parts from the first performance? How many enjoyed the second performance more than the first?]

"Before class is dismissed, let us have a one-minute review of what we have learned so far in this course. In Lesson One, we found out that the same music usually means different things to different people. In Lesson Two, I hope you will understand what is meant when I say, 'Good music is like good friends. Neither one wears out. Each improves as you become better acquainted.'"

LESSON THREE: HOW SHOULD I LISTEN TO MUSIC?

"People who teach music are often asked the question of how to listen to music. Actually, a good answer to that question is, 'Just listen.' But such a short answer might be misunderstood. So let me explain.

"Music says something to each person who listens. The closer you listen, the more you hear. Therefore, the person who makes noise by talking (or even dancing) when music is being played cannot hear as well as the listener who gives his full attention to what is going on. This hardly needs demonstration; but, to make sure, let us try another experiment. I am going to play 'When Johnny Comes Marching Home,' as arranged by the American composer Morton Gould.

"I will play the record all the way through, and I want you to 'listen with your feet.' That is, imagine you *are* Johnny and you *are* marching home. You might want to tap your foot, nod your head in time, or march around the room in time with the music. You may chat with your neighbor or laugh out loud if the music sounds that way. Here we go."

[Play "When Johnny Comes Marching Home."]

"To 'listen with your feet' is not exactly wrong. But there is a better way. The better way is to merely listen. It is better because you will hear more in the music and will get more pleasure out of the music. To make noise during a musical performance is generally bad manners, since the noise of one person prevents another from hearing what he wishes to listen to.

"Let's play the same record the second time. This time, make no noise. *Just listen.* If you wish to think about 'When Johnny Comes Marching Home,' do so. But don't make any noise by tapping your foot or by actually marching. Simply imagine you or Johnny or somebody else named Frank or Mary marching home. Listen for the melody which seems to say, 'When Johnny Comes Marching Home Again, Hurrah! Hurrah! When Johnny Comes Marching Home Again, Hurrah! Hurrah!' Notice that this song or melody is heard almost constantly, although it is varied from one time to another."

[Play recording of "When Johnny Comes Marching Home." This piece was written in 1865 by Patrick Gilmore. Morton Gould's excellent arrangement of it is published and recorded under the title *American Salute.*]

"What have we learned from Lesson Three? One word is a good answer. That word is: *'Listen!'*"

LESSON FOUR: WHAT IS A THEME AND VARIATIONS?

"In Lesson Three, you were told, 'Notice that this song or melody ("When Johnny Comes Marching Home") is heard constantly although it is varied from one time to another.' This point of *variation* needs further explanation.

"In a moment, I want you to listen to a selection which is called a theme and variations. Many composers have written pieces which are constructed as a theme and variations. Here is one called *Carnival of Venice,* written by the American composer, Herbert L. Clarke. J. B. Arban and other composers also wrote variations on this same theme. It is an Italian folk song or theme for cornet solo. Instead of having a pianist play along with the solo instrument, the accompaniment is played by a band. As you listen, notice that the first and principal melody always can be heard in some form or other, played either by the solo cornet or by some part of the band. This is the way a theme and variation works."

[Play recording.]

"Did you notice that the same melody could be heard over and over? It was always the same melody, although it was altered in some way each time. It seemed that the composer was trying to show you how many different ways the same theme or melody could be played. Do you think the theme and variation idea is a good way of writing music? If so, then you agree with most of the world's great composers, for much of the world's music is a theme and variations in one way or another.

"Let us play another number. Here is a famous song which is played by four stringed instruments. It was written by Franz Joseph Haydn. It contains variations on the composer's hymn, 'God Save Franz the Emperor.' Notice that the theme is always played by one of the instruments."

[Play the 2nd movement, the variations from *The Emperor Quartet,* Op. 76, No. 3, by Haydn.]

"Lesson Four has demonstrated one of the most common ways of composing music. The method demonstrated (i.e., the form which was used) is called a theme and variations. Pleasure is increased for the listener when the theme or melody is noticed, and the variations which follow are heard as new versions of the theme.

LESSON FIVE: CAN YOU HEAR MORE THAN ONE MELODY AT A TIME?

"Lesson Four demonstrated one way of listening to music. Lesson Five will explain and demonstrate another. This way will be illustrated by a musical selection usually called *the round.*

"The important thing about listening to a round is that, instead of listening to one melody at a time as in Lesson Four, you are to listen to more than one melody at the same time. We are now going to listen to, and sing at the same time, four different melodies. This means that you, the listener, will have to concentrate more than usual. But don't let this discourage you, because the rewards will be much greater. In a way, this is like looking at a three ring circus, since, at such a show, you are privileged to watch three different performances at the same time.

"Here is a melody we all should know, 'Row, Row, Row Your Boat.' Here is the way it works. The song is made up of four different tunes. The song is sung over and over again. By dividing a group into four sections and letting each begin singing the song at different times, we can hear all four at once."

[Here is a diagram to show how it works. For best results, pitch this song in the key of Bb major.]

Singing Group

#1	#2	#3	#4
START: Row, row, row your boat			
gently down the stream	START: Row, row, row your boat		
merrily, merrily, merrily	gently down the stream	START: Row, row, row your boat	
life is but a dream.	merrily, merrily, merrily	gently down the stream	START: Row, row, row your boat
Repeat to beginning	Etc.	Etc.	Etc.

"See whether you can follow all four parts of the melody at the same time. Here goes."

[Sing several times, stopping the four sections, one at a time, at the end of the verse.]

"To make Lesson Five more understandable, why not sing one or two more rounds? Try these two:

[For best results, pitch this song in the key of C major.]

> Are you sleeping, Are you sleeping,
> Brother John, Brother John?
> Morning bells are ringing, morning bells are ringing,
> Ding, ding, dong. Ding, ding, dong.

[Use key of Bb major for this round.]

> Three blind mice, Three blind mice,
> See how they run, See how they run,
> Etc.

"Now, if you listened to all four melodies at the same time—as well as singing—you were doing extremely well. This is difficult to do. Let us make it easier, and perhaps more understandable, by letting half the class sing one of these rounds while the other half listens. Then we can change sides so we can be sure that every member of the class has listened to four melodies at a time. The trick will be not only to listen to four melodies at a time, but actually to hear four melodies at a time. To be able to do this represents one of the most difficult accomplishments for a listener. This means that you can hear *counterpoint*.

"In Lesson Six you will learn more about counterpoint. Until that time, just remember the word. If you really have begun to hear more than one melody at a time, you really *did* get something. The more you listen to music, the more pleasure and satisfaction you will get out of listening to *counterpoint*."

LESSON SIX: COUNTERPOINT, ROUNDS, CANONS, AND FUGUES

"Lesson Five was so important that Lesson Six has been planned to tell you more about *counterpoint* and how to listen to more than one melody at a time. In this connection, one could describe counterpoint as music in which more than one melody is played or sung at the same time.

"Let us try another experiment. Listen to the first part of the last movement of the *Sonata for Violin and Piano,* by César Franck. See whether you can discover anything unusual about the way this music was composed."

[Play recording.]

"Did you notice that both the violin and the piano play the same melody—only the violin starts later than the piano?

"This movement of this sonata is an outstanding example of the *canon.* A canon in music is a piece where different parts of the same melody are played by two instruments at the same time."

[Play same recording again, at least the first section.]

"Another striking example of counterpoint is demonstrated by performing, all at the same time, the 'Humoresque' (Dvořák), 'My Bonnie Lies Over the Ocean,' and 'Old Folks at Home' (Swanee River).

"Now, for another illustration of counterpoint, let us listen to one of the fugues of Johann Sebastian Bach.[1] Bach is usually considered the best composer of counterpoint and fugues the world has ever known. And fugues usually are considered the most difficult music to listen to. However, since you already have listened to two, three, and four melodies at the same time, the *Little Fugue in G Minor,* by Bach, will not be too difficult.

"Remember the fugue melody. It will be heard first by itself. Then the same tune is played again on a different pitch, at which time the opening melody is changed to a different tune which goes along very well indeed at the same time. This process continues until four different melodies are heard, all going concurrently."

[Play recording of *Little Fugue in G Minor,* by Bach, or the fugue from "Polka and Fugue" from *Schwanda,* by Weinberger.]

"As a conclusion to Lessons Five and Six, it should be pointed out that you learned that music can be made up of more than one melody or tune going simultaneously. This is counterpoint. A round is an example of counterpoint (see Lesson Five); so is a canon; and so is a fugue. To many people who appreciate music, counterpoint is the finest type of music ever written. They will contend that everybody likes a tune, so why not listen to more than one at a time? Other people may not agree because they have not learned to listen to more than one melody at a time. Eventually each person will make up his mind about counterpoint, canons, and fugues. The best way to find a basis for your opinion is to *listen*—and then *listen some more."*

REVIEW LESSONS ONE THROUGH SIX

The first six lessons of this chapter form the basis of the listening program in that a proper approach to listening is established. When the contents of these first lessons are absorbed, the student is prepared to profit more from the many categories of music to be introduced during the next fourteen lessons.

Lesson One pointed out that each person should interpret the music *in his own way.* Lesson Two answered the question, "What is good music?" Lesson Three advised how to listen to it. We noted that the

---

[1] The fugue from "Polka and Fugue" from *Schwanda,* by Weinberger, could be substituted for, or indicated as supplementary to, the Bach *Little Fugue in G Minor* selected here.

same music usually affected each listener differently. The important thing is that the listener respond as an individual. Many adults miss the main point of music appreciation. They seem to think that the listener should know ahead of time how he is expected to react. Such an idea is unfortunate and should be dismissed.

Lessons Four, Five, and Six introduced important forms of composition, the theme and variations, the round, canon, and fugue. Attention was given to the understanding and appreciation of counterpoint.

[A test over the first six lessons would be appropriate at this point. An oral review with the class would be fine, in order to establish more clearly the three cornerstones of music appreciation as indicated in Lessons One through Three.]

LESSON SEVEN: "I'VE GOT RHYTHM"

"In the beginning, music was largely rhythm. This was due to the example of rhythm in nature which early man found all around him—the rolling of waves on the beaches, the sequence of the seasons, days followed by nights, the wind and rain, the pounding of objects together.

"Rhythm is expressed in all of these things as beats, pounding, night and day, year after year—the steady patter of raindrops, the pouring in of water on a beach followed by the rushing back of the same water, and so on and on.

"The way that primitive man used rhythm in his music is indicated clearly in much of his music. This will be illustrated by playing a recording of an 'Indian War Dance.' This particular piece of music was explained to a professor of music by a young Indian student at Haskell Institute. Charles Sanford Skilton, the professor (who was also a composer), then arranged this 'Indian War Dance' for performance by a symphony orchestra."

[Play 'Indian War Dance,' by Skilton, recorded by a symphony orchestra.]

"Let me ask you a few questions about that music. Could you feel the rhythm? Did you respond by wanting to beat your foot? Did you hear a melody? Can you sing it?

"Besides rhythm and melody, there is another musical element. What is it? The harmony you heard was added by Mr. Skilton to make the music sound richer, more resonant, and more exciting.

"For another number, let us listen to a barbaric-sounding piece which is really not authentic primitive music since it was composed during the present century by a young Russian composer named Dimitri Kabalevski. Such a practice is frequently followed by composers of today. A capable composer knows and can write in many styles of music. This is not unlike a dressmaker who can reproduce a primitive dress, or perhaps a seventeenth-century English dress."

[Play "Saber Dance," by Kabalevski.]

"Both of these examples of primitive music demonstrate a very strong rhythm. You may notice that the rhythm has an overpowering effect. Children respond to it. All listeners get a certain type of excitement from it."

LESSON EIGHT: MUSIC GOES TO CHURCH

"In the examples played for Lesson Seven, we heard music which prompted the listeners to move fast and even to jump up and down vigorously. We are going to listen to something entirely different now. Here is music for the church of the Renaissance—around the sixteenth century. It is music from Italy, where the religion was that of the Catholic Church. It is music written for great cathedrals. In most churches, such as the Sistine Chapel, instruments of any kind were not permitted. Therefore, the voice of man, unaccompanied, sang the music of the church.

"The music we are to hear is contrapuntal music. It was composed by weaving together from two to seven different melodic lines. This is called 'polyphony' ('poly'—many, 'phone'—sound; pronounced poll-if-fonny). This music is the finest example of pure, direct religious vocal expression of adoration and contemplation, smoothly blended into beautiful lines of vocal music.

"This is a recording of a cathedral choir not unlike those heard over four hundred years ago in Italy. According to the custom of those times, the text or words were sung in the original Latin. The composer is the most famous composer of Renaissance church music. Much of his music is still a part of the Catholic Mass. His name was Giovanni Pierluigi da Palestrina, but he is known in history by the name of his home town, 'Palestrina.'

"This is the most famous of the ninety Masses by Palestrina. When it was published in 1567, it was dedicated to Pope Marcellus. Therefore, it is referred to today as the *Pope Marcellus Mass*. The original Latin title was *Missa Papae Marcelli*. In listening to this music, remember that it is music for the church—specifically for the Papal Chapel of Pope Marcellus. It was written for a choir 'a cappella.' This means that no instruments were to accompany the voices. The performance you will hear was, of course, recorded in recent years, but its sound undoubtedly resembles closely the original performance in 1565."

[Play recording of *Missa Papae Marcelli,* by Palestrina. Since the entire Mass is about twenty-five minutes long, only portions of it may be possible. An explanation of the sections played will aid the students to understand the music. *Kyrie* means "Lord Have Mercy Upon Us"; *Gloria,* "Glory to God"; *Credo,* "I Believe"; *Sanctus,* "Holy, Holy, Holy"; *Agnus Dei,* "Lamb of God."]

"What is the effect of this music? Does it make you feel differently from the way you responded to the primitive music in Lesson 7?

"Doubtless you will note that the strong, wild rhythm of primitive man has disappeared entirely, whereas the calm, dignified movement of Palestrina's music suggests that we are listening to a church service in a great cathedral.

"Toward the beginning of the sixteenth century, a dramatic event took place within the universal Catholic Church. Martin Luther, a Professor of Divinity at the University of Wittenberg (Germany), rebelled against a number of practices and beliefs embraced by the Catholic Church. This marked the beginning of an age in church history called the Reformation.

"The Reformation began a few years before the birth of Palestrina. Martin Luther was the principal figure of the movement which eventually established a new church (the Lutheran) and effected extensive reform. For instance, Luther decided that the churchgoers should hear the church service in their own native language instead of Latin. He insisted that the official language of the church should be one that could be understood by all people. He maintained, also, that the congregation should be allowed to take part in the music of the service by singing hymns.

"To help carry his point, Martin Luther wrote many hymns using German words instead of Latin. His most famous hymn melody is entitled 'Ein' Feste Burg Ist Unser Gott.' Translated, this means 'A Mighty Fortress Is Our God.' Here is that hymn sung in the original German."

[Play recording.]

"You may have noticed the strong, yet stately, rhythmic movement in the hymn. Hesitancy and uncertainty are completely missing. This is the music of the reformer, Martin Luther, who defied authority in order to establish his right to praise God in his own way.

"This hymn has given man confidence in God for all of these almost three hundred and fifty years. It is probably the most famous of all Protestant hymns. Have you ever sung it? The words, in English, are:

> A mighty fortress is our God,
> A bulwark never failing;
> Our helper He amid the flood
> Of mortal ills prevailing:
> For still our ancient foe
> Doth seek to work us woe;
> His craft and power are great,
> And, armed with cruel hate,
> On earth is not His equal.
>
> Did we in our own strength confide,
> Our striving would be losing;
> Were not the right man on our side,
> The man of God's own choosing:
> Dost ask who that may be?
> Christ Jesus, it is He;
> Lord Sabaoth His Name,
> From age to age the same,
> And He must win the battle.

LESSON NINE: CHURCH MUSIC BY BACH AND HANDEL

"The greatest composer of Christian church music was Johann Sebastian Bach. His life, works, and the times in which he lived are discussed in Chapter Nine. For the present time, we need only to know that Bach was employed for many years as the organist and choir director of the Saint Thomas Church in Leipzig, Germany. One of his routine tasks was to supply the music for the church service each

Sunday. Little music was published in those days (seventeenth and eighteenth centuries), so he usually wrote his own.

"One Sunday he performed one of his own works for choir and organ, 'Jesu, Joy of Man's Desiring.' He probably played the accompaniment on the church's large pipe organ. That performance almost two hundred and fifty years ago must have sounded a great deal like the performance on this recording."

[Play recording, "Jesu, Joy of Man's Desiring" from Cantata No. 147.]

"How did you react to that recording? Did it remind you of church? Would you say that to listen to that music was a religious experience? Music like 'Jesu, Joy of Man's Desiring' expresses man's longing for joy in God. Bach was an inspired composer. That is the reason we still hear so much of his music. In fact, 'Jesu, Joy of Man's Desiring' undoubtedly is heard more often today than in the days of the early eighteenth century. This is quite a record for a rather simple piece of music. Similar recognition has been earned by most of the world's 'good music.'

"All the music played thus far in Lessons Eight and Nine has been slow in movement. This is not always the case. For contrast, let us hear a well-known, fast-moving selection from a tremendously long work called the *Messiah*. This work is an oratorio, which is a vocal composition based on a text from the Bible. The composer of this oratorio was George Frederic Handel. Handel and Bach were born during the same year, 1685.

"The piece we are going to hear is named 'Hallelujah.' It is sung by a large chorus accompanied by a large orchestra. The entire text of the *Messiah* is taken directly from the Bible. You will have no difficulty in discovering why this particular chorus is called 'Hallelujah.' "

[Play recording.]

LESSON TEN: MUSIC FOR DANCING AND DANCE MUSIC FOR LISTENING

"Much music had its origin in connection with dancing. All dancing needs music, but all music does not need dancing. In connection with the relationship between dancing and music, it should be remembered that when music is not being performed for dancing it should be listened to as music in its own right. This holds true even though it might have been composed in a dance style, such as a waltz, a jig, a sarabande,[1] etc. Much 'good music' is written in the style of dance tunes even though it is not expected to be used as music for dancing.

"Practically all music may be used for dancing. As long as there is a 'beat' in music, dancing is stimulated. In the highly developed dancing of the South Sea Islanders, the movements are made usually by the hands rather than the feet. Some outstanding dancers of Europe and America frequently interpret songs, symphonies, and overtures by dancing.

"If you think back to Lesson Seven, you will remember a recording entitled 'Indian War Dance.' This, essentially, was music to be danced, since the American Indian chief used this very music to get his entire tribe of braves stirred up for war. Of course, there was no symphony orchestra to help the Indian. But there were Indian drums for the beats, and there were Indian braves who could, and did, sing the tune. You boys and girls could do this 'Indian War Dance' if you wished. Beat a drum, sing the tune, and make up a war dance step to the music.

"Remember the recording of the 'Blue Danube Waltzes.' This was composed as dance music. It is fun to waltz to, especially if you can do a real waltz step with the large sliding first beat of each measure, as done in the city of Vienna, Austria, where Strauss lived.

"As a new example of dance music (with or without dancing), let us listen to two pieces arranged by Percy Grainger. The first is the 'Irish Washerwoman.' "

[Play recording of "Irish Washerwoman" for String Quartet, by Grainger.]

"Did you have any trouble finding the beat? If you felt like dancing, your answer should be that you *did* find the beat. If you beat your foot—or your big toe, you certainly must have found the beat. If you can find the beat in music, all you need to do to dance to that music is to know the step—or else make up a step that seems to be appropriate. Or, if you prefer just to listen to such music, the music still is essentially 'dance music.'

"Since Percy Grainger enjoyed playing music of a dance style, let us listen to his most popular composition, called 'Country Gardens.' "

[1] A sarabande is a slow, serious dance, popular in Europe about 200 years ago.

This piece was based on an English dance tune very popular in the English countryside."

[Play piano recording of "Country Gardens."]

LESSON ELEVEN: SEVEN PIECES OF DANCE MUSIC FROM THE NUTCRACKER SUITE, BY PETER ILYTCH TCHAIKOVSKY

"All parts of the *Nutcracker Suite,* by Tchaikovsky, are dance music with the exception of the Overture which begins the work. Here are the names of the dance numbers: 'Dance of the Flutes,' 'Dance of the Sugar Plum Fairies,' 'March,' 'Chinese Dance,' 'Trepak,' 'Arab Dance,' and 'Waltz of the Flowers.'

"Do you already know any of these?"

[Play any or all of these. Tell the class that, since the *Nutcracker Suite* is a sort of musical fairy story, each boy or girl can imagine whatever he wishes as he listens to each number.]

[On the other hand, the details of the story may be reported to the class if desired. The following general comments will help in an understanding of the musical characteristics of the various sections of this work]:

"1. 'Overture'—An introduction in the style of the music which follows.

"2. 'March'—A march is a form of dancing. Notice the striking contrasting passages for wind instruments (clarinets, bassoons, French horns, and trumpets) and the strings (violins, violas, cellos, and double basses.)

"3. 'Dance of the Sugar Plum Fairy'—The title tells the story. The solo part is played on a high-pitched metallic-like piano called the celeste, which does have a celestial-like sound. For contrast, a bass clarinet is heard from time to time.

"4. 'Trepak'—A Russian dance which needs only to be listened to in order to understand it.

"5. 'Arab Dance'—Employs the low, tantalizing sound of clarinets and the English horn (a low-pitched oboe). The very soft rhythm of the tambourine, played at intervals throughout the piece, adds a magic touch.

"6. The 'Chinese Dance' is amusing, with the low grunting sound of the bassoons as the accompaniment to the solo of flutes and piccolo.

"7. But in the 'Dance of the Flutes,' the three flutes really come into their own.

"8. The 'Waltz of the Flowers' is the 'grand finale' (big ending). A touch of unreality is added by the harp cadenza, where the harp seems to take off on its own."

LESSON TWELVE: BALLET MUSIC

"When music is written especially for a whole dance group, it is called 'Ballet Music,' since the French word for a dance group is 'ballet.' Many composers have written ballet music. Most ballet music is joyful, since people often dance when they feel happy. However, dancing can portray sadness and even death. Why not try a recording of a dance step entitled in French, 'Valse Triste,' which means, Dance of Sadness. This number was written by the Finnish composer Sibelius."

[Play recording.]

"It would take years and years to listen to all the dance music composed in the Western world alone. Since we do not have that much time in this course, let us end the dance music section by listening to the ballet music named, *Les Sylphides*. The story behind this music is that about a hundred years ago a great Polish composer and pianist wrote this music for performance by a solo piano. Since then, dancers (usually referred to as 'interpretive dancers') have found this music unusually well suited to group and solo dancing. Today, because of the grace, tenderness, and warmth aroused by certain compositions of Chopin, almost every dance group in the world dances to some of his music. If you were a member of a ballet group, do you think you could express by your dancing the same thing that Chopin put into his music?"

[Play recording.]

"There is a new style of ballet today. It is usually referred to as 'modern dance.' It results from the introduction of strong, natural steps —running, jumping, stamping. Whereas the usual ballet dancer wears ballet shoes which are an aid to 'toe dancing,' the modern dancer often wears no shoes at all. When shoes are needed, they are ordinary ones or boots. Boots are worn by all the men when dancing a ballet called *Billy the Kid*. Since this is a story of cowboys, cowboy boots are worn.

"When the American composer, Aaron Copland, wrote the music for the ballet, *Billy the Kid,* he used parts of real cowboy songs, 'The

Old Chisholm Trail,' 'The Dying Cowboy,' and 'Git Along Little Dogie.' The story of the dance follows the life story of William Bonney better known as Billy the Kid.

"The titles of the seven episodes of Copland's *Suite from Billy the Kid* suggests the story. 'The Open Prairie,' 'Street in a Frontier Town,' 'Card Game at Night,' 'Gun Battle,' 'Celebration after Billy's Capture,' 'Billy's Demise,' 'The Open Prairie Again.'"

"Another ballet by Copland is similar in subject and treatment. It is his ballet, *Rodeo*. The titles of this suite are:

"'Buckaroo Holiday,' 'Choral Nocturne,' 'Honky Tonk Interlude,' and 'Saturday Night Waltz,' and 'Hoe Down.'"

[Play parts of all these Copland ballets.]

"In Lessons Ten, Eleven, and Twelve, we have seen the relationship of music and dance. We have heard music which ranged from the light, toe-dancing steps of *Les Sylphides* and 'The Dance of the Sugar Plum Fairy' to the heavy, barbaric pounding of feet on the ground during the 'Indian War Dance.' There was also great difference in the music of the 'Irish Washerwoman,' the 'Country Gardens,' and 'Valse Triste.'"

LESSON THIRTEEN: MARCHES

"When a person marches he really is dancing, since he is moving to the beats of the music. In dancing, he moves in many directions; in marching, he is expected to move forward only.

"All march music has strong beats. This helps to keep the marchers together so each person steps forward at the same time. In this way, no one is expected to step on the heels of the person ahead of him.

"All of us have heard many marches. Perhaps you have noticed the effect of a military march on the listener. How do you feel when you hear the band play the 'Stars and Stripes Forever'? Lots of things happen inside people when they hear march music. Their hearts beat harder and faster, they breathe faster and more deeply. They feel warmer. Their feet seem to be out there marching with the boys.

"The next time you have the chance, check up on those points. See what happens to you. What happens to you probably happens to the person next to you. This is the reason bands participate in parades.

"But all march music does not make you feel the same way. A funeral march is so slow and so gloomy sounding that you probably get a serious and 'let-down' reaction. A good example of the funeral march is the one written by Frederick Chopin."

[Play recording of "Funeral March," by Chopin, 2nd movement, Sonata No. 2 in B♭ minor, Op. 35.]

"For our last march, let us listen to the military march which is the greatest ever written in America, and probably the best in the world."

[Play Sousa's "Stars and Stripes Forever."]

Lesson Fourteen: Folk Songs

"Songs might be said to be words put to music. Why do people sing words instead of just speaking them? This is an interesting question. One question often leads to another. Why do you think the American Indian decided to beat a drum when he sang his War Dance? Why did Handel decide to sing the word, 'Hallelujah' instead of simply speaking it? Anyone listening to those powerful Hallelujahs in his famous chorus will know that the use of melody and rhythm and harmony all help to make a stronger impression on the listener.

"For thousands of years your ancestors have been singing songs. These songs were largely 'folk songs.' This means that they were 'songs of folk' or 'songs of people.' Such music was created by many people, not by only one person. It was made up by people as they sang. The music was not even written down. Instead, it was memorized by one person after another and, in this way, it was passed on (and perhaps changed) from one generation to another.

"Even before they built houses and sang songs, our ancestors probably related stories to one another. Some of these stories were undoubtedly about their own adventures in hunting and fishing. Others were legends and folk lore heard from their fathers and mothers and friends. Over a period of a few years, the stories may not have changed much from one telling to another. But after they had been told thousands of times, over a period of a hundred years or more, the original version was often hardly distinguishable. Stories which last from generation to generation (usually not recorded in writing) are called folk tales.

"Folk tales are still part of our present-day world. What child has not heard the story of 'Jack and the Bean Stalk,' 'The Three Little Pigs,' or 'Little Red Riding Hood'?

"Have you ever noticed that a good story-teller sort of sings some of the words in order to make a better impression on the listener? When you, yourself, tell the story of 'The Three Little Pigs' to your little sister or brother, don't you try to heighten the effect of the words by imitating the deep, mean voice of the wolf demanding entrance to the pigs' house when he says, 'Let me in!' And, when the little pig answers, 'Not by the hair on my chinny-chin-chin!' don't you use a high, squeaky voice to make it sound as though it really were the pig who was answering? This same desire to cause a story to impress is the reason our ancestors began singing stories instead of just telling them. In this way, folk stories became folk songs.

"Folk songs are a natural result of folk tales. In fact, any set of good words, a story or a poem, tends to be put to music in one way or another. Here are three folk songs. No words of explanation are necessary; each one tells its own story":

[Play: (1) "Henry Martyn" (pirate story about sailing). (2) "The Blue Tailed Fly" (humorous story). (3) "Black is the Color of My True Love's Hair" (love song).]

"Attention should be called to another type of folk song. It is a song which has been *composed* in the *style of a folk song*. Some composers have succeeded in capturing the spontaneous earthy expression of folk art. Such a one in America's history was Stephen Foster. This talented and sensitive man seemed preordained to write the songs of America for her. This he did by the hundreds as a means of expressing his love for his country and, incidentally, of earning a living.

"The entire population of the United States as well as millions throughout the world know and love the heart songs of Stephen Foster, 'Swanee River,' 'My Old Kentucky Home,' 'Old Black Joe,' 'Tenting on the Old Camp Ground,' 'Beautiful Dreamer,' 'Camptown Races,' 'Old Dog Tray,' 'Laura Lee' (Love Me Tender, Love Me True), and 'Massa's in de Cold, Cold Ground.' This music is not cast in the large forms of concert music. They are the songs of the American folk, which Foster found in the heart of America. In terms of performances of Foster melodies in American homes, in schools, at picnics, humming and singing together or alone, Stephen Foster is America's most successful composer."

LESSON FIFTEEN: SONGS OF SCHUBERT

"In Lesson Fourteen we found that people have been creating folk songs for thousands of years. The creation or evolution of a single folk song might take fifty to a hundred years or more. Fathers sang their favorite songs to their children who later would sing to their children a version of the same song. Eventually the song would become standardized or established, according to the best version. Then, after printing was invented (by Gutenberg in Germany, in 1450), some of these folk songs were printed. In this way many of the best folk songs have been spread over the world. Other songs, however have a different origin. When a composer decides to compose music for a favorite poem, he simply creates his own melody, harmony, and rhythm.

"Franz Schubert is the world's best-known composer of songs. He was fond of poetry. When he read poetry he seemed to hear melody, harmony, and rhythm. If Schubert liked the music he heard, he often wrote it down. He is said to have written one of his finest songs, 'Serenade,' on the back of a menu after eating a meal in a restaurant in Vienna.

"Schubert was an Austrian. His language was, therefore, German. But his 'Serenade' has become so well known that the words have been translated into many languages, and this song is loved all over the Western world. You have probably heard it on records, in recital, over radio or TV. Whether you heard it sung in the original German or translated into English does not seem to make much difference. No matter which language is used, its message is a love song which appeals to the heart of all people."

[Play "Serenade" by Schubert, original song version.]

"Franz Schubert wrote about six hundred songs during his short life of thirty-one years. All of these are published today, and most of them still are sung. Here is one called, 'Who is Sylvia.' The original title in German was 'An Sylvia,' which means 'To Sylvia.' The words were found in a play entitled, *Two Gentlemen of Verona* by another famous man named William Shakespeare.

"Before listening to 'Who is Sylvia' let us take a look at her record. In the first part of the seventeenth century, William Shakespeare must have known a girl named Sylvia, for he wrote this poem about her:

Who is Sylvia? What is she,
That all our swains commend her?

> Holy, fair, and wise is she;
> The Heav'ns such grace did lend her,
> That she might admired be,
> That she might admired be.

"In the first part of the nineteenth century, Franz Schubert read Shakespeare's poem about Sylvia. Even though 200 years had elapsed since Shakespeare knew Sylvia, her charm appealed to Schubert. He decided, therefore, to compose some music about Sylvia. He did, and called it, 'An Sylvia.'

"One hundred and fifty years later, Schubert's music and Shakespear's words, now 350 years old, are still available to you in print and on record! See what you think of Sylvia."

[Play recording of "Who is Sylvia" in original solo form for tenor.]

"Now you are acquainted with at least two of Schubert's 600 songs. This is only 1/300 of all his songs. If you know another one, your knowledge will be increased to 1/200 of Schubert's complete output of songs. That leaves only 597 more for the rest of your life!

"For our third Schubert song, you will be given an assignment which might be considered gruesome. It deals with death. The subject of death comes up frequently in music, as it does in life. There are good reasons for this. First, it is true that life leads to death. Second, thoughts and feelings about death are usually strong emotions. Sad or tragic feelings are more intense than happy or joyous ones. In spite of the experience of sad feelings, the listener often obtains understanding for those persons who are having trouble through sickness, death of a loved one, etc. There is a certain personal gratification in feeling sympathy and sharing experience. Our third recording of a Schubert song is called, 'Tod und das Mädchen' ('Death and the Maiden')."

The Maiden:

> Go by me, ah go by me,
> Thou spectre wild and grey!
> I am yet young—pass onward,
> And call me not away!
> And call me not away!

Death:

> Give me thy hand, thou maiden young and fair,
> Thy friend I come,
> To hush thy weeping:

Be of good cheer,
Thou shalt not fear,
So soft within my dark arms sleeping.

LESSON SIXTEEN: GRAND OPERA

"Two Italians named Peri and Monteverdi wrote the world's first operas during the first years of the seventeenth century. Their stories were based on the Greek legend of Orpheus and Eurydice. Orfeo, which means Orpheus, was a Greek hero who was an accomplished musician. He was deeply in love with his wife, Eurydice, taken away by death. The miraculous feat of Orpheus was that he brought Eurydice back to life through his songs of love and devotion.

"In 1762 the German composer Christoph Gluck produced what may be thought of as the first modern grand opera. It was entitled *Orfeo ed Euridice,* since it was founded on the same Greek legend.

"Most grand operas deal with stories similar to Orpheus and Eurydice; they are usually full of love, life, and death. The reason for this is not difficult to understand in view of what you found out in connection with Schubert songs (Lesson Fifteen). Grand opera is a dramatic production (or show) in which all words (at least almost all) are sung instead of spoken. An orchestra is required. A conductor is in charge of the singers, the chorus, and the orchestra. Frequently a ballet (Lesson Twelve) is part of the opera. Costumes and scenery are used.

"In order to give you a basis for understanding grand opera, I am going to play some recordings from a very popular opera, *Carmen,* by Bizet. As you might expect, this work is filled with love, intrigue, duels, and death. The year is 1820; the scene is Seville, Spain. Here is a synopsis of the plot involving the three leading characters:

"Carmen, a worker in a cigarette factory, acts as if she were in love with both a soldier named Don José and a bullfighter, Escamillo. At first, Don José does not respond to her charms; but when he is ordered to arrest her because she had stabbed another worker, he falls violently in love with her. At this point, Carmen has a change of heart and repulses his suit. Escamillo, the bullfighter, also falls in love with Carmen; she neither repulses him nor responds to his suit. Instead, she 'strings him along.' Eventually, Don José becomes so enraged with Carmen's fickleness and vanity that he stabs her to death.

"Before the curtain is raised for an opera performance, the orchestra plays an overture. The purpose of this is to introduce the audience to some of the music to be heard later in the show. The overture also transports the audience from the workaday world of work, money, and family, etc., to the world of imagination, story, music, and dance.

"However, the composer of Carmen did not write an overture. Instead, he composed a military march to suggest the nature of the opera. In the middle of the march he wrote an orchestral version of one of the 'hit songs' to be heard later. This is the rhythmic and exciting "Toreador Song.'"

[Play 'Carmen March' recording for orchestra, by Bizet.]

"As the march finishes, the curtain goes up revealing a crowd gathered in a public square in front of a cigarette factory. Carmen shows off by singing and dancing especially for the soldier, Don José. Carmen decides to dance, and sing the 'Habanera,' to the accompaniment of her castanets. Here is her 'Habanera.'"

[Play recording.]

"Carmen's second suitor, the successful bullfighter Escamillo, tries to prove to Carmen and the rest of the villagers (including his opposing suitor) how brave and strong he is. He sings the 'Toreador Song' and invites everybody to attend the bullfight later in the day. Here is Escamillo's proud, haughty, and exciting 'Toreador Song'":

[Play recording.]

"This is only the beginning of the story. During the next two hours, all sorts of intrigue, fights, and plots take place; smugglers against the law, suitor against suitor, etc. The dramatic action is apparent in songs, dances, choruses, in the music of the orchestra, the costumes of the actors, and the lights and scenery on stage.

"The opera closes with a scene near the bull ring. Inside the arena, the crowd (chorus) is praising Escamillo's skill and daring. Outside the arena, Don José is still swearing eternal love for Carmen. Without any sign of mercy, she scorns him, saying, 'No! Never will Carmen consent —Free was I born! Free will I die!" Don Jose implores, 'Now thou refusest my prayers, Inhuman girl! For thy sake am I lost! And then to know thee shameless, infamous! Laughing in his arms at my despair! No, no, it shall not be, by Heaven!'

"Finally, she throws Don José's ring at his feet. Don José goes into a violent rage over the frivolity and faithlessness of Carmen. Maddened with her exclamation of joy over Escamillo's triumph, Don José stabs her in the heart. Carmen falls dead as Escamillo enters. The opera closes as Don José sings, with great feeling, 'I have killed her. Oh, Carmen! My adored Carmen.'"

LESSON SEVENTEEN: LIGHT OPERA (OPERETTA)

"Since 'opera' means 'a work,' 'light opera' means 'a light work.' In Italian, the ending *etta* is a diminutive form; an operetta is 'a little opera.' The text, or libretto (little libro, little book) of a light opera customarily is not as serious as that of the usual grand opera.

"The sharpest difference between the two types of works is the use of the spoken word for the dialogue in operettas, whereas in grand opera the dialogue appears as song or as recitative (pronounced res-sit-ta-teev). (Recitative is a combination of words and music wherein the words are half-spoken and half-sung. The accompaniment of a recitative is a series of chords—harmony.)

"Light opera has become very popular in the United States; in fact, our country has taken world leadership in this field. American musical comedy, light opera, musical plays, or simply musicals, are recognized everywhere. (See Lesson Seven of Chapter Nine.) However, before America achieved her success in light opera, in England a team of writers, Sir William S. Gilbert and Sir Arthur Sullivan, achieved great fame in this field. They firmly established their light opera as a veritable English institution. Together, they produced a series of works, beginning in 1871 and including *The Mikado, The Pirates of Penzance, H.M.S. Pinafore,* and many others. In 1890 they quarreled and the series stopped.

"Gilbert and Sullivan light operas incorporate delightful music with wholesome humor and vigorous satire of English customs. The Savoy Theater in London was built especially for performances of their works, and, at one time, as many as ninety opera groups were touring England presenting performances of *Pinafore*.

"A glance at the list of characters in *The Mikado* (first performed in 1885) will give a clue to the delightful and humorous nature of the work:

Nanki-Poo . . . . Son of the Mikado (Emperor of Japan), disguised as a wandering minstrel and in love with Yum-Yum

Ko-Ko .... Lord High Executioner of Titipu
Pooh-Bah .... Lord High Everything Else

Yum-Yum
Pitti-Sing }....... Three Sisters, Wards of Ko-Ko
Peep-Bo

[Play selections, from *The Mikado,* particularly "Three Little Maids," "The Flowers That Bloom in the Spring," "Willow Tit-Willow."]

"Irish-born Victor Herbert established light opera in America, following the failure of his grand opera *Natoma.* During the first twenty-five or thirty years of this century, his operettas became Broadway hits in rapid succession: *Gypsy Love Song, The Fortune Teller, The Red Mill, Sweethearts, Babes in Toyland,* and especially *Naughty Marietta.*

"Herbert's operettas, like those of Gilbert and Sullivan, have lost some of their great popular appeal, but the delightful music contained in the scores lives on in individual selections. From *Naughty Marietta* alone, present-day repertoires still feature 'Ah! Sweet Mystery of Life,' 'I'm Falling in Love with Someone,' and the exciting 'Italian Street Song.'"

[Play the above selections from *Naughty Marietta.*]

"In recent years, a series of 'musical plays' by a team of Americans has made box-office history in the United States. The vocal scores for these works bear this inscription, 'Music by Richard Rodgers—Book and Lyrics by Oscar Hammerstein, 2nd.' Their *South Pacific* ran continuously on Broadway for 1,925 performances, *Oklahoma* for 2,246 performances. Little wonder, because almost every musical selection is a hit tune. *Oklahoma* opens with the fresh and enthusiastic song, 'Oh, What a Beautiful Morning,' and closes with the stirring,

> Oklahoma, where the wind comes sweepin' down the plain,
> And the wavin' wheat can sure smell sweet,
> When the wind comes right behind the rain. . . .
> We know we belong to the land,
> And the land we belong to is grand. . . .

"Other successful shows of Rodgers and Hammerstein include *Carousel, The King and I,* and *The Sound of Music.* The collaboration of Rodgers and Hammerstein ended abruptly with the death of Oscar Hammerstein in 1960."

[Play selections from *Oklahoma.*]

LESSON EIGHTEEN: DESCRIPTIVE MUSIC FOR THE SYMPHONY ORCHESTRA

"Until late in the nineteenth century, practically all music written for the symphony orchestra was referred to as pure music or absolute music. Lessons One, Two, and Three showed that the listener was not restricted, or even expected to respond in any particular way, to the various parts of the music. In other words, the listener was free to hear, feel, imagine, interpret, or even see whatever he found to be his sincere reaction to the music. However, in the nineteenth century, Hector Berlioz of France, Richard Strauss of Germany, and Camille Saint-Saëns of France popularized a type of music which is called *descriptive*. It was so named because the composer attempted to *describe* in music a particular event or scene. Another name for descriptive music is *program music,* because it is necessary to print notes in the program in order to guide the audience in listening for certain things.

"An easily understood example of descriptive or program music is *The Carnival of the Animals,* by Saint-Saëns. It is not difficult to know what the composer had in mind by such a title, but Saint-Saëns decided to help the listener further by making sure that he would be thinking about a particular animal in connection with each of the ten short pieces in *The Carnival of the Animals.*

"The music was written for, and performed by, a small orchestra of strings, woodwinds, and brass and percussion instruments with two solo pianos. Here is the 'program' the composer wrote for *The Carnival of the Animals.* As you listen you are supposed to keep the right animal in mind."

Le Carnaval Des Animaux, Grande Fantaisie Zoölogique

Introduction and Royal March of the Lion	Aquarium
Hens and Cocks	Personages with Long Ears
Wild Donkeys	Cuckoo in the Woods
Tortoises	Pianists
The Elephant	The Fossils
Kangaroos	The Swan
	Finale

[Play *The Carnival of the Animals,* reading the name of each selection before it is played. If the recording includes the humorous verses of Ogden Nash, the names of the various animals will not be necessary.]

"Did you have trouble identifying the animals?

"The one piece called 'The Fossils' might have given some trouble. Of course, a fossil could be the remains of an ancient animal, but, in this instance, Saint-Saëns was playing a joke on his fellow pianists. He was jokingly referring to them as sort of 'old fogies' who like to practice scales. You will note that the scales up and down are the only thing these two fossil-like pianists seem able to play!

"The finest selection of *The Carnival of the Animals,* as far as music is concerned, is undoubtedly 'The Swan.' This is considered by posterity (i.e., the mass of people who really are the judges of what is ultimately good or bad in all the arts) to be a little masterpiece of composition. In fact, it is so fine that, whether it were called 'The Swan,' or 'The Swallow,' or 'A Day in June,' or simply 'Etude,' or 'Contemplation,' or 'Piece for Cello and Piano,' it would be just as beautiful.

"Descriptive music is usually what might be called 'fun music,' because it is sporting for the listener to let the composer try to describe something in music. Practically all descriptive music tends to get monotonous when the test of good music is applied. According to Lesson 2, that test is, 'The more one hears it, the more he enjoys it.' 'The Swan' is the only part of *The Carnival of the Animals* which is played frequently as a separate solo work. The reason is that it 'wears well.'

"You can test the rule of good music by playing 'Hens and Cocks' or 'The Kangaroos' several times in succession. Then compare your reaction to listening to 'The Swan' the same length of time."

LESSON NINETEEN: PURE MUSIC FOR THE SYMPHONY ORCHESTRA

"*Pure music* was explained at first in Lesson Eighteen. Pure music is often called *abstract music* because it does not represent any particular story or picture. Rather, it is simply and directly music for people to listen to. Each listener is expected to listen discriminatingly and to respond sincerely in his own way. As one becomes more experienced in the field of music, he learns more, of course. This should give him new and better ideas about music and its meaning. He probably will hear much more in repeated hearings of good music or in subsequent hearing of new music.

"During Lessons One through Eighteen, this class already has heard much music which is considered pure or abstract music. Lessons Eight and Nine offer good examples.

"*Symphony No. 5 in E minor,* by Anton Dvořák, is another example of pure music. Most symphonies have similar titles which indicate the number and principal key or tonality of the work. In this way, one can identify a particular work. This *Symphony No. 5* by Dvořák specifies the symphony as the fifth one composed by Dvořák, and the E minor indicates the key of the symphony. This is not unlike the name of kings and queens, i.e., King George V or Queen Elizabeth II.

"A symphony is an extended work, usually in four movements. It is written to be performed by a symphony orchestra. The symphony orchestra is made up of four families of instruments—strings, woodwinds, brasses, and percussion instruments. Since there are four or five different members of each of these families, the number of different instruments usually totals fifteen to twenty or more. [Detailed information on the symphony orchestra will be found in Chapter Five.]

"Usually the composer of a symphony merely indicates the Italian tempo mark for each movement. Such marks are given in Italian, since all music of the Western world uses these same Italian words in giving instructions to the conductor and players regarding the proper tempo or rate of speed.

"The following information shows what the composer, Dvořák, wrote to help the performers understand each movement of his *Symphony No. 5 in E minor.*"

Movement	Italian Tempo Terms	English Translation
1st Movement	Adagio, Allegro molto	At ease, then very cheerful or fast
2nd Movement	Largo	Broadly
3rd Movement	Scherzo molto vivace	A joke, a playful piece; vivaciously
4th Movement	Allegro con fuoco	Fast, with fire and animation

"However, Dvořák wanted his readers, or players and listeners, to know something characteristic about his Fifth Symphony. Therefore, since it was composed while he was a visitor in the United States, he named this work, *Symphonie Aus der Neuen Welt* (in German), or *Z Moveho Sveta* (in the Czech language). Both of these titles, translated into English, mean *Symphony from the New World.*

"Let us hear this work. Knowing that it was written in the United States (actually in a small town, Spillville, Iowa, in the year 1892), the listener will be apt to note American influences, for Dvořák composed his principal tunes in the style of American folk melodies. Therefore, you may expect to feel that this symphony is quite American-sounding, and really comes from the New World."

[The recording should be played, and even repeated, movement by movement, with an interval for comments by the members of the class. Encourage each student to be frank in the expression of his reaction to the music. This will result in each boy or girl feeling a vital part of the music. Some healthy disagreement may be expected, regarding the meaning of various passages and melodies.]

"The melody of the largo movement may be recognized as the same as the song, 'Goin' Home.' This is due to the fact that the composer of 'Goin' Home' used the principal melody of this largo movement for his song. The words he wrote tell us what the melody meant to him. Actually, the meaning of the music, as far as other people are concerned, might as well be titles such as 'Stayin' Home,' 'I Love You,' 'Sleepy Time,' or what not. But such titles as 'Fightin' You,' or 'Runnin' Wild' would not be at all appropriate. Why?

"The experienced listener of music probably would prefer not to associate any words with the music, since words tend to limit his response. He would prefer to assimilate and enjoy the many moods of the music in his own way, with thoughts directed by his own imagination and intellect."

LESSON TWENTY: CHAMBER MUSIC

"A review of the other lessons in this chapter will reveal that a number of different locations for the music heard seems to be indicated by the different types of music. For instance:

Marches—Out of doors
Symphonies—Concert hall
Opera—Opera house
Religious music—Church or cathedral
Ballet music—Theatre
Songs and Instrumental pieces—Recital hall

"However, chamber music is different from all of these in respect to the appropriate location. Chamber music, by its name, specifies that the performance should be in a chamber or room. Chamber music is room music. There is a reason.

"To understand why a composer writes chamber music instead of concert music, put yourself in his place. Imagine that you wish to write about something very personal. If you were telling such a story to a thousand people in a large auditorium, you would do so with a loud voice, very slowly and very distinctly, and you would be forced to omit intimacy of expression. But if you were telling the same thing to one person or a small group of people, in a drawing room or living room, your approach would be different. In a relatively small room, your discussion would be much more intimate and personal. Instead of carrying out the role of an orator in a large auditorium, you would discuss your message 'man to man' in a living room. Many composers prefer the living room approach for their finest music. Thus, add to the above list: 'Chamber music—The living room of a home.'

"Most composers write a great quantity of chamber music. Much of it is scored for (written for) small groups of instruments, usually including stringed instruments and piano.

"The first selection of chamber music you will hear is the second movement for a composition written for a string quartet consisting of two violins, a viola, and a cello. These four instruments are similar to the four singers in a vocal quartet. The usual assignment of parts for both groups is: first and second soprano, tenor, and bass.

"The name of the selection to be heard is 'Andante Cantabile,' by Tchaikovsky. Again we find the title to be an Italian tempo term, the translation of which is 'a slowly walking song.'"

[Play recording.]

"Did the 'Andante Cantabile' sound as if it were a personal conversation? Does this music fit best in a large hall or in a room in a residence? Is there much feeling in it? Did you feel that more than one person was communicating ideas and feelings? Why has 'Andante Cantabile' become a number frequently played before the present-day public?

"The concluding selection for this chapter is a work composed by Joseph Haydn. Haydn was born the same year as George Washington, 1732. Strangely enough, both men earned the honored name of 'Father.' Washington is called the 'Father of his Country,' and Haydn is called the 'Father of the Symphony.' In musical circles, he is often referred to as 'Papa Haydn.'

"Joseph Haydn wrote 82 complete string quartet works, most of which have four movements each. The duration of an average Haydn quartet is approximately twenty to thirty minutes. He was the first composer to devote so much effort to composing for the string quartet. These 82 Haydn quartets are still among the best and are frequently played 'in the chamber' or in recital.

"In listening to Haydn's string quartet, *The Horseman,* Op. 74, No. 3, note the conversational style employed. Each instrument seems to have its say, although the first violin holds forth more frequently."

[Play recording.]

THE STORY OF MUSIC

The purpose of Chapter Nine is to tell the story of musical development in the history of man. A knowledge of history is not essential to the enjoyment of music, but music cannot be fully understood until its historical setting has been established. Conversely, no historical period can be fully understood until its music is known.

Almost without exception, histories of music begin with man's early music. Each successive development is described. Eventually, the music of today is revealed as the culmination of an evolutionary process. Such an approach is systematic and logical for the mature individual.

However, this usual approach to the history of music contains certain difficulties for the boy or girl of junior high school age, since the music which is the most difficult to understand and appreciate is studied first.

The reason for this difficulty is that the music of Ockeghem, Orlando Lassus, Palestrina, Bach, and Handel, as well as the other pre-Bach and Baroque composers, is not set in a background as familiar to youngsters of today as is the music of the present. This is the primary reason that junior high school students understand better and respond better to the music of George Gershwin, Morton Gould, and the romanticists, Sibelius, Tchaikovsky, and Mendelssohn.

For this reason, this chapter will approach the history of music more or less in reverse—by beginning with music which the student *already* knows and working back toward earlier musical eras. Thus the music of Stravinsky or Debussy will be explained in terms of

361]

Gershwin and Gould rather than the reverse. Likewise, Brahms and Mendelssohn will serve as stepping stones to Beethoven and Mozart—and they, in turn, to Handel and Bach. By this process, instead of studying the pre-Bach period of counterpoint at the beginning of the course, it is taken up near the end, after the youngsters will have had the advantages of eighteen lessons to help them understand this important era of music. As background information for the course, the first two lessons are devoted to an explanation of music as a natural phenomenon and as an activity of primitive man.

Ample opportunity to help the story of music come to life has been planned through the use of carefully selected recordings. Obviously, these recordings are not the only ones which can serve as examples and illustrations. The ingenuity of the teacher may bring forth other music, on records, on tape, or "alive," for use throughout the course.

The system of the two preceding chapters will be followed again, using square brackets to indicate specific suggestions to the teacher, and quotes for explanations to the students. Class assignments will be found at the conclusion of each lesson. It is imperative that each student keep a comprehensive, up-to-date notebook.

LESSON ONE: WHERE DID MUSIC COME FROM?

"Some people assume that music was thought up by wise philosophers or invented by great composers. This is not true. Music was merely brought into focus when man found out how to use that which was already present in the natural world of musical sound.

"Ask a science teacher, physicist, or some other informed person, 'What is the scientific explanation of a musical sound?' You may not understand the answer of a scientist to this question, but you will realize that there *is* a scientific explanation of music:

"1. A *musical sound* is sound which has *pitch*. An example is the sound of a piano when a key has been struck, or the sound which comes out of a musical instrument when it is properly blown or played upon. Other musical sounds which are familiar are singing, humming, and whistling.

"2. Every musical sound is a combination of many sounds. This combination is called the overtone series.

"3. Points 1 and 2 mean that every time we hear what we think is one musical sound what we actually hear is a whole *series* of musical sounds.

"Here are the first sixteen sounds we hear every time we hear a single musical sound:

Partials:	1st	2nd	3rd	4th	5th	6th	7th	8th	9th	10th	11th	12th	13th	14th	15th	16th
	or															
	fundamental															

THE PARTIALS OR OVERTONE SERIES
(The number and pitch of the first sixteen partials)

A closer examination of this series of sounds reveals a pattern of tones that bears a striking resemblance to the history of music. Man's first harmony was the result of singing the first three partials together. This practice was originated by the Greeks centuries before Christ and was continued by the Romans for hundreds of years after the advent of Christ.

"Partials 4, 5, and 6 (C-E-G) form the major triad which is the basis of the harmonic system used by the Western world. Partials 7, 8, 9, 10, and 11 form the whole-tone scale, the harmonic basis of impressionism popularized toward the close of the nineteenth century by the French composer Claude Debussy."

Such comparisons between the nature of musical sound and the history of music suggest that music has been discovered by man instead of being created by him.

[Demonstrate the overtone series on the piano and on any brass instrument (without using its valves) or on any stringed instrument by lightly touching the 'open string.' Run the left hand up and down the full length of the string, thus producing the natural harmonics. In all demonstrations, it will be noted that the series of intervals produced is always the same.

[Remind the class that the letters of the alphabet are employed to name the spaces and lines above C, i.e., D, E, F, G, A, B, C, D, etc. By reading the names of sixteen notes, the highest and last note will be found to be a C. The highest, or top one, is three octaves above the first. Other points of musical notation may be indicated as deemed advisable by the teacher. One such item of interest is to point out that "middle C" rests between the two staffs. This is to be expected, since the staff originally consisted of eleven lines with the middle one colored for ease of identification. Today we still use these same eleven lines, except that the middle line is left out. When it is necessary to write "middle C," a short line is inserted for "middle C" between the two staffs of five lines each.

[Some of the students who are informed regarding the structure of sunlight may recognize the similarity between light and sound, because the colors of a rainbow (or spectrum) blend together to make colorless sunlight in a way very similar to the blending of many sounds to produce a single musical sound.]

Assignment: Study Lesson Five, "Reading and Writing of Music," from Chapter Seven.

LESSON TWO: PRIMITIVE MUSIC

"The history of the earliest music of man is unknown. There seems no doubt that early man did sing, hundreds of thousands of years ago. Today we can only surmise how or what he sang. Also, we may assume that, as primitive man sang, he also beat various rhythms on drum-like instruments, and sometimes he moved around in a dance-like fashion. But there are no records to prove it. A curtain of darkness hangs over the beginnings of man's musical activity.

"Man is thought by anthropologists to have lived on this earth for about five million years, although remains of human-like creatures have been found dating back only about one million years. It is shocking and humbling to realize that so little is known about the development of our ancient ancestors. Not until man was able to leave records of his life in hard materials (such as stone and metals which resisted the deteriorating effects of water, snow, and ice) does his story become known.

"Through the study of stone instruments, some earthern objects and metal-like artifacts found in deposits of sand and silt around the world, the archaeologist of recent times is able to describe characteristics of the life of early man. Scientists have pointed out that, by comparison with the animal kingdom, man's genus, *homo sapiens,* developed rapidly. For instance, much animal life is older by millions of years than man; yet, today, man alone is capable of creating and producing his own thoughts in writing and in works of art and music.

"Curt Sachs, the eminent musicologist (a musicologist is a scholar who scientifically studies the history of music), writes in his *Our Musical Heritage* regarding the music of primitive man:

But not even the earliest civilizations that have left their traces in the depths of the earth are old enough to betray the secret of the origins of music. Moreover, the digging spade yields little in the field of music: the songs of stone-age men have faded away, and their instruments were probably, in the majority of cases, made of wood or cane and other materials too perishable to resist decomposition in ten or a hundred thousand years of interment.[1]

Assignment: Write a report on primitive man and show how he lived.

Lesson Three: Music Today

"The story of music in history will be told to you by beginning with music of today. This is music with which you are already familiar. It is the music you understand best. It forms a basis for you to understand the music which preceded it. In this way, the story of music in history will be unfolded all the way back to the beginning of Christian music around the time when Christ was born.

"By comparison with the musical accomplishments of early man, the present-day standards of music are impressive indeed. For instance, today, in the United States alone, there are over 1,000 professional or semi-professional symphony orchestras, about 750 opera companies, and in the schools there are approximately 25,000 orchestras and 48,000 bands. One of our largest industries is the production and selling of recorded music. Radios and television sets by the millions transmit music every day. Most school children receive daily music instruction, and now, music is heard even in banks, stores, factories, taxicabs, and buses.

"Another area of music is found in the home and in the church. It is in the home that the mother sings to her baby, and the children hum, whistle, and sing as they play. Hymns of praise to God are heard each Sunday in churches and in Sunday Schools everywhere.

[1] Curt Sachs, *Our Musical Heritage: A Short History of Music 2nd.* © 1955. Prentice-Hall, Inc., Englewood Cliffs, N.J.

"The American poet, Walt Whitman, writes regarding the American musical scene,

I hear America singing, the varied carols I hear, . . .
The delicious singing of the mother, or of the young wife at work,
  or the girl sewing or washing,
Each singing what belongs to him or her and to none else,
The day what belongs to the day—at night the party of young fellows,
  robust, friendly,
Singing with open mouths their strong melodious songs.

"It might be interesting to know how many times each of you heard music yesterday." [Ask those who did to hold up their hands. Call on a few to explain.]

"Also, it will be interesting to know how many minutes or hours it has been since last you heard music." [Ask for hands up of those who recall. Call on some, asking each not only when it was, but to explain the occasion.]

"For the rest of the period, I am going to play a recording for you. It is music of the 20th century. All of you have heard at least part of this music. The performance you are going to hear is played by an orchestra under the direction of Paul Whiteman, with the composer as piano soloist. It was written in 1923 by a twenty-five year old American. The music is the *Rhapsody in Blue;* the composer was George Gershwin. How many of you already know this music? And how many knew the name of its composer?"

[Play *Rhapsody in Blue* by George Gershwin.]

Assignment: Listen to another selection by Gershwin. Write a report comparing it with the *Rhapsody in Blue.*

Lesson Four: The Music of George Gershwin

"The music of George Gershwin is enjoyed by all Americans. Gershwin is America's most popular composer. The mere mention of the titles of some of his works recalls them as favorites: *Rhapsody in Blue;* 'Summertime'; *Of Thee I Sing;* 'Bess, You Is My Woman Now'; 'It Ain't Necessarily So'; 'I Got Rhythm'; *An American in Paris; Porgy and Bess,* etc.

"America knows Gershwin because he wrote as an American about America. The sounds of present-day life abound in his music. Many of these sounds are everyday sounds—snapping fingers while dancing and singing, the song of a man saying, 'I Got Plenty o' Nuttin,' the lament of a wife who is blue, the sound of a jazz pianist, a night club entertainer, or children playing amid noises of traffic.

"Gershwin knew the sounds of America well. He was born and raised in Brooklyn. His first professional music assignment was to play the piano in a music store to demonstrate new popular songs. At the age of nineteen, he wrote a song entitled 'Swanee' which sold over a million copies and over two million records. Contrary to the inability of most great composers to make a good living from the sale of their publications, Gershwin never failed to derive a fine income from music royalties.

"Even after he became established as a famous composer, he continued to study harmony and counterpoint wtih private teachers. His special talent was his ability to create melodies which Americans like to sing. Gershwin also possessed a great gift for hard work. He wrote musical comedies in rapid succession, employing the popular jazz idiom of the day. Starting in 1920, he wrote one or more complete shows each year until his early death due to a brain tumor in 1937. His most ambitious work was his American folk opera, *Porgy and Bess.*"

[Give the class an idea of the plot of *Porgy and Bess,* and play some of the well-known selections from it.]

Assignment: Write a report on *Porgy and Bess* as an example of American music of the twentieth century.

LESSON FIVE: WHAT HAPPENED TO MUSIC IN 1913?

"The answer to the question of what happened to music in 1913 involves the name of a famous composer Igor Stravinsky. This is what happened.

"A ballet company in Paris, France, employed a young Russian composer from St. Petersburg to write original music for a ballet to be scheduled in 1913. The composer's name was Stravinsky. At that time, he was not well known. Young Stravinsky was a person who had been serious about his musical studies. He had worked hard to learn the craftsmanship necessary to write music of a high order. He had studied the music of the great composers. He was, in short, exceedingly well-schooled.

"Among the musical studies of young Stravinsky were the art and science of orchestration. This means knowledge of what instruments make up the orchestra and how they can be used for the best results. This subject he had studied under a famous Russian composer named Rimsky-Korsakov. He had learned to write for the group of orchestral instruments employed by Papa Haydn, the Father of the Symphony. He had learned that Haydn recognized four families of instruments for his orchestra.

The Symphony Orchestra
Established in the Eighteenth Century
By Joseph Haydn

Family of Woodwinds .... Flutes, Oboes, Bassoons
(Made of wood and played by blowing)

Family of Brass .... French Horns and
Trumpets
(Made of brass and played by blowing)

Family of Percussion .... Pair of Kettle Drums
and occasionally other
percussion instruments
(Instruments played by hitting)

Family of Strings .... 1st and 2nd Violins,
Violas, Cellos, Bass
Viols
(Made of wood with strings which are
fingered with the left hand and made
to vibrate by bowing)

[Play all or any part of a Haydn Symphony calling attention to the simplicity of the orchestral sound. The slow movement of the *Surprise Symphony* is a good example of the orchestra described above.]

"Stravinsky was familiar also with the expansion which had taken place in the orchestra since the days of Haydn. For instance, the youthful composer, Mozart, who startled the world even as a boy by his genius for musical accomplishments, had favored and added two new instruments to the orchestra. These newcomers were the clarinet (a woodwind) and the trombone (a brass instrument).

"Well, this process of evolution had continued through the next hundred and twenty-five years. By the time Stravinsky began to compose his ballet music in 1909, he had many new instruments to choose from and many novel ways to write for them. Of particular importance to him as an example of modern orchestration were the Frenchman, Hector Berlioz, the German, Richard Strauss, and his own teacher, the Russian, Rimsky-Korsakov. (See Lessons 9, 10, and 11 of this chapter.)

"What happened? Stravinsky wrote his music not for just sixteen different instrumental parts as did Haydn, but for fifty-one! Furthermore, Stravinsky was able to write in a much more free way for each instrument, and since manufacturers had improved most of them, virtuoso players of each had demonstrated (during the 125 years since Haydn) new ways of obtaining better and more varied effects.

"Here is a comparison of the orchestral instruments found in the symphonic scores of Haydn and Stravinsky:

Haydn Orchestra	*Stravinsky Orchestra*	
2 Flutes	3 Flutes	
	1 Piccolo	
	1 Alto Flute	
2 Oboes	4 Oboes	
	1 English Horn	*Woodwinds*
	1 Small Clarinet	
	3 Clarinets	
	1 Bass Clarinet	
2 Bassoons	4 Bassoons	
	1 Contra Bassoon	
2 French Horns	8 French Horns	
	1 Small Trumpet	
2 Trumpets	4 Trumpets	*Brass*
	3 Trombones	
	2 Tubas	
1 Pair Kettle Drums	8 Percussion Instruments	*Percussion*
2 Violins	2 Violins	
1 Viola	1 Viola	
1 Cello	1 Cello	*Strings*
1 Bass Viol	1 Bass Viol	
16 Different Parts	51 Different Parts	

"What else happened? In addition to the greatly expanded orchestration and the new ways of writing for the instruments, there were three more surprises for the Paris audience on that night in 1913 when Igor Stravinsky startled the world of music with his *Rite of Spring*.

There was a new type of *melody* and a new type of *harmony;* and there were also new and more complicated *rhythms.*

"You will hear the startling result of these elements as we listen now to Stravinsky's history-making composition, *Le Sacre du printemps,* which is the French title for the English translation, the *Rite of Spring.*"

[Play selection from the *Rite of Spring.*]

"Do you like this music? Do you notice ways that this music differs from other music? Are the melodies different? Are they easy to sing and whistle like American folk songs? Is the harmony pleasing like church hymns, or is its effect startling and exciting? Can you understand why this first performance of the *Rite of Spring* was an important step in ushering in modern music? Do you hear any relationship between the sound of the *Rite of Spring* and the sound of the *Rhapsody in Blue?*"

Assignment: Prepare a written report on your impressions of the *Rite of Spring.*

[The *Rite of Spring* score was used in Walt Disney's movie, *Fantasia.* The orchestra for this film was directed by Leopold Stokowski. *The Fire Bird* suite (by Stravinsky) could be used instead of the *Rite of Spring,* although its impact on the development of modern music was not as significant. It was given its premiere three years earlier, in the same city, Paris.]

LESSON SIX: WHAT IS MODERN MUSIC?

"Igor Stravinsky was perhaps the most important composer of the first part of the twentieth century. His music has influenced most other composers from that time till today. Since the *Rite of Spring,* music has not been the same!

"Much of the music since the *Rite of Spring* is referred to as 'modern music' or 'contemporary music.' Here are some of the characteristics of modern music:

1. The sound of the *harmony* used is made up of many different notes; often the effect is strident or disturbing. Usually it is not soothing and smooth sounding, like a church hymn.
2. The *melody* does not sound like the usual melodies that people hum or sing. Large, and even awkward, skips replace smooth progressions.

3. The *rhythm* of the music is often complicated. Sometimes it is the most important element. Because of the prominence which the rhythmic elements have assumed in modern music, the percussion section of the orchestra has taken on a prominent role (i.e., drums of all sorts in addition to tympani, bells, gongs, cymbals, rattles, marimba, xylophone, celeste, etc.).

4. The size of the orchestra has increased, a number of new instruments having been added. The sound is much more intense, loud, and varied.

"Another characteristic (not music, but related to it) is the type of dancing suggested by it.

"The type of dancing suggested by modern music is not traditional ballet. 'Modern dance' goes with 'modern music.' The ballet slippers are discarded; dancers are often barefooted. Gliding steps have been replaced by running, jumping, and walking. Pirouettes (spinning or whirling on the toes) have given way to jumps and leaps. Modern dance is more natural and down to earth than classic ballet, which strives to present the beautiful and the graceful even though detached from the workaday world.

"In order to understand the music of all composers, one must listen to it. One must listen 'with wide-open ears and wide-open mind.'"

"Don't make up your mind immediately that you do or don't like the music. Give the music a chance to speak to you. Music is communication. But all human communication requires at least two persons: the one who is speaking and the one who is listening. If the listener closes his ears and mind, it is impossible for him to receive any message or impression or feeling.

"Have you ever listened to a conversation in a foreign language? If so, your first reaction was probably, 'That doesn't make sense!' Actually, what you should have thought was, 'I don't understand.'

"Music from different countries is not exactly like language from different countries, but at times it may seem that way. In order to understand a foreign language, it is necessary to study it for a long time. But with music, although studying helps in understanding, the real necessity for enjoyment is merely to listen with wide-open ears and wide-open mind. A good rule is to listen to at least two performances of a new piece of music before beginning to form your opinion about it.

"The best way to learn the music of any or all composers is to get a recording of the work you are concerned with. Play it. Listen to it at least two times. If you find interesting sounds in it, if you respond to it in a satisfying way, if you become curious about it, if you find yourself wondering what it means, if you feel that you want to share it with others, then play it some more times. It is like a new friend.

"As you listen to the first, second, or tenth performance of a piece of music, you will help the process of communication, understanding, and enjoyment.

"As an example of learning the music of one of our contemporary or present-day composers, listen to Morton Gould's arrangement of 'When Johnny Comes Marching Home' (*American Salute*). Here is a description of it following the four points of listening which have just been explained.

"1. The harmony of Gould is not as strident as that in the *Rite of Spring*. But it is not hymn-like, either. It reflects a harmonic influence from Stravinsky and other similar composers, but it does not go so far toward the modern sound.

"2. The melody is strong and easy to sing; it is an American folk song known to practically every citizen. Melody is the 'backbone' of this piece. It is heard over and over, with considerable variation of notes, rhythm, harmony and orchestration.

"3. Gould's rhythm is strong and important, but not nearly so complicated as the rhythm found in the *Rite of Spring*.

"4. Gould's orchestration is not as large and varied as Stravinsky's.

"The *dancing style* suggested is not traditional ballet. The prevailing feeling indicates march steps, humorous moods, heavy beats, large strides, and other modern motions.

"It will be noted that Gould does not go as far into the modern style as Stravinsky did some twenty-five years earlier. This is not unusual, since all composers do not *take off* where the other composer *left off!*"

[Again play the recording of Gould's arrangement of "When Johnny Comes Marching Home." His title for it is *American Salute*.]

The four points for listening represent changes in much of the music of the twentieth century when compared with earlier music. Stravinsky alone did not cause all these changes, but his impact on the musical scene carried a large influence toward modern music.

"Many other composers also have contributed their influence to the changes in the way music was composed during the first half of the twentieth century. Among them are found these very prominent men, with diverse national backgrounds:

Béla Bartók (Hungarian)
Sergei Prokofiev (Russian)
Arnold Schoenberg (Austro-American)
Jean Sibelius (Finnish)
Ralph Vaughan Williams (English)
Paul Hindemith (German-American)

"Here is another group of well-known composers, Americans who wrote in the present century and whose music has been given popular support through many performances, particularly in the United States.

Leroy Anderson
Irving Berlin
Ernest Bloch (Swiss-American)
Hoagy Carmichael
Aaron Copland
Norman Dello Joio
Ernst von Dohnanyi (Hungarian-American)
Carlisle Floyd
Rudolf Friml (Czech-American)
Samuel Gardner
George Gershwin
Percy Grainger (Australian-American)
Morton Gould
Charles Griffes
Howard Hanson
Roy Harris
Victor Herbert (Irish-American)
Jerome Kern
Edward MacDowell
Gian-Carlo Menotti (Italian-American)
Walter Piston
Cole Porter
Richard Rodgers
Sigmund Romberg (Hungarian-American)
Roger Sessions

Assignment: Have each member of the class write his own impressions of Gould's *American Salute,* with reference to the four points for listening, plus any other points which occur to him.

LESSON SEVEN: LIGHT OPERA IN THE UNITED STATES

"God gave man a voice. Man has learned to talk and to sing with that voice. He has learned, also, to imitate or supplement his voice with man-made instruments.

"The voice is the most natural musical expression of man. Although instrumental music has risen to a high degree of excellence during the nineteenth and twentieth centuries, vocal music is still primary. This is natural, since the voice is actually a part of man himself. If man were a manufactured instrument such as a violin or a trombone, he would probably respond more to the violin or trombone than to the voice. But he isn't. Man is a voice.

"Historically speaking, the United States never has fully realized the potential of the vocal element in her cultural activities. Other countries have done so, particularly Italy. Through its emphasis an opera, long tradition of *bel canto* (beautiful singing), and the widespread support of the vocal art, Italian vocal performance and opera composition have gained a world-wide reputation of distinction for Italy.

"Other countries have made their places in vocal music history. During the time of Queen Elizabeth, the English school of madrigal singing achieved a degree of perfection never surpassed elsewhere. The Russian Orthodox Church religious choral music of nineteenth- and twentieth-century Russia is another high point in vocal music.

"Although the United States never has realized the full potential of the vocal expression, it has achieved a position of world leadership in light opera, which depends primarily on singing. Light opera is referred to also as musical show, musical comedy, and operetta.

"In the United States during the first part of the twentieth century, serious opera (usually called 'grand opera') was not particularly popular among the masses. Performances were limited to the large cities, with the exception of a repertoire of opera presented by several traveling companies. Few Americans heard more than one or two operas.

"The word *opera* means 'a work' in the Italian language. Since the most successful grand operas have been written by European composers, the languages used have been, almost without exception, European. However, the custom in Europe has been that an Italian opera would be translated into French when sung in France, or into

German when presented in Germany. But in America, this was not the case; German opera produced here was sung in German, French opera in French, and Italian opera in Italian.

"This situation began to change in America with the advent of Victor Herbert, a composer of operetta in English. Herbert was born in Ireland; thus his native tongue was English. When he was in high school, his family moved to Germany. Shortly after his marriage to a Viennese opera star, he moved to America because she was engaged by the Metropolitan Opera Company.

"Victor Herbert tried the grand opera medium only twice. These efforts were unsuccessful, but he attained great renown as a composer of light opera. One after another, the works of Victor Herbert became 'hits' on Broadway—*Babes in Toyland, The Red Mill, Naughty Marietta, Sweethearts,* etc.

"Other nations began looking toward the United States for leadership in the field of operetta. They still do. For after Victor Herbert came these:

Oscar Straus (*The Chocolate Soldier, All Around Love, My Lady's Glove*)
Rudolph Friml (*The Firefly, Rose Marie, Vagabond King,* etc.)
Sigmund Romberg (*Blossom Time, The Student Prince, The New Moon,* etc.)
George Gershwin (*Lady Be Good, Oh Kay, Girl Crazy, Of Thee I Sing, Porgy and Bess,* etc.)
Cole Porter (*Anything Goes, Mexican Hayride, Kiss Me, Kate, Can-Can, Silk Stockings,* etc.)
Richard Rodgers and Oscar Hammerstein II (*Oklahoma, Carousel, South Pacific, The King and I, The Sound of Music,* etc.)

"The partnership of light opera with the ingenuity and resources of Broadway was indeed a fortunate wedding. When you read the list of American operettas, you read a veritable 'Who's Who' of light opera for the world. Although the prestige from this medium does not indicate a standard of culture as serious as that ˙for grand opera, symphony, art song, or chamber music, this attaining of world leadership in light opera is nevertheless a point of national pride and prestige." (See Lesson Seventeen, Chapter Eight.)

Assignment: Select a light opera and write your opinion of the music in one or more of its selections, basing your judgments on the four points for listening, Lesson 6.

LESSON EIGHT: IMPRESSIONISM IN MUSIC

"Almost a hundred years ago, a new movement in art aroused so much support among certain writers, painters, composers, and sculptors that it took on the dimension of a French school of arts. In the beginning, this development was centered almost exclusively in one city of France, Paris. Gathered there, as artists for centuries had been, were those who felt moved to discard the heritage of classic and romantic art. They were searching for something other than the strong, bold lines of the classic concept; they were striving to escape from the intellectual and emotionally dramatic attitudes of the romantic style.

"The new school of thought in the arts may be exemplified by such paintings as "Sunrise—An Impression," by Edouard Manet, and the vague, dreamy, and sensuous pastel-colored works of Pissaro, Degas, and Claude Monet; by the vague symbols and images in the lyric poetry of Mallarmé, Maeterlinck, and Rimbaud; and by the first great piece of impressionism in music, *Prelude to the Afternoon of a Faun,* by Debussy.

"The music of Claude Debussy is impressionism. He, almost alone, is the prophet of this new musical epoch. Like the other impressionistic arts of the last half of the nineteenth century in France (and in other lands somewhat later), the music of Debussy is characterized by the iridescent color of muted strings and brass, the chromatic sound of the harp, the vagueness of sensuous themes devoid of precise meter.

"Impressionism is found in many of Debussy's titles, *Reflections in the Water, The Submerged Cathedral, Images for Piano, Veils, What the West Wind Saw, The Terrace of Audiences of Moonlight,* etc.

"Today, I want you to imagine yourself sitting in a music hall in Paris, France. The date is December 23, 1894. It is 9:30 P.M.

"The large symphony orchestra of ninety players is ready; the conductor mounts the podium. The audience is quiet though concerned. The name of the next number on the program is, *Prélude à l'Après-midi d'un faune (Prelude to the Afternoon of a Faun).*

"In order to help you understand this music, let me give you the dictionary definition of a faun, 'One of a class of rural Italian deities represented as of human shape, with pointed ears, small horns, and sometimes a goat's tail.' Webster does not tell what a faun does. But Debussy does give you his impressions of the afternoon of a faun.

[Play from the recording of *Prelude to the Afternoon of a Faun* by Debussy. Judge by the reaction of the class how much of the record should be heard at this time. If interest in the music lags, try one or two other spots in the record so that a typical reaction to the music can be counted upon. Remind the class to listen with wide-open ears and mind.]

"How do you like it? If this is the first time you have heard music of this kind, your reaction is probably similar to the reaction of that audience of French people back in 1894; for that was the first performance of impressionistic music, and the music you have just heard is the music they heard. Do you have a definite idea of what the music was about? Did it say something definite to you? Or did you feel that it was a dreamy piece of music about something from the world of fantasy, filled with unworldly animals and mysterious incidents? These could not be *seen* clearly, but they could be imagined if you allowed the music to stimulate your 'mind's eye.'

"Let's try a few more measures of the music and just 'let yourself go.' Let the music suggest things to you. In music of this sort, the listener is certainly the most important person—because who knows any better than you do what a faun does on an afternoon?"

[Play some or all of the same record a second time.]

"Now, before discussing impressionistic music any further, I want you to listen to a small work of Debussy's. Since this piece is extremely popular, you may already know its French name and the translation of it."

[Play "Clair de lune" (Light of the Moon) by Debussy.]

"From a scientific viewpoint, the harmony of impressionism can be explained by pointing to overtones 8, 9, 10, 11, and 12. These five notes are each one whole step apart. In other words, there are no half-steps. (See Lesson One of this chapter.) The effect of this 'five-tone harmony' is quite different from the major scale. This can be demonstrated by playing the five-tone scale in sequence and contrasting it with the major or minor scale. The five-tone scale is used in most impressionistic music, because its sound is illusory and without focus.

"A visual explanation of impressionism can be seen and felt by looking at paintings by artists such as Monet, Degas, and Renoir. These men were doing the same thing in painting that Debussy was doing in music. The objects, or subjects, of their paintings were shown only as impressions: hazy, blurred, or frequently distorted, with a certain touch of fantasy. Actual likeness to life was neither sought after nor recorded with any degree of accuracy.

"The viewers of impressionistic paintings or the listeners to impressionistic music were to fill in the gaps in the pictures or the music with ideas and thoughts of their own. The work of art (painting or music) was to serve merely as a suggestion or impression, with a great deal left to the ingenuity and interpretation of the 'looker' or 'listener.'

"The same approach through impressionism came about in the field of writing. One of these poets was named Stéphane Mallarmé. He was a friend of Debussy, and he wrote the poem upon which *Prelude to the Afternoon of a Faun* was based. Another poet friend of Debussy was a Parisian named Paul Verlaine whose poetry inspired Debussy's 'Clair de lune.'

"Debussy's mastery of music, with his devotion to the principles of impressionism, had great influence on other composers at home and abroad. Among these are such important persons as Maurice Ravel and Arthur Honegger of France, Ottorino Respighi of Italy, Isaac Albéniz of Spain, Charles Griffes of the United States, and Frederick Delius of England.

"Impressionistic poetry, like impressionistic music and painting, suggests impressions, establishes moods, is often dreamy, and seems to take place in a sort of twilight zone."

Assignment: Write a paper comparing the sound and ideas found in the music of Debussy with the music of Gershwin, Stravinsky, or Morton Gould.

LESSON NINE: THE ROMANTIC PERIOD AND RICHARD STRAUSS

"The nineteenth century was a golden age for music. The economic life during the first half of the century was a flourishing one for the states of northern Europe which later formed the German Empire. In the 1870's, Bismarck, who became chancellor, formed the German Empire amid prosperity and great interest in the cultural life of the country. The seven fine arts flourished: painting, sculpture, architecture, drama, poetry, dancing, and music.

"Romantic music was largely the product of the late eighteenth and early nineteenth centuries. The musical aspects were, however, only a part of man's reconstruction of European politics and society. The French Revolution eight years before the turn of the century was the first of a number of upheavals in France, Germany, England, and Italy. The importance of the individual as a member of society emerged simultaneously with revolutions through central Europe in 1830, in France and Poland in 1848, in Germany in 1848 and 1851, and in the new French Empire under Napoleon III. The Industrial Revolution was another powerful force for nineteenth-century man. The new condition under which he worked and the new products available to him redirected his efforts.

"In America, the North and South engaged in a War Between the States which sealed the fate of the country as a United States. In subsequent European upheavals, the English and French fought the Crimean War in defense of Turkey against Russia, and the Franco-Prussian War of 1870 united all Germany into one empire under Bismarck. Italy became free in 1871, and the British Empire under Queen Victoria flourished as a colonial power over the face of the globe. All of this stimulated the mind, spirit, and imagination of nineteenth-century man.

"Music naturally reflected the new spirit of these times. Romantic music was popular because it satisfied the new outlook of man in society. Expansion in his physical world stimulated his musical life.

"Romantic music evolved from the music of the Classic period which preceded it, but it was altered and expanded in a number of ways. In Romantic music, *melody* is freer, it skips around more, and it changes according to the mood of the music or the meaning of the words. *Harmony* is complicated, and rich and resonant, but not as complicated as the harmony used by Stravinsky, Prokofiev, Copland and Gould. *Rhythm* is clear cut and strong, but it rarely dominates the other elements. Generally speaking, the elements of music develop from one age to another.

"The next four lessons will deal with the romantic music of the nineteenth century. This span of time was rich in great music. This was the period which produced Mendelssohn, a highly cultured individual, the son of a wealthy Jewish banker, and leader of the Romantic school; the great composer-pianist, Franz Liszt; and Robert Schumann, a highly imaginative composer, influential critic, and forceful writer. This was the era of Chopin, the greatest composer of virtuoso piano music; Berlioz and Rimsky-Korsakov; the French and Russian masters of the art of orchestration—i.e., how to write for the symphony. And this was the day of Wagner, the leading composer of German opera. These and many other musical giants made the romantic period one of tremendous achievement and impact upon the music and musicians which followed.

"Here are several selections typical of the Romantic period of music. Listen to them. As you listen, decide whether the music is formal or informal; conservative or exciting. Is it confined by set patterns of rhythm and harmony and 'well-behaved' melodies or free to follow almost any path or rhythm, harmony, and melody as long as the message is one of beauty and intensity? Do you feel the personality of the composer behind the work? Do you believe the performers are expressing something personal and highly imaginative?"

[Play the Scherzo from *A Midsummer Night's Dream* by Mendelssohn, *The Variations on a Nursery Rhyme* by Dohnanyi, the *Hungarian Rhapsody No. 2* (for piano solo) by Liszt, and *The Revolutionary Etude* (for piano solo) by Chopin.]

"Richard Strauss served as a bridge between the modern music of the twentieth century and the romantic school of the nineteenth century. He employed many principles of the romantic style, but he substituted other principles which later became part and parcel of what is now called 'modern music.' His life of approximately forty years in each century paralleled his influence on both periods.

"Richard Strauss should not be confused with Johann Strauss, who composed so many of the world's favorite Viennese waltzes. Johann, who was not related to Richard, was a popular composer in Vienna before and after the period of the Civil War in America. But Richard was not born until 1864 and lived and composed through both World Wars.

"By the time Richard Strauss began his creative period of music, the romantic period had already reached its full bloom. Strauss was a romanticist in the sense that he employed the dramatic plot for his operas; he wrote free and luscious melodies, and he used his orchestra to create theatrical effects. But he apparently felt the need to add something new.

"He often expanded the harmony toward the modern dissonant trend instead of following the style of the romantic school. Instead of casting his symphonies in the accepted form of four movements, he followed the lead of Franz Liszt by unifying the entire work into a single long movement uninterrupted by any of the usual breaks; he also chose to use a legend or a poem as a subject for his music. This approach was, therefore, a form of 'descriptive music.' (See Chapter Eight, Lesson Eighteen). Usually, Strauss wanted the music to be the most important part of the work, so he merely applied a literary title without giving details of the story. Perhaps he used this plan to help establish the proper mood. Works by Strauss which illustrate this practice are *The Merry Pranks of Till Eulenspiegel, Don Juan, Don Quixote, Death and Transfiguration,* and *A Hero's Life.*

"Richard Strauss wrote for a very large orchestra; a hundred or more players are needed for some of his symphonic poems. With the improved instrument manufacture of the time, Strauss was able to make many additional demands on the orchestral performers."

Assignment: (1) Give the class a project to listen several times to *The Merry Pranks of Till Eulenspiegel,* asking each to write his reaction to the music in relation to the story. (2) Almost all of the compositions of Mendelssohn, Schumann, Liszt, Wagner, Tchaikovsky, and Rimsky-Korsakov are typically romantic in style. Have each member of the class select one of these men's works (several are mentioned earlier in this Lesson). Then have each student listen three or four times to the work he has chosen, and write an opinion describing its meaning to himself.

Lesson Ten: The Romantic Period, Sibelius and Saint-Saëns

"The compositions of Sibelius, Saint-Saëns, Grieg and their predecessors are examples of Romantic music. Although other composers also made important contributions to this phase of the history of music, the selection of these names will serve to represent the many.

"Jean Sibelius was born in Helsinki, Finland, in 1865, the year after Richard Strauss, and he lived eleven years longer, to 1957. Throughout his long and distinguished career as a composer he remained true to the traditions of the romantic school of composition. He also carved a reputation as a staunch nationalist devoted to the character of his native land.

"The music of Sibelius was enthusiastically endorsed by the people of Finland. He wrote on Finnish subjects, treating many themes in the style of his country's folk music, and he was granted a sizable stipend by the government for ten years. His music aroused so much national fervor that, under the Czarist government which controlled Finland at the turn of the century, performance of some of his music was forbidden.

"One of his most popular and stirring works was called *Finlandia*. Though forbidden by the Russian government it became a Finnish national anthem. Other works which remain popular with both Finnish and American audiences are his seven symphonies, *The Swan of Tuonela*, and "Valse Triste."

"A sympathetic understanding between Sibelius, as a cultural representative of his homeland, and the United States developed before World War I. Two months before the outbreak of the War, Sibelius made one of his rare journeys away from Finland. In Connecticut, he conducted the premiere of a symphonic poem commissioned by an American admirer. This affinity grew stronger after World War I, when tiny Finland paid back its war debt to the United States.

"Camille Saint-Saëns' career as a French composer somewhat paralleled that of Sibelius in Finland. Both men lived long lives amid great honors, and both remained true to the romantic tradition. While Sibelius was always a great favorite with the Finns, it remained for the German people to acknowledge the greatness of Saint-Saëns before and more intensely than did his own French countrymen. This was due in part to a Germanic trend in his composition which led him toward a heavy, dramatic treatment of his thematic materials—more like the German music of that day than like the French.

"Saint-Saëns' fame has not lasted as well as his great reputation during his lifetime would indicate. He was an inspired composer, and he had complete command of his craftsmanship, but much of his best work seems to have been surpassed by similar works of other composers. In cases such as this, the work of art which is the best is the one which endures.

"The works which remain in the present-day repertoire (i.e., which are still performed) are some of his concertos for piano and organ; his stylish *Rondo Capriccioso* for violin solo; 'My Heart at Thy Sweet Voice,' from his opera *Samson and Delilah;* and the beautiful little number for solo cello, 'The Swan,' from his descriptive suite, *The Carnival of the Animals*. (See Lesson Eighteen of Chapter Eight.) He remained active as a conductor and pianist almost to the time of his death in 1921."

Assignment: Write a paper on the works of one of these composers. Play the recordings, listening attentively to meaning, mood, and expressive qualities in relationship to the four specific musical characteristics listed in Lesson Six (harmony, rhythm, melody, and orchestration). Also, describe any other distinguishing qualities you discover in the music.

LESSON ELEVEN: THE ROMANTIC PERIOD AND GRIEG, DVOŘÁK, AND TCHAIKOVSKY

"Music always takes on certain international meanings; it speaks to all peoples. The music of the Western World tends to bring its peoples together in that common interests, feelings, and understandings are established. This is illustrated in a personal way when an acquaintance becomes a friend by telling you why he is unhappy or why he is jubilant. When you know what has caused his feelings and what directs his actions, you acquire an understanding of him which usually brings you closer.

"The Norwegian composer Edvard Grieg did much to create an understanding of his country. Most of his music is definitely nationalistic. This is particularly true of his music for *Peer Gynt,* written for performance during a drama with the same title by the prominent Henrik Ibsen, a fellow national.

"Grieg used many themes which he composed in the style of Norwegian folk melodies. A glance at his voluminous output reveals such nationalistic titles as *Norwegian Dances, Two Norwegian Melodies, In the Style of a Folksong, Cowkeeper's Tune, Peasant Dance, Evening in the Mountains, Norwegian March,* and *Six Norwegian Mountain Tunes.*

"The Norwegian Government recognized Grieg's contribution as a 'cultural ambassador' and honored him with an annuity of 1600 crowns from an early age until his death. This enabled him to devote most of his time to composition.

"Most Americans are acquainted with Grieg's first *Peer Gynt Suite* ('Morning,' 'Aase's Death,' 'Anitra's Dance,' and 'In the Hall of the Mountain King'). Many have played or heard his brilliant Concerto in A minor for piano and orchestra. His 'Heart Wounds' and 'The Last Spring' are songs of and from the heart, not easily forgotten. His three very popular sonatas for violin and piano remind listeners of the landscape of his country. When you listen to the music of Grieg, you will find the spirit of romanticism. The melodies, the harmony, and the rhythm all respond to the beauty of the natural world about us; they turn man toward the spiritual and away from prosaic materialism.

"Though not as nationalistic as Sibelius, Antonin Dvořák was a composer who was deeply imbued with the spirit of his homeland, Bohemia. (After World War I, Bohemia became known as Czechoslovakia.) Dvořák freely employed the colorful folktunes of his country in his works. These fill to overflowing the measures of his numerous *Slavonic Dances*. However, he composed his most famous piece, a symphony *From the New World* (Lesson Nineteen, Chapter Eight) while living in America. During his time here he served as director of a music conservatory in New York.

"The music of Dvořák has a universal appeal. His melodies are dynamic and exciting; his harmony sparkles intensely and his rhythmic treatment is often electrifying. The *Carnival Overture* and his symphonies illustrate these characteristics. Other works played frequently in the United States include the *American String Quartet in A Minor,* the short violin solo *Humoresque,* and his large choral work, *Stabat Mater* ('Standing Mother,' referring to Holy Mary at the crucifixion of Christ).

"Piotr Ilyitch Tchaikovsky was a famous Russian composer. Like Rimsky-Korsakov, he was a true romanticist. The Tchaikovsky melody is a trademark; his themes are strong, lyrical, romantic, luscious, and sometimes rather sentimental. (There is a difference between sentiment and sentimental. The former means rich in sentiment, a highly complimentary statement, whereas 'sentimental' is not complimentary, since it implies exaggerated emotion.)

"The music of Tchaikovsky has always been well-received in America. This is true also in Russia; but in Germany, where the public prefers a more virile, vigorous melody, performances of his music are comparatively rare.

"The great output from Tchaikovsky's pen was made possible by a very unusual arrangement. A wealthy widow, Nadezhda von Meck, paid Tchaikovsky a sizable subsidy of 6,000 rubles annually.

This made it possible for him to keep up a steady flow of compositions without troubling about making a living, a matter which is very difficult for any composer.

"A list of his best-known works sounds like a record of American symphony programs: *Symphonies 4, 5,* and *6, The Nutcracker Suite,* Concerto No. 1 in B minor for piano and orchestra, *Romeo and Juliet Overture,* the Violin Concerto in D minor; considerable ballet music, including *Swan Lake* and *The Sleeping Beauty;* not to mention the Andante Cantabile movement from one of his three string quartets.

"In October of 1893, Tchaikovsky had just completed his Sixth Symphony *(Pathétique).* He journeyed to St. Petersburg to conduct the premiere performance. An epidemic of cholera was currently raging in St. Petersburg. In spite of specific warnings, and in spite of the memory of his mother's early death of cholera when he was fourteen, Tchaikovsky carelessly drank unboiled water. It was contaminated, and he fell a victim to the dread disease; he died within a few days.

"Under present-day Communist Russia, his music is widely accepted in official circles. The Soviet government supports an annual Tchaikovsky International Competition, and his home in Klin (not far from Moscow) is a national shrine. It was here that Tchaikovsky composed, simultaneously, his saddest music, Symphony No. 6 *(Pathétique),* and his happiest work, the suite from the ballet *Nutcracker."*

Assignment: Look up the dates for Grieg, Dvořák, and Tchaikovsky. Write an outline of the important historical events which occurred in the United States during the period between the year of the birth of the first of these composers and the death of the last.

LESSON TWELVE: THE ROMANTIC PERIOD AND LISZT, CHOPIN,
AND SCHUMANN

"Liszt, Chopin and Schumann were romantics who wrote for the piano. Each began as a pianist. The temperament of each was attuned to the piano, not to its predecessor the harpsichord. The invention of the piano 100 years before their births made possible not only their successful careers as virtuosos of the keyboard, but also served as a great stimulation to the Romantic period of music itself. The harpsichord belonged to the Classic age as surely as did the piano to the Romantic. It was the sonority, the expanded responsiveness of pedal and key that served as the expressive medium for the emotion, the individuality, and the rhapsody which were Liszt, Chopin, and Schumann.

"Liszt, Chopin, and Schumann were the greatest composers of virtuoso piano music the world has ever known. (A virtuoso is one highly skilled in technique.) They were born within a few months of each other in 1810–1811. The similarity of their artistic interests and the prominence of their genius brought them together as colleagues and, in the case of Liszt and Schumann, made them intimate friends.

"Franz Liszt created a new piano technique. Piano playing, until his time, was attuned to the spirit of the classic style which preceded it. Liszt caught the new spirit of the nineteenth century. He strove to expand the horizon of music in accordance with the broadened outlook of man in a more individualized environment.

"Sometimes great men are remembered by posterity for the little things they did. Liszt is no exception. The composition which practically every person in the Western world knows is his short work. *Liebestraum* (*Dream of Love*). Another very popular number of his is *Rhapsody No. 2*, one of twenty Hungarian rhapsodies. His large works which established his fame as a composer are the two concertos for piano and orchestra, his piano sonata, several symphonies, and the symphonic poem, *Les Préludes*. Liszt is considered the creator of the symphonic poem, which Richard Strauss developed to its present proportions. (See Lesson Nine.)

"Frédéric François Chopin was born near Warsaw in 1810. His father was a teacher and ran a private school. Frédéric was a pupil there. His unusual gift for music and for the piano was discovered at an early age, and he played a concerto in public in his seventh year. By the time he was fifteen he had published a rondo. When he was nineteen he had earned sufficient prestige as a composer and pianist to win high praise in concerts at the German music centers of Leipzig and Dresden, and in Austria and Vienna. Two years later he was received with such acclaim in Paris that he remained there, never to return to Poland.

"Liszt and Schumann praised the genius of Chopin. He was admitted as an equal to the society of the leaders in literature, Balzac and Heine. Schumann, who had established renown as a critic of new music, wrote, 'He [Chopin] is indeed the boldest and proudest poetic spirit of the time.'

"Such an estimate of Chopin's ability also might have been made of Robert Schumann himself, for Schumann was indeed a bold and poetic spirit. His opinions of music were acknowledged to be of highest authority. His creative output, after almost one hundred and fifty years, remains as romantic, poetic, spiritual, and expressive as it was when it was first written. This is a form of immortality earned by few men, and, among composers, earned only by those of his great stature.

"Both Schumann and Chopin lived short lives, but the heritage of their music is long lasting. There is a saying in Latin which brings out this truth, *Ars longa, vita brevis.* Can you translate this into English? Chopin died from tuberculosis at the age of thirty-nine, and Schumann died in his forty-sixth year. Liszt lived many years longer. But the important thing about all of these men is their music. Do you think the world is a better place as a result of Schumann's tender and touching *Traumerei (Dreams)* and Chopin's lyrical *Nocturnes?*

"Chopin was fond of the dance forms. He wrote volumes of mazurkas, polonaises, tarantelles, and waltzes. His largest works were his three immortal sonatas. The slow movement from his Sonata in B♭ minor is his familiar 'Funeral March.' The large works of Schumann are his most distinguished—the Sonatas, the remarkable Concerto in A minor for piano and orchestra, and the Piano Quintet for piano, two violins, viola and cello. All composed symphonies, chamber music and songs.

"When assembled into large-sized books in which one copy of each work is included, the total output of the three amounts to:

> Liszt: 38 Volumes
> Chopin: 26 Volumes
> Schumann: 34 Volumes"

Definitions

Sonata—A large work for one or two instruments (solo or duet). It is usually in four movements. The first movement is always in the Sonata-Allegro form.

Waltz (valse)—A graceful dance in three-four time with a strong beat on the first of the measure.

Polonaise—A stately Polish dance in moderate three-quarter time.

Tarantella—A rapid Italian dance, popularly believed to be a remedy for the bite of the poisonous tarantula spider.

Assignment: Write a review (your opinion) of your favorite piece by Liszt, Chopin or Schumann, after listening to it several times.

LESSON THIRTEEN: THE UNIQUE ROLES OF BRAHMS AND MENDELSSOHN

"In the preceding lessons the scope and intensity of romantic music during the nineteenth century was apparent. Schumann, Chopin, Liszt and Wagner in Germany, Berlioz and Saint-Saëns in France, Dvořák in Bohemia (now Czechoslovakia), Rimsky-Korsakov and Tchaikovsky in Russia—all were widely accepted as leaders of the romantic school of music composition.

"In the midst of this most glorious age of Western music, there appeared a man who was soon to rise to a position challenged by only a few of the greatest. That man was Johannes Brahms, born 'on the other side of the railroad tracks' in Hamburg, Germany. Brahms became so widely recognized during his lifetime that he was frequently referred to as the successor to Beethoven, generally regarded as the greatest composer of all time.

"An interesting observation about Brahms and Beethoven illustrates this point. Beethoven's outstanding contributions to music literature were his nine symphonies. Brahms, on the other hand, failed to write a single symphony during the first forty-two years of his life. While younger composers were writing symphonies during their immature years, Brahms (who had already earned widespread fame) held back. Finally, in 1876 (twenty-one years after he began it), his *Symphony No. 1 in C minor* was given its premier (first) performance. It was heralded by the conductor Hans von Bülow as 'Beethoven's Tenth Symphony!'

"Another epoch-making remark by von Bülow created the most famous group of composers in the world, 'The Three B's,' referring to Bach, Beethoven, and Brahms.

"This symphony of Brahms is indeed a monumental work. Even today, it remains one of the most frequently performed items on the programs of symphony orchestras. It seems to express the strength and yearnings of a people full of energy and ambition, in their struggle to achieve the 'super' in a world of opportunity. But it was cast in the classic form of earlier composers.

"Contrary to the aims of his fellow-composers who were his friends and colleagues, Brahms seemed to have no desire to be an innovator as were the Romanticists of his day. He seemed satisfied with the classic approach, and he strove to master it despite the general belief that the set classic forms had been exhausted by the titanic Beethoven. This makes the position of Brahms unique in the history of music.

"His next three symphonies followed in less than ten years. Occasionally a concession was made to the romantic style—here and there the form was expanded or altered and sometimes his themes burst into great leaps of melody. Elsewhere the harmony became strident and tenuous, but, for the most part, Brahms composed as if he were born in the eighteenth century along with Beethoven and Schubert. However, what Brahms wrote was great and important music. His message appealed to men everywhere. The content was there, and he said it well.

"Another distinctive talent was born a few years earlier in the same city of Hamburg. This child lived on 'the right side of the railroad tracks,' for he was the son of a well-to-do banker, Abraham Mendelssohn. The boy was named Jacob Ludwig Felix Mendelssohn-Bartholdy, paying full homage to the forebears on both sides of his illustrious family. The wealth and attention might have spoiled young Felix. Fortunately, this did not happen; Mendelssohn remained a congenial person and a serious student. He had the best teachers in Hamburg and in Paris, and his work and views were recognized by the important people with whom he had contact. He traveled widely for professional reasons (as composer, conductor, and pianist) and for pleasure. He received widespread honors, recognition, and few disappointments.

"In 1818, at the age of nine, he played in a public concert; two years later he was composing regularly. When he was seventeen, he wrote the dazzling Overture to a *Midsummer Night's Dream,* a work which is still in the standard repertoire of the symphony orchestras of today.

"The earmarks of his music are also the characteristics of his personality and of his success. His personality was delightful. He was cheerful and attractive. He expressed himself well and was popular among the people of his day. For sheer joy and delight, his Scherzos are the best. (A literal translation of scherzo is 'a joke.') His Concerto in E minor for violin and orchestra is today the most widely played concerto for violin. Its melodies are as romantic as springtime.

"Mendelssohn was a voluminous writer. He created profusely in all fields except opera, and he was eagerly looking for a suitable opera libretto when he died at the early age of thirty-eight. During his life-

time, and for years after, Mendelssohn was thought to be the leading
light of the Romantic Period. The passing of a century, however, indicates that his high rank has given way to others—Schumann, Chopin,
Liszt and Wagner."

Assignment: (1) Listen to, and write a comparison of, the *Academic Festival Overture* of Brahms (based on college songs of his
time) and Mendelssohn's Overture to *A Midsummer Night's Dream.*
(2) Describe the "Lullaby" of Brahms and the "Wedding March" of
Mendelssohn according to Four Points for Listening (Lesson Six)
and give your reasons for each of these compositions still remaining so
popular a hundred years after they were written.

Lesson Fourteen: Nineteenth-Century Opera and Wagner

"Opera is a European art. It started there, it has flowered there, and
it remains to this day one of the most popular forms of cultural activity.
The city and village opera houses of Europe still are found across the
continent. By tradition, opera has become a part of the life of most
Europeans—Italians, Germans, Frenchmen, Austrians, Hungarians,
Englishmen, and Scandinavians alike know and love and attend grand
opera. When wars broke out, opera continued even through bombard-
ments from the enemy. When wars ended, the opera houses were
among the first buildings to be rebuilt.

"During the World Wars of the twentieth century opera continued
in production. Opera every night was the rule in the cultural centers of
countries at war. Civilian morale apparently received needed support
from hearing and seeing productions of drama in music. Some famous
opera houses like the Staatsoper (State Opera) of Vienna were de-
stroyed by enemy bombing, but they were among the first buildings to
be rebuilt after the war ended.

"Nineteenth century opera in Europe was in the Grand Tradition. It was conceived as romantic music and presented in the romantic
tradition of the theater. (The romantic tradition is sometimes called
'the grand tradition.') Generally speaking, the romantic school emphasizes love, conflict, adventure, etc., as the principal elements in a work
of literature, drama, or music. This style of creativity differs from the
concept of the earlier classic school, which stressed the *form* as the con-
trolling element in a work of art.

"With few exceptions, opera in Europe was sung in the native language of the country in which it was performed. The action and setting of grand operas were usually familiar to the audience. They knew the plots, customs, settings and even the language employed because the histories and legends of European countries were part of the opera tradition. Wagner based some of his principal operas on the legendary origins of the German people, and Hitler hoped that such music would maintain the morale of the German people and thus help win the war.

"Wagner's life was, in itself, dramatic. Family troubles besieged him from youth until his marriage to his second wife, in 1870. Shortly before this time, King Ludwig of Bavaria requested him to flee to Switzerland because of the constant opposition of his numerous enemies. His lifelong ambition was to build his own theater—the Wagner theater to be ideally suited to the performance of his own works. This was finally realized when the German city of Bayreuth offered him a site as a gift, but this did not end his ever-present problem of finances.

"Wagner changed the form of traditional grand opera; he found a new form, the music drama. By writing his own text (libretto) he overcame the problem of searching for a literary work suited to the intent and temperament of the composer. A long line of music dramas was the result: *Rienzi, The Flying Dutchman*, the *Ring* (four powerful operas planned for production for four consecutive evenings), *Lohengrin, Tannhäuser, The Mastersinger, Tristan and Isolde*, and his last, the monumental *Parsifal*. These works rise as mountains of creativity and strength to stand as symbols of man's determination to make a place for himself in this world despite the many difficulties which deter him."

Assignment: Read the story of a Wagner opera. Listen to a recording of one or more selections from it and turn in a report which tells how the selection fits in to the action of the opera.

Lesson Fifteen: Nineteenth Century Opera in Italy, and France

"While Wagner composed and produced his massive operas in Germany, scores of other opera composers were busy in other European countries. Opera houses were the rule even in the small cities and towns of Europe. Opera in those days served somewhat the same purpose as the movies of today. The principal difference is that singers and instrumentalists in opera were people in the flesh engaged in presenting works of proven artistic value—whereas the movies of the next century are mechanized reproductions of shows of all caliber, including some works of art.

"The names which would have been 'up in lights'—had electric lights been available—were Puccini's *La Bohème,* Verdi's *Aïda,* Bizet's *Carmen,* and Gounod's *Faust.*

"Italy has always served as the comfortable home of opera. The Italian people like to sing, and they are enthusiastic about the singing of others—particularly when it is part of a dramatic show complete with costumes, scenery, orchestra, and sometimes ballet. Giacomo Puccini and Guiseppe Verdi together are largely responsible for most of the Italian operas. They wrote the Italian operas which have become standard in that country—with the exception of the very popular *I Pagliacci* of Ruggiero Leoncavallo. (Puccini is best known for *La Bohème, La Tosca* and *Madame Butterfly,* and Verdi for *Rigoletto, La Traviata, Aïda, Otello,* and *Falstaff*).

"Georges Bizet and Charles Gounod were natives of France. Bizet composed the most widely performed opera of all, *Carmen.* It is a story of intrigue and love (Lesson Sixteen, Chapter Eight). Bizet wrote many other operas, *Carmen* remains his only hit.

"Charles Gounod was born in 1838, twenty years earlier than Bizet. He, too, wrote a number of operas which enjoyed a certain amount of popularity at first but have since been dropped, but like Bizet, Gounod produced one tremendous hit. It was *Faust,* the story of Dr. Faust, who gave the devil (Mephistopheles) his soul in exchange for the love of the beautiful Marguerite. The libretto was taken from the masterwork of Germany's leading author and philosopher, Wolfgang Goethe."

Assignment: Read carefully a synopsis of an opera composed by one of the men discussed in this lesson. Then listen to as much as possible of the music of this opera. Try to procure a recording in English, but, if this is not available, use a foreign language recording. A libretto which has a translation into English should eliminate difficulties in understanding the plot and feeling of the work.

LESSON SIXTEEN: THE ROMANTIC-CLASSIC TRANSITION, BEETHOVEN
AND SCHUBERT

"Styles in music are somewhat like styles in architecture; the changes that take place occur gradually. The Gothic cathedral is an example of a style of architecture which developed over hundreds of years. It frequently took fifty years or more to build one.

"When the style of composing changed from the classic tradition to the romantic, this, too, was a long and gradual process. Romantic elements appeared during the decades which came before the final turning point. It is generally accepted that the transition from the classic to the romantic took place from about 1800 to 1820. At that time, Beethoven and Schubert were influencing the trend in composition through their freer and more individualized approach and the emotional intensity of their expression. Although both belonged to the classic period, their genius knew no bounds.

"Ludwig von Beethoven was born in 1770 in Bonn, Germany (now the capitol of West Germany). He was a victim of bad health leading to total deafness (by 1820), a lover of independence and freedom, a possessor of deep emotion, painstaking in craftsmanship, and endlessly devoted to the art of music.

"He died in the spring of 1827, but not until he had heard the harmonies, rhythms, and melodies of ages beyond his own. The works of his third period were composed with the hearing of the inner ear only. Though deaf, he heard better than any other living person. The third period includes music of the future—his 9th Symphony, five of his 38 piano Sonatas (Op. 101, 106, 109, 110, 111), the *Missa Solemnis* (*Solemn Mass*) and his last six monumental string quartets—all works which stretched the established classical boundaries beyond the point of no return.

"Franz Schubert was born of lowly ancestry three years before the advent of the nineteenth century. He was jovial and filled with the spirit of camaraderie for his close friends—musicians, artists, and writers. He never achieved any degree of polish or poise for other social occasions. The young women who attracted his admiration thought of him only as a friend.

"His life was composition. He began serious writing at fourteen years of age, wrote his first symphony at sixteen and a Mass at seventeen. One of his masterpieces (after four revisions) 'Erlkönig' (Erl King) was completed in the same year. A year later in 1815 (the year Napoleon 'met his Waterloo') Schubert triumphed with the creation of 144 songs.

"Schubert taught elementary school for three years. His 'schooling' as a composer was meager, but his talent was tremendous. He simply poured out music. Ninety-three of his 634 songs were written to poems by the great German poet, Goethe.

"Schubert died from an attack of typhus before his 31st birthday. His compositions were scattered everywhere. About 70 years later, manuscripts of a hundred of his songs were located, and on the shelf of his home was found the score of his masterpiece, the *Symphony in B minor,* 'the Unfinished.' Only the first two movements were complete, and it was never performed during his lifetime. As the creator of the modern German *lied* (song), Schubert pushed far beyond the traditional way of writing. The spirit of Romanticism showed through much of his music. (See Lesson Fifteen of Chapter Eight.)

"Beethoven and Schubert ushered in the new era, the Romantic Period of music composition, a fertile field for the inspiration of the following age. Beethoven, the creator, was the prophet of great music."

Assignment

1. Play an early work of Beethoven: the "Minuet in G," the *Military Marches,* the twelve *Contretänze* (*Country Dances*), the two *Romances for Violin and Orchestra,* or the First Symphony.

2. Contrast the music listed above with that from his third period. Write a description of the differences, keeping in mind the harmonic, rhythmic, and melodic development and the expanded intensity of expression, use of instruments and meaning in terms of the listener.

3. For a better understanding of some of Beethoven's masterpieces, listen to *Symphonies No. 3, 5,* and 7 and the *Moonlight Sonata,* Op. 27, No. 2 and the *Appassionata Sonata,* Op. 57.

4. Listen to Schubert's *Unfinished Symphony* (in B minor) and his song 'Erlkönig.' Write a commentary on elements of Romanticism apparent in these works. (See item 2 above.)

LESSON SEVENTEEN: THE CLASSIC STYLE (MOZART AND HAYDN)

"Although the classic style, the style of symmetry and balance, can be found in all the arts at various times, it is characteristic of eighteenth century music.

The composers of the century succeeded in creating much of the world's best music with the beautiful but simple harmonies of the classic period, with its positive, virile rhythms, its melodious tunes, and its available instrumental resources.

"Among the finest composers of this period were Wolfgang Mozart and Joseph Haydn.

"Mozart was probably the most musically talented child in the history of the world. He began composing at the age of four. At six, he went on his first concert tour. At fourteen, he was recognized as a conductor, composer, harpsichordist, violinist and a 'wunderkind.'

"The German word 'wunderkind' sounds like the English words, 'wonder kid,' and that is what it means. With such great talent, Mozart learned at an unbelievable speed. His production of a tremendous quantity of music was exceeded only by its quality: 49 symphonies, 46 concertos, 42 violin and piano sonatas, 15 masses, 20 operas, and countless other compositions—all written within a short life-span of fewer than 36 years. All of his compositions are available in print today. They are found together in 46 volumes averaging about 200 pages each.

"Another unique fact about Mozart was his personal acquaintance with kings, queens, and other members of the aristocracy. These people who were accustomed to supporting musicians, writers, and artists, but for one reason or another, he failed to profit from the offers. He remained poor most of his life. There seemed to be a strong will in Mozart which kept him from accepting aid which might control his spirit.

"He and his family suffered from poor health; never did they have enough money to maintain an adequate standard of living. Mozart became discouraged, but he continued to compose. When his sadness was at its height, he retreated alone to a little house in the hills around Vienna. Despondent and all but completely forgotten, he worked in solitude. After a few weeks, he completed the world's happiest opera, *The Magic Flute*. He wrote only one more composition, the *Requiem* (Mass for the Dead). A few weeks later, he died so poor that he was buried in an unmarked pauper's grave.

"In contrast to Mozart's bad fortunes, another great composer and friend lived a long life of financial security, happiness, and good fortune. He was Joseph Haydn. Haydn earned the titles 'Father of the Symphony' and 'Father of the String Quartet' because he did more than any other person to establish the symphony orchestra, the symphony as a composition, and the string quartet in their present form. (See Lessons Four and Twenty of Chapter Eight.)"

Definitions

The Seven Fine Arts: architecture, painting, sculpture, poetry, drama, dancing, music.

Assignment

1. Listen to *Eine Kleine Nachtmusik* (*A Little Night Music*), by Mozart, as an example of classic writing for the string quartet (first and second violins, viola and cello).

2. Listen to one of the symphonies of Mozart—the invigorating Haffner *Symphony in D major,* or his masterpieces, the Jupiter *Symphony in C major,* or the *G minor Symphony.*

3. Listen to one of the Haydn symphonies, noting the similarity of style to that of Mozart. (The *Surprise Symphony* is a representative work and has a humorous surprise in the slow movement.)

4. Write a report of your reaction to the music.

Lesson Eighteen: The Classic Style (Oratorio of Handel and Bach)

"The life of eighteenth century man centered around the church. Great cathedrals, larger than those of today, were dedicated to the glory of God. Choir schools for young boys and men were established to produce the best music for the services. The position of 'Kapellmeister' (chapel or choir master) was sought after by the best organists of the day. Little wonder that the oratorio flourished, since it is an extended choral work composed to a text from the Holy Bible. The two finest writers of oratorio were Bach and Handel. To the basic classic style, they added ornamentation and embellishments.

"George Handel's most widely known composition is his oratorio, the *Messiah.* Today, after two and a half centuries, Christmas would not be complete without hearing a performance of this powerful religious music.

"Johann Sebastian Bach was born in the same year as Handel, 1685. His greatest works were also oratorios, the *Passion of Christ According to the Gospel of St. Luke, St. Matthew,* and *St. John.* Other monumental compositions were his masses and church cantatas. This music reaches the most lofty aspirations of religious man.

"Bach seemed to do for music what Luther did for the church. Both were completely dedicated souls. Each strove to find the truth according to the strong earthy convictions of the German people. Bach's dedication to the church was through church music. So powerful and important is Bach's religious music that, by comparison, his personal life seems unimportant. He was an outstanding organist, he composed much of the music for his weekly Sunday services at the Saint Thomaskirche in Leipzig, he taught music, and he was the father of twenty-one children."

[Play portions of the *Messiah* by Handel and excerpts from the Mass in B minor or one of the other Passion oratorios by Bach.]

Assignment: Ask each student to copy the text of one portion of the music heard in class, and to comment on the effect of this text when set to music by Bach or Handel.

LESSON NINETEEN: THE PRE-BACH PERIOD

"Bach was such a monumental figure in the world of music that the period previous to his birth is often referred to as the 'Pre-Bach Period.' However, this does not indicate that the Pre-Bach Period was unimportant. Bach would have accomplished much less, had he not had the good fortune to be born after such masters as Ockeghem, Orlandus Lassus, and the Italian masters, Palestrina, Scarlatti, Corelli, and Vivaldi.

"From about 800 A.D. to the middle of the eighteenth century (Bach's death in 1750), the art of counterpoint flourished. Counterpoint is polyphonic writing, because *poly* in Greek means *many* and *phone* is *sound*. Counterpoint, or polyphony, is the art of combining melodies. One melody is heard against another (point against point). (See Lessons Five and Six of Chapter Eight.)

"The remarkable quality of counterpoint is its reliance on tunes or melodies as the basis of musical expression. A purely contrapuntal composition is the result of melodies woven together like the colored threads in a tapestry. People respond to counterpoint because everybody likes a tune. When a composer has mastered the art of counterpoint, he can write music consisting of a number of tunes to be played or sung simultaneously. The experienced listener will receive intense satisfaction from such luxury of melody.

"The contrapuntal concept of music is, in the opinion of many musicians, the most rewarding. Song is the natural musical expression of man. Counterpoint is the fullest utilization of song; therefore, it should be pointed out that counterpoint represents the most complete medium of man's musical expression. But, counterpoint demands concentration. Counterpoint requires musical talent from both the performer and the listener.

"Counterpoint differs from the so-called 'popular tunes from Tin-Pan Alley' which usually consist of 'catchy' rhythms and melodies repeated over and over with a monotonous chordal accompaniment. This type of music requires little concentration on the part of the listener. Counterpoint represents a long-term investment. It may not appeal to you on first hearing, but the beauty of well-written counterpoint becomes apparent with subsequent performances. As one experienced musician put it, 'Every time you hear it, you will hear something new.'

"The purest form of counterpoint is to be found in the writing of Palestrina, the greatest composer of Catholic Church music. He composed 93 Masses for the Catholic Church of the sixteenth century. His exalted music still embodies the highest musical meaning of the church. It is performed by voices only because instruments were not allowed to participate in the church service."

[Play one or more of the five sections from the *Mass for Pope Marcellus,* by Palestrina. At times there are seven different voice parts. Then play it a second and third time, till the class becomes more familiar with it. As an example of secular (non-church) counterpoint, play one of the concertos of Vivaldi; then repeat it for a second and third time. For other examples of counterpoint see Lesson Six of Chapter Eight.]

Assignment: Have each member of the class record changes that took place in his reaction to repeated performances of contrapuntal music.

LESSON TWENTY: EARLY CHRISTIAN AND ANCIENT GREEK MUSIC

"Lessons One through Nineteen contain an outline of musical history. The composer of today learns from the composer of yesterday. Thus the Americans, Gershwin, Gould, Copland, and MacDowell, profited from the example of Debussy, Strauss, and Brahms who learned from the Romanticists, Liszt, Chopin, Mendelssohn, and Schumann. In turn they were inspired by the Classic masters, Beethoven, Schubert, Mozart, and Haydn; these latter could have never created their everlasting works of art without the knowledge of the great contrapuntalists, Bach, Handel, Vivaldi, and Palestrina. The music of today seems only a few steps away from ancient music.

"The art of counterpoint flourished from the ninth century A.D. Little did the Christians of that century realize that the adding of a second melody (an interval of a fifth above or a fourth below) was a giant step forward from the reverent single melody of the Gregorian chant and would lead eventually to counterpoint. Between this first example of counterpoint and the music of primitive man are the Roman and the Greek eras. The Roman period preceded the general acceptance of Christianity by 500 years. The Age of Greece began another 500 years earlier.

"Here are steps in the history of music which will take us back to that earliest known poet-musician, Homer.

"In the sixth century A.D., St. Gregory, Pope of Rome, sponsored the establishment of music for the Universal Catholic Church. Up to this time the single melody chant was slow and labored. Pope Gregory's music emerged as Gregorian chant, wonderfully wrought from the meaning of the sacred word. Each syllable possessed its individual tone. The key of the entire chant was based on eight scale-like modes of ancient origins. The Gregorian chant still remains the official music of the Catholic Church. Derivations of it are found in other present-day Protestant churches and known as plainsong, plainchant, or Anglican chant."

[Have the class sing and listen to Gregorian and Anglican chant.]

"The fourth century marked the triumph of Christianity in the Roman Empire. Persecution of the followers of Christ ceased, and Christianity was legalized under Constantine. These events marked the formation of a new government, the Holy Roman Empire. Coincidental with these dramatic events, St. Ambrose, Bishop of Milan, composed and introduced Christian hymns into the church service. Before this time, the music of Christendom reflected the agonies of the catacombs where the faithful were forced to flee from persecution by the Romans. The early chants were settings of the Psalms of David, but they were limited in musical character and possessed no definite feeling of key.

"Before the Christian era for a period of approximately two centuries (beginning about 500 years before Christ), the glory of ancient Greece shone like a light over the world. Athens, the capitol of the Greek republic, prospered as did her great philosophers, Socrates, Plato, and Aristotle. During this Golden Age of Greece, music was highly developed and widely performed. Its theoretical phases had been formulated by the philosopher-scientist Pythagoras. Every freeman of Ancient Greece was expected to study music and sing the epic songs of the land as he accompanied himself on the lyre.

"Nine hundred years before the birth of Christ, lived the first great Greek poet and musician. Today, he is referred to simply as Homer. His two epic poems are the *Iliad* and the *Odyssey*. Homer might be considered the first professional musician in the history of the world, since he sang his poems to the accompaniment of his lyre at banquets and civic events. He also participated in national contests. He toured and gave recitals in crowded arenas. Homer's writings are still read and studied all over the Western world, but his music has been lost. Only eleven fragments of Greek music have been preserved either on stone or other hard material. The curtain of darkness which has separated present day man from the music of his ancient and primitive ancestors has never been completely opened."

Assignment: Hand in your notebook. For a term project make a chart showing the chronological development of music from the present day back to the earliest period of primitive man. Write in the representative names studied in this course. Add other composers, whose contribution to music history was significant.

CHAPTER TEN

RESPONSIBILITIES OF THE TEACHER

There are many phases of general music teaching at the junior high level which, though of paramount importance to the success of the total music program, do not merit individually an entire chapter of discussion. It appears a desirable procedure to isolate this information from direct identification with any other specific phase of the music program.

Lesson Planning

USE OF MUSIC LESSON TIME

The continuity of an organized general music or school chorus program is contingent on careful lesson planning. Work to be covered by the chorus during any week should be planned not later than the preceding weekend. The director needs an approximate time breakdown as a guide for every lesson, but it must be sufficiently flexible to permit sectional extension or contraction in accordance with class progress toward the desired lesson objective. At no point in any lesson will the competent choral teacher experience a moment's hesitation as to what comes next.

A sample time breakdown for a junior high school chorus, meeting three or five periods a week, might be:

10 A.M.	Roll call
10:05	Warming up with a song already learned. Stimulate the chorus to a fine effort, do not tolerate casual singing.
10:10	Music reading. Start with review, and proceed quickly to instruction of the new material. Keep a running log in order to assure cumulative continuity.
10:20	Transfer music reading activity to learning new music, using a simple well-known song or an exercise. The teacher should be completely familiar with new selection.
10:30	Drill for tone quality, illustrate by means of fine choral recordings.
10:35	Work on a number already partly rehearsed, with a view to eliminating errors and gaining a more thorough grasp of notation, blend, and general import.
10:45	Refinement of a number already learned, diction, interpretation, phrasing, etc.
10:55	Progress appraisal given the chorus by the teacher and dismissal.

The above is not a stereotyped time breakdown for every chorus meeting, but it will serve as a guide for apportioning blocks of time for whatever specific activity is proposed for the lesson. On occasion it might be desirable to use the entire lesson period for refining the performance of several numbers for use at a coming performance. In this event the time breakdown should list songs to be rehearsed and the order of their appearance during rehearsal. However, even in a lesson of this sort some music reading activity should take place in accordance with the dictates of the cumulative learning program. Use of a system of lesson plans, with accompanying progress logs, will assure the choral director that at concert time he will not be unprepared. The same system assures the general music teacher of cumulative continuity of the entire program.

The total program presented in this volume represents an ultimate ideal which under present conditions, i.e., insufficient schedule time, may not be fully reached. According to schedule time at his disposal the general music teacher should decide which of the phases of the total program he will use; after reaching this decision he should not change the pattern of instruction for the remainder of the semester. Certain basic phases which should be included: song singing, music reading, ear training, and instruction in such fundamentals of music theory as are requisite to understanding the symbols appearing on a one-line vocal score. Music reading is necessary in every lesson, but the teacher may wish to alternate the other phases in the class schedule.

Therefore the sample lesson plan presented below is a time breakdown for a general music class scheduled for one period of music per week. The only difference between a one-semester or two-semester program will be that the students on the latter schedule cover about twice as much material as do those limited to one semester participation.

10 A.M.	Roll call
10:05	Warm-up using song previously learned, preferably a lively tune.
10:10	Music reading
10:15	Ear training
10:20	Introduction of new song or new section of a song, or work on a song not yet thoroughly learned.
10:40	Perfection and refinement of specific choral repertoire items.
10:55	Evaluation and dismissal.

The evaluation is an estimate of progress achieved during the lesson, addressed to the class by the teacher. Wherever possible this should be favorable, communicated with an air of satisfaction and concluding with remarks which indicate pleasurable anticipation of the next meeting. A little praise goes a long way in promoting willing, cooperative effort at the junior high school level.

A schedule permitting two general music periods per week is highly desirable and worth pressing for with the school principal, for then ear training may alternate with listening, and theory fundamentals may alternate with history. If this is possible the time allotment for listening will be longer and might well be taken from the last portion of the period. Undoubtedly the music teacher's special interests will govern the balance of the lesson plan.

The practice of consistently evolving lesson plans gives direction to the entire general music program, contributes to cumulative continuity, and makes it possible to maintain a class progress log; students, sensing orderliness of presentation, acquire a more responsive attitude. The lesson plan in itself is futile, however, unless it contains the ingredients to promote musical growth which will lead to music literacy and understanding.

PUBLIC PERFORMANCE AND ASSEMBLIES

At various times during the course of the school year it is wise to find performing outlets for both school chorus and general music classes. There is much more zest in a singing lesson or choral rehearsal if the singers know their achievement will be displayed before an audience. This is not a trait peculiar only to junior high personnel, it is common to all performing groups at any level.

The school chorus should be involved in at least two major ventures during the year, a Christmas concert and a Spring concert, with additional appearances at PTA meetings, one or two service club meetings, and occasional church affairs. Radio and television provide other useful performance outlets. In some areas there is also the district or county junior high choral festival.

General music class students also need the stimulation of one or two performing outlets; this need is well-satisfied by singing at school open assemblies, or maybe by combining two or more classes for a small section of the Spring concert.

To ensure well-balanced choral programs at major performances a tentative repertoire should be selected well before the school year opens and a provisional rehearsal schedule drafted. Selected repertoire numbers can be injected into the schedule in such a manner that there is constant variety of style in every rehearsal. Stress is constantly being laid on planning. Pre-planning for every activity is one of the secrets of a successful music program.

SAMPLE CHORAL REPERTOIRE FOR FIRST YEAR

A sample repertoire schedule for junior high school chorus appears herewith. Items referred to in this schedule are selected from four octavo collections, *Tunetime for Teentime*,[1] *Accent on Singing*,[2] *Sing*

[1] Irvin Cooper, *Tunetime for Teentime* (New York: Carl Fischer, Inc., 1952).
[2] _____, *Accent on Singing* (New York: Hansen Music Co., 1954).

One, Sing All,[1] and *Yuletime for Teentime.*[2] Prefixes refer to "easy," "moderately difficult," "difficult."

E	Jacob's Ladder	
E	The Old Gray Mare	
E	Aunt Dinah's Quilting Party	
E	The Ash Grove	
E	Were You There?	
E	Alouette	
Md	Beautiful Savior	*Tunetime for Teentime*
E	Clementine	
E	How Can I Leave Thee?	
E	Silent Night	
Md	Baby Jesus Soundly Slept	
Md	Veni, Veni, Emmanuel	
Md	The First Noel	
E	Lully Thou Little Tiny Child	
E	Joy to the World	*Yuletime for Teentime*
Md	Bring a Torch Jeanette, Isabella	
Md	Jingle Bells	
E	Campus Serenade	
D	Crawdad Song	*Accent on Singing*
Md	Song for America	
Md	Lonesome Valley	
E	Polly Wolly Doodle	*Tunetime for Teentime*
D	Sands of Dee	
E	A Capital Ship	
D	Now Thank We All Our God	*Sing One, Sing All*
Md	Michael Finnigan	
D	Battle Hymn of the Republic	

A more complete list of other choral materials commensurate with vocal limitations of junior high voices will be found in Appendix A. One of the most serious factors delaying development of junior high choral music is the sparse amount of literature available, singable by groups which include boys with changing voices.

To return to the sample repertoire schedule. The selection of songs presented in the above schedule has been made according to three criteria, (1) progressive difficulty of learning, (2) variety of style to retain rehearsal interest, (3) period of the school year during which

---

[1] Irvin Cooper, *Sing One, Sing All* (New York: Bourne Co., 1955).
[2] _____, *Yuletime for Teentime* (New York: Carl Fischer, Inc., 1954).

songs are likely to be rehearsed. Criteria one and two are fairly obvious to interpret; criterion three might bear a little clarification.

At the beginning of the school year the chorus will have regressed in choral accomplishment, and will have acquired at least one-third new grade seven members. The grade nine chorus will have new students. A period of rehearsing easy-to-learn music is recommended, not only to build a feeling of confidence and achievement, but to provide a small repertoire of songs, to which the chorus may revert as a change of pace from learning more difficult numbers.

By the time the first group of numbers has been learned, the Christmas season will be approaching. Selecting music appropriate for Christmas requires some thought and care, inasmuch as this is a *one performance* preparation; the same music cannot be performed again until the following Christmas. In view of this it behooves the choral director to select music which is easy to learn, yet which is effective chorally and of sound musical value. Incidentally, it is a very worthwhile experience for the school chorus to share its Christmas music with inmates of hospitals and homes for the aged. In Southern states where climate is favorable, carolling is an excellent, enjoyable performing outlet.

Following Christmas vacation the choral repertoire schedule changes to meet the serious business of the school Spring concert, and perhaps county or district festivals. Music proposed for this period is of a more challenging nature, on the assumption that the choral ability of the students has developed considerably as a result of Fall and pre-Christmas training. Proceeding to a more involved type of music learning further assumes the chorus has been exposed to regular and cumulative music reading experiences.

Choral festivals at the junior high level can often provide very rewarding experiences for the singers; they can result also in frustrating experiences, depending on the type of festival in which they participate.

FAINTING

A director can be reasonably certain that if the youngsters stand for any length of time during the course of a public performance someone is going to faint. Instruct the group on this matter, that if anyone suspects the inclination to faint or otherwise be sick he should ask his neighbor to help him off stage immediately. Once the spell has passed he should return to the group.

School Assemblies

Assemblies are excellent outlets for general music performance. The general music class develops much more interest and enthusiasm in its work if there is to be a public performance of it. Although singing is not the sole objective, it is nevertheless a major activity, and the standard of performance, while not being at the level of the school chorus, should be of such excellence that students can take pride in their choral achievements. The music teacher is advised to find several occasions during the school year when a very short interlude of choral music performed by a general music class, or a combination of two such classes, will be welcomed by the teacher in charge of assembly programs.

Selection of music for these occasions would be made from the repertoire being studied as a regular part of the general music program. Choice must be made from numbers which the class performs very well, leaving no chance for even the slightest embarrassing moment. In schools where there are several general music classes, healthy rivalry develops between groups in producing a superior performance.

A further outlet for exceptionally good classes is the PTA meeting at which the teacher might offer a brief discussion on the composition of his group, stressing the part which boys play in creating the *new* sound. Parents react with great interest to a clinic type of performance in which the teacher reenacts the procedures followed in Lesson One of the *Singing Program*, culminating with a review of the method used in teaching "Santa Lucia."

Discipline

One of the prime worries of the college music education major is whether or not he will be able to maintain class discipline when he takes his first job in junior high school. There should be little difficulty, however, if the teacher is interested in the subject, is assertative, and is able to generate and retain class interest.

Character Traits of Junior High Students

What are some of these character traits which the music teacher might use to good advantage? Desire to belong to a peer group is one. Fine achievement in musical performance is not the sole prerogative of the bright student. A slow learner in other subjects may quite reasonably prove to be a stalwart in chorus or general music singing, and many a tough student, frustrated and hostile as a result of inability to keep pace with friends in academic disciplines, becomes docile and cooperative in a good singing group, where he is sometimes not only an equal, but superior to his classmates in his contribution to the group achievement. Another heart warming character trait of junior high youngsters is affection and loyalty lavished on the music teacher who can lead them to a group achievement.

Desire for strong inspiring leadership, while not exactly in the category of a character trait, nevertheless is an attribute on which the smart teacher will capitalize in building a tradition for good discipline in music activities. Instruction should be given in terms of clear, concise information with an aura of firm authority. Such approaches as "how do you think we should sing this song?" are a clear invitation to trouble. It leaves the way open for any blythe spirit to inject his particular brand of adolescent humor into the situation, and the teacher has no redress. He has invited open opinion and has got it. The teacher is the only person in the room with the background to determine ways and means of procuring a sensitive interpretation for the song under rehearsal.

The best way to ensure good discipline is to concentrate on it the very first lesson, aggressively yet genially. Do not meet your first class in a spirit of love and sunshine. This may be and often is effective at the elementary school level, but is fatal at the junior high level. Commence your year's teaching with a tight, aggressive, but benign control, and as soon as you sense a cooperative response ease up in your control and adopt a more relaxed attitude. Students will know you are capable of control, and if occasion arises when it is necessary to tighten the reins, it will be a simple matter to do so.

A companionable let's-love-music-together approach in the early part of the semester is an ideal concept, but the youngsters do not know this. Awed by the new experience of being freshmen in secondary school, grade seven youngsters are unsure as to the consequence of being discovered in overt acts, and they feel their way cautiously for a few days. This might lull the teacher into a false sense of security. Then one day love and sunshine are of little avail and a firm hand and some scolding are completely out of character with the image the teacher has created. It sometimes even amuses a group to witness the teacher's desperate attempts to change the image in a matter of a few moments. This can be avoided if a policy of tight control is exercised in the first lesson.

Here is a proposed opening address to a new class. It must be delivered with authority.

Teacher: "Some very interesting and exciting things will happen in this room this year, and *you* will make them happen. However, there are one or two points to make quite clear concerning fine achievement in any group. The football team, basketball team, or baseball team have each their head coach whose word is law, or you do not play anymore. I am your singing coach, and I work on the same idea. We have a great deal of work to do this first lesson, work which I know you will like, but I must first give you a few instructions which I expect to be observed by everyone in the class.

"First, a sharp clap of my hands means I expect instant attention, no matter what you are doing. Let us try this quickly. You may start talking with each other, but when I clap my hands once there must be instant silence."

Students talk for a few seconds, then teacher claps his hands with a noisy slap.

"Not good enough, try again." (Procedure is repeated) "Much better, I do not expect complete silence throughout an entire lesson, there will be talking opportunities, but the moment I clap my hands *there must be complete silence."*

"Next rule, there will be no calling out. Anyone wishing to say something to me will raise his hand and permission will be given to speak aloud. Another rule, no one approaches my desk to speak to me or for any other reason, without my invitation. These are all the rules you need just now. During the first few days you will probably forget, but make no mistake, I will remind you."

The teacher should immediately proceed to a very brief discussion of the vocal characteristics of junior high students, administer the voice classification routine, regroup the students as sopranos, cambiate, baritones, then teach "Santa Lucia" in four parts as presented in Chapter Three (the first song).

Eyebrows may be raised questioningly as to the appropriateness of the procedure proposed above in terms of the intimate teacher-pupil relationship advocated by many authorities. But the system works, and the youngsters, sensing a leader who will stand no nonsense, fall into line and respond with confidence and enthusiasm. Always be consistent in enforcing the rules. Do not relax one day and bear down the next. Treat every student equally, favoring none more than others.

Unfavorable discipline situations are sometimes originated unwittingly by the teacher, consequently a few *don'ts* are offered for the new teacher.

1. *Don't* ask a general question of the class which evokes mass vocal response. "What song would you like to sing?" "Would you like to listen to a phonograph recording?"

2. *Don't* ask a student *if* he will do something for you, such as cleaning the chalkboard. Instruct him to do it, followed by the word please.

3. *Don't* turn your back on the class for more than a few seconds.

4. *Don't* ever promise retribution you are unable, or not disposed, to carry through.

5. *Don't* ever get angry or show temper. If punishment is unavoidable, exact it in a regretful manner.

6. *Don't* send a nonconforming student to the principal's office for disciplinary treatment. The moment you do this you have admitted personal defeat, a fact known to the class, and your prestige is lowered.

7. *Don't* listen to tales or gossip about other members of your chorus or class, or about other members of the faculty.

8. *Don't* make any special student friends or try to be casual with your class or chorus. Being a good fellow and one of the gang sometimes gets you into a situation in which it is impossible to assert yourself with any authority.

9. *Don't* allow your class to dismiss noisily. Let the students move out one line at a time.

Following a profusion of negatives, surely there are some positive actions to recommend in the matter of ensuring good discipline. To offset the list of *don'ts* here is a parallel list of *do's*.

1. Always exude enthusiasm and pleasure during your teaching. This is important; even in your sterner moments a smile should never be far away.

2. Know your work thoroughly, especially a new song, and begin every lesson with a clear lesson plan in mind.

3. Be quick to recognize and praise fine effort. Be proud of your singers, and tell them so.

4. Lighten the lesson occasionally with appropriate humor. Expect and ignore raucous response, using a double clap to restore quiet.

5. Dress neatly and conventionally, clean shoes, tidy hair.

6. Find what popular school sport interests prevail. Learn about these sufficiently to discuss them with the students. Attend school games regularly and be sure you are noticed.

7. Meet each incoming class at the door of the music room and establish order and quiet before you admit students to the room. This is especially necessary after recess or if boys are coming from a physical education activity.

8. At the end of a lesson reaffirm your control. Dismiss the class or chorus one row at a time, no running, no talking.

9. Be ever ready to admit a personal error, such as an indefinite lead-in, insufficiently clear instruction, uncertain starting pitch, etc., and avoid placing blame on the singers for your error.

Junior high students are somewhat insecure in themselves; their aggressive and sometimes clownish activities are frequently a cloak to cover this insecurity. They much prefer to follow strong leadership if the goals are worthwhile to floundering around trying to make their own decisions about most things.

Give to the oversized or overaged boy, who feels he has to demonstrate some sort of superiority, a regular job to make him feel necessary and important, such as that of music prefect who brings his class quietly into the music room and conducts the class quietly away from the music room. He might be responsible for roll call, or as librarian he might hand out music books and see that they are returned in good condition at the end of the period.

Giggling is a minor disturbance which cannot be stopped by a command. Sympathize with the victim and tell her (it is rarely a boy) to step outside the room until she has regained control. Do not scold.

The potential music teacher must know that certain kinds of problems sometimes arise and that there is some technique available for handling them. As a matter of fact the ingenious teacher will probably devise many more effective measures than are mentioned here.

FACULTY AND PUBLIC RELATIONS

To assure smooth, effective operation of a music program it is essential that your principal and faculty colleagues understand the nature of your program, sense your sincerity and consider your work a strong component of the total school effort.

There is sometimes an aggressive selling job to be done here; unless your principal and faculty are with you, students will not enroll for your activities. Ask your principal if you may be given five minutes at the first faculty meeting when you will present your philosophy and your proposed plans for various music activities during the coming school year. Plan your talk effectively under the following headings:

1. The importance of music as a school subject.
2. Your keen desire to reach as many students as possible.
3. Your plans for a strong cumulative general music program, stating that while you are more than willing to help other teachers select music appropriate for enriching their own particular discipline, your course will stress the intrinsic value of music.
4. Make clear your plans for public performance and assembly cooperation.
5. Ask for their cooperation and support in realizing your objectives, admitting frankly that these cannot be reached without faculty support.

The above procedure is necessary only when starting in a new school situation.

Good public relations are much easier to obtain than faculty relations. With permission of your principal, seek an interview with the music reporter, social reporter, educational reporter, or other appropriate writer in the local press. Tell him of your new plans for building a strong music program and ask help in communicating this to parents. Be specific in your information and avoid vague generalities. It is a good investment to discuss this at a meal sponsored by the music teacher.

PARENT RELATIONS

There are two groups of parents whose good will is of great value to the junior high music teacher, parents of school chorus members, and parents of students in general music.

Again with consent from your principal invite parents of your chorus group to a brief meeting some evening early, but not too early as very often parents have younger children to put to bed. Discuss your plans, objectives, public performances, needs for equipment, uniform dress or gowns, etc., possible future need for chaperones, and ask for support, particularly in home attitude toward music participation. Suggest that they at least consider forming a chorus parents' association as a type of *booster* club, and invite them as individuals to visit during a chorus rehearsal, giving times, days, and location of rehearsals.

Invite open discussion of a chorus parents' association idea, and if a favorable climate appears to be developing, ask if anyone would care to set the discussion on a firmer basis by making a motion which proposes the formation of the association. When this has been accomplished ask for a second to the motion, and from this point work by usual procedure towards a favorable adoption of the motion.

This done, select the most voluble of the scheme's supporters, ask him or her to take temporary chairmanship of the meeting to elect officers: president, vice-president, treasurer, secretary. Officers duly elected, the new president should assume permanent chairmanship of the group, and from this point on you are a spectator, present in an advisory capacity only. They will decide on regular meetings, committees (as they become desirable and necessary), but you must always be ready to suggest ways and means of supporting your activities.

You may be asked what types of committees might be appropriate. Here are a few: (1) by-laws committee to draft suitable constitution for the new association; (2) telephone committee to contact parents concerning meetings; (3) business committee to assist with business matters pertaining to public performance, travel, etc.; (4) social committee.

If your chorus has two or three choral numbers in good shape for performance, use them for entertainment and instruction at some time during the meeting. Preface the performance with a very short talk, drawing attention of parents to the use of boys' voices during mutation and the choral function of cambiate. Serve light refreshments.

Concerning good public relations with parents of the general music classes, a modified version of the chorus parents' meeting is a good idea. Combine two general music classes for a demonstration clinic and invite parents of all your general music students to attend.

Start the meeting with a brief but concise statement relative to junior high vocal problems, giving special attention to cambiate and baritones. Use chalk board illustrations. Stress the fact that cambiate have been neglected in past years; boys, as a result, were eliminated from choral activity during their junior high school years. In recent years, however, new information has become available concerning range, scope and limitations of boys' voices during the changing period. Tell parents present you are about to show them how voices are discovered and classified, regroup them, and demonstrate the teaching of a four-part song. This, of course, is merely a repeat of what you did with the boys and girls during their first lesson.

It is assumed your clinic class will be seated in a strategic position where parents can see and hear what is happening. Girls should be grouped in their regular blue or green blocks, but cambiata, baritone and soprano boys should be *carefully scrambled* to avoid obvious blocks of similar voice types.

Begin the voice classification procedure outlined in Chapter Three, instructing parents as to the rationale behind each phase of your procedure. Do not rush. Deliberate convincingly in assigning various boys to their respective parts. When classification has been completed regroup the boys into choral formation and ask parents for questions concerning what you have done.

The next step is to demonstrate boys and girls singing as a chorus by teaching "Santa Lucia." Use the method proposed in part two of Chapter Three. Direct parents' attention to the sound of cambiata, frequently classified as non-singers and rejected from choral participation. Be prepared for applause when parts two, three, and four are combined for the first time.

Now, turn your attention to parents. Talk about the innate musicianship of junior high boys and girls, enter a plea for recognition of this, and for the desirability of regular music instruction to develop this musicianship to a point where appreciation and understanding of good music might enrich leisure hours the remainder of their lives. Tell parents you will prove your statement on innate musicianship by asking boys and girls to sing "Santa Lucia" once more, without giving them any starting notes. Turn to the class, instruct them to sing "Santa Lucia," give three silent beats, then lead in confidently and very strongly. Do not hesitate if there is a preliminary faltering; it will quickly straighten out.

If your general music group has one or two songs sufficiently well prepared, this is a good time to let parents hear the kind of choral achievement which develops during the semester.

Following the vocal portion of your presentation, take time to out-line other phases of music instruction you offer to general music students. The objective of the general music program is not to develop performers, but to make the youngsters musically literate. The teacher may want to conclude with the thought that if any parents are inter-ested in becoming acquainted with the fine literature of music, there might be an evening class where recordings will be discussed and played.

There is no point in trying to form a general-music parents' associ-ation. As a matter of fact it is quite probable that some parents of general music students are already members of the chorus parents' association. The purpose of this particular meeting is solely to inform parents about the worthwhile nature of your program, and to foster attitudes of approval among the local population.

One more factor to consider in organizing types of meetings here discussed. If your principal is a strong supporter of the school music program, and is also a convincing speaker, ask him to act as chairman. Should he accept, give him a typed copy of your proposed agenda and discuss it with him.

What is to be gained by all this? What are the foreseeable out-comes which justify all this effort? There are many advantages to be gained. (1) You meet in a somewhat intimate manner the people who help to supply your salary, and give them an informed exposition of what you are doing to merit your appointment; (2) you are dispelling the *frill* concept of school music and establishing your subject as a strong curricular component; (3) for a few days at least your demon-stration is likely to be a talking point with neighbors and the news will spread; (4) you have established your reputation in the immediate neighborhood as a competent music teacher with a fine contribution to offer to the community.

Equipment and Materials

An expert garage mechanic may understand all the mysteries of an internal combustion engine and be quite capable of diagnosing malfunctions of an automobile, but without the special tools of his trade he could not effect the simplest repair. So it is with the school music teacher, who may be an excellent musician and fine teacher, but without specific equipment his work is impossible. Absolutely necessary are the following:

1. A wall-length chalk board, half of which contains systems of permanent painted stafflines, the other half being blank.
2. One staff liner and an ample supply of white chalk, kept in the teacher's desk and dispensed one stick at a time. Do not leave chalk lying around when you are out of the music room.
3. A large-size music stand, a good-size desk, two chairs, blotting pad, class register book, log book for keeping accurate up-to-date information of class or chorus progress. The extra chair is advisable for individual counselling.
4. A reasonably good piano, tuned three times a year, September, December, and March. A small grand is preferable; apart from richer sonority, the teacher can play and keep every member of the class in view.
5. A sufficient quantity of sheet music or books should be available to permit each singer a personal copy of all songs in the year's repertoire, plus extra copies for teacher and accompanist and reserves to replenish loss. This particular item needs clarification. Two or more singers on one copy usually results in building an interdependence, the weaker singers or readers lean heavily on the more secure readers and do not develop their own skills. They merely listen and imitate. This works to the detriment of the music reading program.

A popular, seemingly innocent, subterfuge is to buy one copy of music and provide multiple copies for classes through school multigraphing services. Many school music teachers fail to realize this is illegal; discovery and prosecution bring severe retribution. This activity has become so widespread that publishers are alarmed and are on the lookout for violations of the copyright act. Publishers are also constantly speculating in an effort to provide up-to-date materials for the use of the music educator and they are entitled to a reasonable return on their investment.

The latter is an excellent point to present to your administration when budget is discussed. School boards are reluctant to stand behind a music teacher who becomes legally involved in a copyright suit.

6. For chorus members it is advisable to have individual large, strong folders in which are kept all choral items presently in rehearsal. Each folder will bear a student's name, and he or she will be responsible for loss or excessive wear and tear of music contained therein. Folders will be issued each rehearsal and collected for filing at the close of the rehearsal.

7. A steel filing cabinet for storing sheet music, music books, and chorus folders. The chorus student librarian will be responsible for care of the music library, periodically checking student folders for items missing or ill-used.

8. High fidelity record player, preferably portable in order that teachers of other subjects may use it.

9. A set of fine recordings commensurate with the needs of the listening or ear-training programs you intend to offer.

10. A cabinet in which to store records. This should also have a padlock attachment.

11. A modulator[1] for spontaneous syllable practice. This is in the form of a chart which may be hung over the chalk board, rolled up and stored when syllable practice is ended.

12. One set of music reading books, sufficient in quantity to provide one book for each member of the largest general music class.

13. Wall chart pictures of the instruments of the orchestra.

14. A bulletin board on which to place rehearsal schedule, news items of topical interest, appropriate magazine illustrations, etc.

The foregoing list of equipment and materials represents minimum requirements for operating a satisfactory general music and chorus program. There are, however, other desirable pieces of equipment and materials which add strength to the program and will help in giving more meaning to your teaching.

1. A good tape recorder to help in promoting higher standards of singing performance. Whereas the director, standing in front of the group, hears the total sound of his group in terms of balance, tone quality, diction, phrasing, interpretation, etc., the individual singer hears only what is happening in the immediate vicinity. By taping classroom performance and rerunning the tape for class listening, the music teacher is able to demonstrate his points much more effectively than by words only. Surprising as it may seem, these youngsters are highly self-critical while listening to a recording of their own performance.

2. One dozen tapes. This may seem excessive, but there is a great deal to be gained by dating a tape, storing, and rerunning some weeks later to evaluate progress.

3. A series of student work books relating to fundamentals, listening, history of music. Many types of excellent publications are available from which the teacher may select one suitable to his presentation of these aspects of the general music program. Inasmuch as these books contain a good deal of space in which the student writes, they cannot be

---

[1] *Classroom Music Modulator,* produced by John Curwen, Ltd. London, England. Distributed in the United States by G. Schirmer, Inc., New York.

transferred from one class to another, or from one year to the next, therefore students should purchase them.

4. One autoharp for use in demonstrating harmony and occasionally as an accompaniment aid for the singing class. Due to its limited chordal resources, the autoharp can only be used to accompany simple folk songs; further, due to the unusual voicing of junior high choral groups and the necessity for selecting appropriate keys, these keys do not always coincide with those available on the autoharp. Performing keys must be selected in accordance with junior high vocal ranges and cannot be changed to accommodate limitations of the autoharp.

5. One very useful piece of equipment is a high stool similar to that used by band directors. The music teacher is on his feet a good deal of the time and this can be very tiring with a full teaching schedule. An ordinary chair is useless; the choral director needs to be elevated. If the budget is insufficient to provide a standard-model conductor's chair, an efficient substitute is an ordinary kitchen stool.

6. A pitch pipe for Christmas carolling or other performance for which a piano may not be available.

No mention has been made of a sound-movie projector. This piece of equipment is too expensive and is used too infrequently to be the sole prerogative of the music department. Most schools now possess this equipment for use by any faculty member. The music teacher will, however, be well advised to include twenty-five dollars in his budget for film rentals.

At some time during his interview with the principal, an applicant for a school music teaching position should make sure that minimum equipment prescribed above is either available or will be procured. If the request is not favorably received this is a portent which indicates a dubious situation to accept.

SUMMARY

It is impossible to write a book such as this so that it is applicable to every type of general music program, every type of curricular schedule allocation, every level of junior high school student competence and every type of music objective. Neither is it possible to write a book about general music which will satisfy the needs of all junior high music teachers, or agree with all basic assumptions of all music education teachers at the college level.

Musical competencies of freshmen entering junior high school vary from state to state, county to county, city to city, and even school to school. Some areas provide an excellent elementary school music program taught by music specialists, while in some other areas significant music help is given the classroom teacher through regular and frequent visits made by a qualified music consultant.

Students entering Grade 7 after passing through such an elementary school music program will be acquainted with portions of ear-training or fundamentals section presented in this book. Such instances, however, are very rare. Even in some areas where such elementary music programs were operative on paper, clinic music has had to be taught by rote.

Most school systems provide sparse music consultant help for elementary classroom teachers. Teachers may even have difficulty reading music well enough to learn a new song for presentation to their children, and they are certainly not sufficiently equipped to teach their classes the skills of music reading. This is not a criticism of the hard-working, dedicated classroom teacher; it is a straight statement of fact concerning a situation which merits serious consideration, investigation, and remedial action.

Such change will take some years to materialize. When that time comes, much of this present book will become obsolete at the junior high level and become operative at the elementary level. In the meantime, however, there is a very definite need for the type of program proposed herein for Grades 7, 8, and 9.

Instruction begins with the assumption that the youngsters have been exposed to some music experiences in singing songs in elementary grades, but that reading skills are not strong. Any junior high music teacher may select any point of entry into the instructional sequence commensurate with his class's ability to cope with the information offered. The authors have endeavored to provide a text which will meet the needs of teachers whose general music responsibilities involve teaching students in their first organized music learning experience. At the same time, they have tried to provide a course of instruction which terminates at a sufficiently high level of achievement to challenge the attention of the best teacher and the best music student.

Obviously, a music teacher with a meager schedule allocation for general music activities cannot possibly attain the final goals presented herein; he will need to select certain aspects of the program and eliminate the remainder. Singing and music reading should, however, be mandatory.

Every general music lesson should involve the class in a good deal of singing, using material carefully selected to meet the range limits of all voices. In singing, class participation is clearly visible and audible to the teacher. To realize worthwhile achievement and complete satisfaction, however, the finest possible performance must be called for, even with a small group. Every song should be treated as though it were a concert performance; desultory or commonplace singing should not be tolerated. Artistic and interpretive singing should ever be the goal, even in a simple song.

It is often easy to drift into a casual demeanor not only in the singing lesson but also in the listening program. Interesting, tuneful music should be used, and the listening lesson should be well organized, continuous, and cumulative.

The total content of this course of instruction will require a minimum of two consecutive semesters of at least two forty-five minute periods per week. The teacher is advised to select which portions of the program he will adopt and plan a broad tentative outline of instruction well ahead of the first lesson. For instance, a teacher with only one general music period per week might decide to use the singing program, the music reading program and parts of the listening program, or perhaps singing, music reading, and that part of the ear training program presented in "The Exciting Sounds of Music." There are many combinations of music activities available, but singing songs should always be an important part of every lesson.

The first few lessons of the semester should be devoted to the voice classification procedure defined herein and to the rote teaching of some four part songs. Once the youngsters have experienced the satisfaction of choir singing and the enjoyment of really belonging to a group which produces this kind of music, they are easily persuaded that their choral achievements can be much finer and greatly accelerated by learning to read music.

When Phase Two of the music reading program is completed the information thus assimilated may be correlated in learning new choral selections. As each new complexity is mastered in the ensuing phases it may be illustrated in the choral music being studied and incorporated into the song learning process. Music reading per se has little to commend it unless skills are transferred to song learning.

Correlation between the music reading and ear-training programs is essential for parallel growth in both areas. The ear-training program should lag one lesson behind the music reading program.

One point mentioned earlier in the presentation of both these programs needs stressing again. This work should not be overlabored to secure perfection, nor should it ever occupy more than one-quarter of the general music period; that is, approximately one-eighth for music reading and one-eighth for ear training.

Correlation between the foregoing programs and the fundamentals program is also recommended. The study of fundamentals of music should not be isolated from other areas of music study. It is advisable however to defer this study until Lesson Ten of the music reading program has been completed.

The history program obviously correlates closely with the listening program and The Exciting Sounds of Music portion of the ear training program. Correlation here, however, does not need to be so tightly organized as it was in music reading, ear training, and rudiments.

In conclusion, mentioned in the foreword and considered worthy of repetition, the authors do not presume to suggest that the foregoing pages constitute the sole method for planning and teaching a junior high school general music program.

Many teachers who are interested in using this approach will modify and improve procedures presented herein. Others who might not favor the music syllable approach may arbitrarily reject it. In many years of teaching experience the authors have used numbers, letters, fixed *doh* and moveable *doh* syllables in teaching at elementary or junior high level and decided on the moveable *doh* system as the most reliable beginning teaching medium. It was found to be the only system which does not break down when simple chromatics are introduced.

Reluctance to use music syllables as an aid to early music reading experiences has been encountered in some clinics and workshops. Enquiry concerning reasons for this reluctance has revealed that nonfavoring teachers were not acquainted with the system or its benefits. The moveable *doh* music syllable system is so very easy to learn, and it is an invaluable aid in teaching rote songs, unison or parts, also for initiating music reading activity. A music teacher can master the system merely by guiding his students step by step through Lessons One to Ten in Chapter Five.

The use of syllables may be discarded when students have completed Phase Five of the music reading program, but the teacher will want to make use of them frequently to overcome reading problems in more difficult choral music.

A final word of advice to the teacher. Keep track of the progress of every general music class and the chorus by maintaining a log. Keep it up to date every lesson.

Appendix A

JUNIOR HIGH SCHOOL CHORAL PUBLICATIONS BY IRVIN COOPER

SONG BOOKS, SSCB*

Bourne Co.; New York, N.Y.
   Sing One, Sing All; 1954

Carl Fischer, Inc.; New York, N.Y.
   Teen-Age songs; 1942
   Tunetime for Teentime; 1952
   Yuletime for Teentime; 1954
   Songs for Pre-Teentime; 1956
   Hymns for Teentime; 1957
   Sing, Boys, Sing; 1957
   Cantate Deo (Catholic); 1960
   More Tunetime for Teentime; 1962
   Descants for Junior High Singing; 1962
   The Junior High Choral Concert; 1964

Charles H. Hansen Music Corp.; New York, N.Y.
   Cambiata Hymnal; 1954
   Cambiata Easter Hymnal; 1955
   Accent on Singing; 1955
   General Music Singing; 1956

Gordon V. Thompson, Ltd.; Niagara Falls, N.Y.
   The Singing Teens; 1952
   Unison Songs for Teen-Age Boys; 1953

Silver Burdett Co.; New York, N.Y. and Morristown, N.J.
   Music the World Sings; 1952 (contributor)
   Music in our Life (part author); 1959
   Music in our Times (part author); 1959

SHEET MUSIC, SSCB*

Carl Fischer, Inc.; New York, N.Y.
   D   At Last; 1955
   MD   The Arrow and the Song; 1955
   MD   Exposition; 1955
   MD   Young and Old; 1955

   * SSCB—Soprano I, Soprano II, Cambiata, Baritone
   E—Easy
   MD—Medium difficulty
   D—Difficult (concert material)

Charles H. Hansen Music Corp.; New York, N.Y.

MD   The Lost Lamb; 1954
MD   Move That Mountain; 1954
MD   These Things Are Known; 1954
E   Rudolph, the Red-Nosed Reindeer; 1954
MD   His Hands; 1955
MD   Yellow Rose of Texas; 1955
MD   He; 1955
E   Little White Duck;
E   Autumn Leaves; 1955 (also CCB and CCBB)
E   Hi! To You; 1955
E   Alma Mater; 1956 (also SATB)
E   Will Ye No' Come Back Again; 1956 (also SATB)

Cromwell Music, Inc.; New York, N.Y.

MD   I Believe; 1953

Frank Music Co.; New York, N.Y.

E   Stranger in Paradise; 1954 (SSCB)

SCB AND SACB*

Bourne Co.; New York, N.Y.

MD   Square Dance; 1954 (SACB)

Carl Fischer, Inc.; New York, N.Y.

D   The Lost Chord; 1951 (SACB)
D   When the Foeman Bares His Steel; 1953 (SACB)

Charles H. Hansen Music Corp.; New York, N.Y.

E   On Top of Old Smoky; 1954 (SCB)
MD   Down by the Riverside; 1954 (SACB)
MD   Campus Serenade; 1954 (SCB)
E   Young at Heart; 1954 (SACB)
E   That's Amore; 1954 (SACB)
MD   Stranger in Paradise; 1954 (SACB)
MD   Kentucky Babe; 1954 (SACB)
D   One God; 1954 (SACB)
MD   Man with a Banjo; 1954 (SACB)
MD   The Night Before Christmas; 1954 (SCB)
E   Sleepy Suwanee; 1954 (SCB)
MD   This Ole House; 1954 (SCB)
MD   My Bambino; 1954 (SCB)
MD   Little Marguerite; 1954 (SCB)
E   Song for America; 1955 (SACB, also SATB)
MD   Old Johnnie Goggabee; 1955 (SCB)

* SCB–Soprano, Cambiata, Baritone
SACB–Soprano, Alto, Cambiata, Baritone

SSA

Carl Fischer, Inc.; New York, N.Y.

D   I Have Done; 1951
E   Lullaby; 1951
E   Petals; 1951
D   Serenade for Spring; 1951

Some other choral publications compatible with tenets of the Cambiata Concept of junior high school voices:

Living With Music, Volumes I and II, by Allen L. Richardson and Mary E. English, published by M. Witmark and Sons, New York.

Patterns in Songs, by Allen L. Richardson and Arthur R. Frackenpohl, published by M. Witmark and Sons, New York.

Let's Sing Parts, Books I and II, by Rj Staples, published by Mills Music Co., Inc., New York.

Sing Praises, by Walter Ehret, published by Broadman Press, Nashville, Tennessee.

Time for Music, by Walter Ehret, E. Lawrence Barr, and Elizabeth Blair, published by Prentice-Hall, Englewood Cliffs, New Jersey.

Music for Everyone, by Walter Ehret, E. Lawrence Barr, and Elizabeth Blair, published by Prentice-Hall, Inc., Englewood Cliffs, New Jersey.

Appendix B

Report on Authors' Activities with Early-Adolescent Voices

Table of Clinic-Demonstrations and Festivals

State	Location	Activities Number	Type	Sponsor	Students Participating	Teachers Present
Alabama	Bay Minette	1	clinic-demonstration	City schools	84	8
Arizona	Tempe	1	clinic-demonstration	Arizona M.E.A. (state)	97	247
Florida	Chipley	1	clinic-demonstration	Florida M.E.A. (district)	60	14[1]
	Crawfordville	1	clinic-demonstration and festival	Local schools	94	22
	Daytona	1	festival	Florida M.E.A. (district)	436	5[1]
		1	festival	All State Chorus	420	30[1]
	Fort Lauderdale	1	clinic-demonstration	Florida State University (ext.)	85	84
		1	television		40	3
	Gainesville	1	clinic-demonstration	City schools	132	6
		1	clinic-demonstration	University of Florida	180	8
	Greenville	1	clinic-demonstration	Florida State University (lab.)	46	23
		1	clinic-demonstration	Florida State University (lab.)	80	24
	Jacksonville	1	television	Florida State University (lab.)	42	2
		1	festival	Florida State M.E.A.	644	6[1]

[1] It is not possible to estimate total number of teachers present, number given refers to participating teachers.

State	City	No.	Type	Organization		
	Miami	2	clinic-demonstration	Florida M.E.A. (district)	112	15
				Southern M.E.N.C.	92	163
	Tallahassee	37	see footnote[2]	Florida State University (lab.)	3125	8
				Tallahassee M.E.A.		⎫
				M.T.N.A.		324 student teachers
				F.S.M.E.A.		⎭
	Tampa	2	clinic-demonstration	Florida M.E.A. (state)	545	64
		1	festival	Florida M.E.A. (state)	385	4[1]
		1	clinic-demonstration	Florida S.M.E.A.	140	12
	West Palm Beach	1	clinic-demonstration	Rosarian Academy	120	14
Georgia	Atlanta	1	clinic-demonstration	Georgia M.E.A. (state)	91	46
Illinois	Chicago	1	clinic-demonstration	M.E.N.C. (national meeting)	120	2500 (approx.)
Indiana	Bloomington	7	workshop	Indiana University	290	217
	Columbus	1	festival	County schools	930	11[1]
	Greenfield	1	festival	County schools	1040	10[1]
	Indianapolis	1	clinic-demonstration and workshop	Indiana M.E.A. (state)	84	72
		1	workshop	Butler University	36	24
Iowa	Cedar Falls	1	clinic-demonstration	Iowa State Teachers College	87	23
Kentucky	Lexington	1	clinic-demonstration	Kentucky M.E.A. (state)	98	84
	Louisville	2	clinic-demonstration	City schools	76	6
		1	workshop	University of Louisville	82	14
Louisiana	New Orleans	1	clinic-demonstration	City schools	34	28
					121	19
Maine	Portland	1	clinic-demonstration	New England Music Festival	88	43
Maryland	Baltimore	1	clinic-demonstration	M.E.N.C.-Eastern division	116	650 (approx.)

[2] Tallahassee has been research and experimentation center since 1950. Totals include clinics, festivals, but not monthly checks on some groups.

Appendix B (continued)

State	Location	Activities Number	Activities Type	Sponsor	Students Participating	Teachers Present
	Upper Marlboro	1	clinic-demonstration	County schools	91	22 24 student teachers
Massachusetts	Boston	1	clinic-demonstration	In and about Boston M.E.A.	76	82
Minnesota	Minneapolis	1	clinic-demonstration	Minnesota M.E.A. (state)	119	186
	Mankato	1	workshop	Mankato State Teachers College	68	38
Mississippi	Jackson	1	clinic-demonstration	Mississippi M.E.A.	115	320
New Hampshire	Concord	1	clinic-demonstration	New Hampshire M.E.A.	86	41
New Jersey	Atlantic City	1	clinic-demonstration	M.E.N.C.-National meeting	94	350 (approx.)
New York	Avon	1	clinic-demonstration	County schools	124	4
	Buffalo	1	clinic-demonstration	Catholic M.E.N.C.	90	240 (approx.)
	Caledonia	1	clinic-demonstration	County schools	105	3
	Fredonia	1	clinic-demonstration	Fredonia State Teachers College		
	Geneseo	1	clinic-demonstration	County schools	98	2
		1	festival		360	8[1]
	Potsdam	2	clinic-demonstration	Potsdam State Teachers College	205	41
	Rochester	1	clinic-demonstration	New York M.E.A. (state)	87	240 (approx.)
	Syracuse	1	clinic-demonstration	New York M.E.A. (state)	68	147
North Carolina	Durham	1	clinic-demonstration	North Carolina M.E.A. (district)	56	14

State	City		Type	Host		
Ohio	Columbus	1	all boys' festival		820	14[1]
	Columbus	1	clinic-demonstration	Ohio M.E.A. (district)	82	42
	Mansfield	1	clinic-demonstration	Ohio M.E.A. (district)	88	22
	Sandusky	1	clinic-demonstration	Ohio M.E.A. (district)	78	34
Oregon	Eugene	3	clinic-demonstration	University of Oregon	325	27
Pennsylvania	Allentown	1	clinic-demonstration	County schools	98	14
	Bellefont	1	clinic-demonstration	Pennsylvania M.E.A. (district)	48	8
	Harrisburg	2	clinic-demonstration	Pennsylvania M.E.A. (state)	196	520 (approx.)
	New Castle	1	clinic-demonstration	Pennsylvania M.E.A. (district)	68	14
	Philadelphia	1	clinic-demonstration	M.E.N.C. (national)	108	2500 (approx.)
South Carolina	Clemson	6	clinic-demonstration	Clemson College	630	12
	Spartanburg	1	clinic-demonstration	Converse College	82	31
Tennessee	Knoxville	2	clinic-demonstration	City and county schools	620	34
		2	festivals	City and county schools	3000 (approx.)	24[1]
	Memphis	3	festivals	City schools	3500 (approx.)	36[1]
Texas	Austin	1	clinic-demonstration	City schools	94	12
	Austin	1	festival	City schools	1100 (approx.)	9[4]
	Carthage	1	clinic-demonstration	City schools	83	8
	Corpus Christi	1	clinic-demonstration	City schools	124	11
	Dallas	2	clinic-demonstration	City schools	438	15
	El Paso	1	clinic-demonstration	City schools and Texas Western College	98	24
		4	festivals	City schools	4000 (approx.)	48[1]
	Galveston	1	clinic-demonstration	Texas M.E.A. (state)	92	83
	Huntsville	1	workshop	Sam Houston State Teachers College	47	24
	Kilgore	1	festival	Texas M.E.A. (district)	360	11[1]
	San Benito	1	clinic-demonstration	City schools	64	5
	Temple	1	clinic-demonstration	City schools	102	8

Appendix B (continued)

State	Location	Activities		Sponsor	Students Participating	Teachers Present
		Number	Type			
	Waco	2	workshops	Baylor University	235	34
	Weslaco	1	clinic-demonstration	City schools	83	6
Vermont	Burlington	1	clinic-demonstration	Vermont M.E.A.	76	22
	Newport	1	clinic-demonstration	City schools	64	3
Virginia	Arlington	1	clinic-demonstration	City schools	88	5
	Massanetta	1	workshop	State Department of Education	126	64
	Richmond	1	clinic-demonstration	Southern M.E.N.C.	131	350 (approx.)
Washington	Seattle	1	clinic-demonstration	City schools	93	24
West Virginia	Bluefield	2	festivals	County schools	1657	261
	Charleston	1	clinic-demonstration	M.E.N.C. (Southern)	98	650 (approx.)
	Huntington	1	clinic-demonstration	County schools	243	8
Wisconsin	Madison	1	clinic-demonstration	University M.E.A.	93	114
	Mequon	1	workshop	School Sisters of Notre Dame	88	257
Province (Canada)						
British Columbia	Vancouver	1	clinic-demonstration	Canadian M.E.A. (national)	78	104
New Brunswick	Moncton	1	clinic-demonstration	City schools	103	4
Nova Scotia	Halifax	3	clinic-demonstration	City schools	615	6
	Truro	1	clinic-demonstration	City schools	38	2
Quebec	Stanstead	1	year research project	Stanstead College	173	3

RANGE, SCOPE-LIMITATIONS OF EARLY ADOLESCENT VOICES
REPORT OF INVESTIGATIONS IN MONTREAL, CANADA, 1939-47

Year	Number	Activities Type	Girls	Boys	Total	Teachers Involved
1939-40	41	voice classifications	3002	2741	5743	27
	23	school concerts	1423	1142	2565	18
1940-41	40	voice classifications	2875	2776	5651	27
	26	school concerts	1684	1230	2914	20
	1	all-city festival	2062	1784	3846	25
1941-42	40	voice classifications	2870	2755	5625	26
	28	school concerts	1741	1495	3236	24
1942-43	41	voice classifications	3059	2742	5801	28
	25	school concerts	1545	1341	2886	20
	1	all-city festival	2074	2006	4080	26
1943-44	41	voice classifications	2965	2809	5774	28
	29	school concerts	1741	1286	3027	25
1944-45	40	voice classifications	2832	2785	5617	28
	23	school concerts	1462	1178	2640	19
1945-46	41	voice classifications	2971	2749	5720	28
	24	school concerts	1344	1188	2532	19
1946-47	41	voice classifications	2980	2813	5793	28
	4	voice classifications (French speaking schools)	1214	1164	2378	68
	17	school concerts	1003	939	1942	14
	1	International Festival	2114	1850	3964	43
			42961	38773	81734	

Composer Index

Subject Index

fications of voters shall be regulated by by-laws to be adopted by the Community.

In the trustees, so elected, we the undersigned members do hereby vest all the powers, rights of action and privileges granted to corporations by the laws of this state, and also all requisite power and authority to arrange, control and manage, in brotherly concurrence according to our order of grace, or by a majority of votes, all the affairs and concerns of this corporation whatsoever; to receive new members under this constitution; to assign to the members their work, labor and employment; to fix the amounts of the yearly allowances for the support of the members; to exclude, order away and remove such members who are unruly and resisting, and who will not mend themselves after repeated admonition; to settle and liquidate the accounts of those members withdrawing from the Society, either by their own choice or by expulsion; to receive and to administrate all the active and passive capital stock and personal estate of the Society; to keep books and accounts of every thing; to buy and to sell; to make, fulfill and revoke contracts, to carry on agriculture, the rearing of cattle, manufactures, mills and trades of any kind, to erect buildings, to improve and take down the same; to make inventories; to appoint attorneys, agents and managers; to borrow, lend and safely invest funds and moneys; also in the corporate name of the Society, or in the name of the trustees, or of any member thereof to ask, demand, levy, recover and receive all kinds of goods, moneys, principal and interest, effects, debts, demands, inheritances and legacies, wheresoever and whatsoever; to receive, execute and deliver all deeds, mortgages, notes, bonds, power of attorney, receipts, discharges, and all other documents and accounts whatsoever; and to do, transact and carry out all needful, beneficial, legal, proper, just and equitable acts, matters and things in general of all and every kind whatsoever, all for and in the name, behalf and benefit of this corporation.

In the event however of matters of great importance and responsibility it shall be the duty of the trustees to hold special meetings and to decide therein either by unanimous concurrence or by a majority of votes whether or not such matters shall be submitted for counsel and decision by vote to all the elders of the Community and to the members entitled to vote.

All resolutions of the board of trustees relating to the sale of the Society's lands situate within the Town of Amana require the consent of two-thirds of all the trustees and of two-thirds of all the elders in the Community, as also the consent of a majority of the members entitled to vote.

The lands now owned by the Society lying beyond the Town of Amana shall be under the administration of the trustees with power to sell, exchange or rent the same, as they shall find best in the interest of the Society.

Vacancies in the board of trustees occasioned by withdrawal, sickness or death of any of its members, may be filled for the intervening time until the next annual election by the remaining trustees themselves, out of the number of the elders in the Community, not being members elected to the board.

In the month of June in each year the trustees shall exhibit to the voting members of the Society a full statement of the real and personal estate of the Society.

The trustees shall annually elect out of their number one Director, one vice-director and one secretary, and shall procure a seal, which shall be the corporate seal of the Society.

All public and legal documents and instruments emanating from the Society by a resolution of the trustees, in conformity with this constitution, shall be signed by the director, countersigned by the secretary, and the corporate seal of the Society affixed thereto.

On the application of any three members of the board of trustees it shall be the duty of the director to call an extra or special meeting of said board.

ARTICLE V.

Every member of this Society is in duty bound to hand over his or her personal and real property to the trustees for the common fund, at the time of his or her acceptance as a member, and before the signing of this constitution.

For such payments into the common fund each member is entitled to the credit thereof in the books of the Society and to a receipt signed by the director and secretary of the board of trustees, and is moreover secured for such payments by the pledge of the common property of the Society.

Article VI.

Every member of this Society is, besides the free board and dwelling, and the support and care secured to him in his old age, sickness and infirmity, further entitled out of the common fund to an annual sum of maintenance for him or herself, children and relations in the Society; and these annual allowances shall be fixed by the trustees for each member single or in families, according to justice and equity, and shall be from time to time revised and fixed anew.

And we, the undersigned members of this corporation in consideration of the enjoyment of these blessings in the bond of our Communion, do hereby release, grant and quit-claim to the said corporation, for ourselves, our children, heirs and administrators all claims for wages and interest of the capital paid into the common fund, also all claims of any part of the income and profits, and of any share in the estate and property of the Society separate from the whole and common stock.

Article VII.

All children and minors in the Society, after the death of their parents or relations, shall as orphans be under the special guardianship of the trustees of the Society, during the time of their minority. In case of such parents or relations deceased having a credit on the books of the Society, without their leaving a will or testament for the disposition of the same; or in case such parents or relations are indebted to the Society for advances made them, then the children or minors of such parents and relations shall at the time of their majority, in regard to such credits or debts, enter into the rights and into the liabilities of their deceased parents and relations, as their natural and lawful heirs, and the credits or debts of members so deceased shall then be transferred on the books of the Society to such heirs, according to the proper share of each, under the direction of the trustees. Such personal estates or credits as may be left by members, dying in the Society, without having made any will or testament for the disposition of the same, and without leaving any lawful heirs, shall revert to and vest in said corporation.

ARTICLE VIII.

Such members as may recede from the Society, either by their own choice or by expulsion, shall be entitled to receive back the moneys paid into the common fund, and to interest thereon at the rate not exceeding five per cent. per annum, from the time of the adjustment of their accounts until the repayment of their credits, which rate is to be fixed by the board of trustees.

Such receding members shall however not be entitled to any other allowance for any services rendered to the Society during their membership, but to such, as may be granted them by the board of trustees, on the settlement of their accounts, as a gratuity and not as a legal claim.

To enable however the Society to make such repayments to receding members, as also eventual payments of legacies and inheritances of members deceased in the Society, to relations or heirs thereto entitled beyond the Society, without loss and oppression, it has been agreed on between ourselves, that such payments shall be made in the following manner, viz: of all sums up to $500, one-fourth part on the adjustment of the claim, and the remainder within four months thereafter; of all sums over $500 up to $20,000, and over, the sum of from $200 to $600 at the time of settlement, and the remainder in three, four, six, nine, twelve, fifteen, eighteen and twenty-one equal four-monthly installments, in proportion to the amounts to be paid.